Tourist Experience and Fulf

What makes life worth living? Many people would argue that it is fulfilling experiences. These experiences are characterised by feelings of joy and pleasure, positive relationships and a sense of engagement, meaning and achievement. Tourism is arguably one of the largest self-initiated commercial interventions to promote well-being and happiness on the global scale but yet there is absence in the literature on the topic of fulfilling tourist experiences from psychological perspectives.

Drawing on insights and theories from the research field of positive psychology (the study of well-being), this is the first edited book to evaluate tourist experiences from positive psychology perspectives. The volume addresses the important topic of fulfilment through the lens of the world's largest social global phenomenon, tourism. In doing so, the book refreshes and challenges some aspects of tourist behaviour research.

The chapters are grouped under three broad parts which reflect a range of positive psychological outcomes that personal holiday experiences can produce, namely: happiness and humour, meaning and self-actualisation, and health and restoration. The book critically explores these fulfilling experiences from interdisciplinary perspectives and includes research studies from a wide range of geographical regions. By analysing the contemporary fulfilling tourist experiences the book will provide further understanding of tourist behaviour and experience.

Written by leading academics, this significant volume will appeal to those interested in tourism and positive psychology.

Sebastian Filep, PhD, is Honorary Research Fellow, Victoria University, Australia and Lecturer at the Department of Tourism, University of Otago, New Zealand. Dr Filep is a co-author of *Tourists, Tourism and the Good Life* (Routledge, 2011) and a co-author of *Vacation Rules*, a popular market e-book.

Philip Pearce, PhD, is Foundation Professor of Tourism at James Cook University, Australia. He has published a number of books in tourism including two sole author works on tourist behaviour in 2005 and 2011.

Routledge advances in tourism
Edited by Stephen Page
School for Tourism, Bournemouth University

1 **The Sociology of Tourism**
   Theoretical and empirical investigations
   Edited by Yiorgos Apostolopoulos, Stella Leivadi and Andrew Yiannakis

2 **Creating Island Resorts**
   Brian King

3 **Destinations**
   Cultural landscapes of tourism
   Edited by Greg Ringer

4 **Mediterranean Tourism**
   Facets of socioeconomic development and cultural change
   Edited by Yiorgos Apostolopoulos, Lila Leontidou and Philippos Loukissas

5 **Outdoor Recreation Management**
   John Pigram and John Jenkins

6 **Tourism Development**
   Edited by Douglas G. Pearce and Richard W. Butler

7 **Tourism and Sustainable Community Development**
   Edited by Greg Richards and Derek Hall

8 **Tourism and Political Boundaries**
   Dallen J. Timothy

9 **Leisure and Tourism Landscapes**
   Social and cultural geographies
   Cara Aitchison, Nicola E. MacLeod and Stephen J. Shaw

10 **Tourism in the Age of Globalisation**
    Edited by Salah Wahab and Chris Cooper

11 **Tourism and Gastronomy**
   Edited by Anne-Mette Hjalager and Greg Richards

12 **New Perspectives in Caribbean Tourism**
   Edited by Marcella Daye, Donna Chambers and Sherma Roberts

13 **The Advanced Econometrics of Tourism Demand**
   Haiyan Song, Stephen F. Witt and Gang Li

14 **Tourism in China**
   Destination, cultures and communities
   Edited by Chris Ryan and Gu Huimin

15 **Sustainable Tourism Futures**
   Perspectives on systems, restructuring and innovations
   Edited by Stefan Gössling, C. Michael Hall and David B. Weaver

16 **Advances in Tourism Destination Marketing**
   Managing networks
   Edited by Metin Kozak, Juergen Gnoth and Luisa Andreu

17 **Drive Tourism**
   Trends and emerging markets
   Edited by Bruce Prideaux and Dean Carson

18 **Tourist Customer Service Satisfaction**
   An encounter approach
   Francis P. Noe, Muzzafer Uysal and Vincent P. Magnini

19 **Mining Heritage Tourism**
   A global synthesis
   Edited by Michael Conlin and Lee Jolliffe

20 **Tourist Experience**
   Contemporary perspectives
   Edited by Richard Sharpley and Phillip Stone

21 **Sustainable Tourism in Rural Europe**
   Edited by Donald Macleod and Steven Gillespie

22 **The Critical Turn in Tourism Studies**
   Creating an academy of hope
   Edited by Nigel Morgan, Irena Atelkevic and Annette Pritchard

23 **Tourism Supply Chain Management**
   Haiyan Song

24 **Tourism and Retail**
    Edited by Charles McIntyre

25 **International Sports Events**
    Impacts, experience and identities
    Edited by Richard Shipway and Alan Fyall

26 **Cultural Moment in Tourism**
    Edited by Laurajane Smith, Emma Waterton and Steve Watson

27 **Contemporary Tourist Experience**
    Richard Sharpley and Philip Stone

28 **Future Tourism**
    Political, social and economic challenges
    James Leigh, Craig Webster and Stanislav Ivanov

29 **Information Communication Technologies and Sustainable Tourism**
    Alisha Ali and Andrew J. Frew

30 **Responsible Tourist Behaviour**
    Clare Weeden

31 **Tourist Experience and Fulfilment**
    Insights from positive psychology
    Edited by Sebastian Filep and Philip Pearce

Forthcoming:
Dark Tourism and Crime
Derek Dalton

Tourist Experience and Fulfilment

Insights from positive psychology

Edited by Sebastian Filep and
Philip Pearce

LONDON AND NEW YORK

First published 2014
by Routledge
2 Park Square, Milton Park, Abingdon, Oxon OX14 4RN

Simultaneously published in the USA and Canada
by Routledge
711 Third Avenue, New York, NY 10017

First issued in paperback 2017

Routledge is an imprint of the Taylor & Francis Group, an informa business

© 2014 Sebastian Filep and Philip Pearce for selection and editorial matter; individual contributors their contribution.

The right of Sebastian Filep and Philip Pearce to be identified as the authors of the editorial material, and of the authors for their individual chapters, has been asserted in accordance with sections 77 and 78 of the Copyright, Designs and Patents Act 1988.

All rights reserved. No part of this book may be reprinted or reproduced or utilised in any form or by any electronic, mechanical, or other means, now known or hereafter invented, including photocopying and recording, or in any information storage or retrieval system, without permission in writing from the publishers.

Trademark notice: Product or corporate names may be trademarks or registered trademarks, and are used only for identification and explanation without intent to infringe.

British Library Cataloguing in Publication Data
A catalogue record for this book is available from the British Library

Library of Congress Cataloging in Publication Data
Tourist experience and fulfilment: insights from positive psychology / edited by Sebastian Filep and Philip Pearce.
   pages cm. – (Routledge advances in tourism; 31)
   Includes bibliographical references and index.
   1. Tourism–Psychological aspects. 2. Tourists–Psychology.
   3. Self-realization. I. Filep, Sebastian.
   G155.A1T39825 2013
   910'.019–dc23   2013006786

ISBN 13: 978-1-138-08192-5 (pbk)
ISBN 13: 978-0-415-80986-3 (hbk)

Typeset in Times New Roman
by Wearset Ltd, Boldon, Tyne and Wear

Contents

List of illustrations ix
List of contributors x
Foreword xii
MIHALY CSIKSZENTMIHALYI
Acknowledgements xiii

1 **Introducing tourist experience and fulfilment research** 1
SEBASTIAN FILEP AND PHILIP PEARCE

PART I
Happiness and humour 15

2 **Humour, tourism and positive psychology** 17
PHILIP PEARCE AND ANJA PABEL

3 **Walking the talk: positive effects of work-related travel on tourism academics** 37
MIEKE WITSEL

4 **Travel as a factor of happiness in Hungary** 54
TAMARA RÁTZ AND GÁBOR MICHALKÓ

5 **Tourism, wellness and feeling good: reviewing and studying Asian spa experiences** 72
JENNY PANCHAL

PART II
Meaning and self-actualisation 89

6 Meaning making, life transitional experiences and personal well-being within the contexts of religious and spiritual travel 91
GLENN ROSS

7 Experiencing flamenco: an examination of a spiritual journey 110
XAVIER MATTEUCCI

8 Personal transformation through long-distance walking 127
ROB SAUNDERS, JENNIFER LAING AND BETTY WEILER

9 The development of self through volunteer tourism 147
ZOË ALEXANDER AND ALI BAKIR

PART III
Health and restoration 165

10 How does a vacation from work affect tourists' health and well-being 167
JESSICA DE BLOOM, SABINE GEURTS AND MICHIEL KOMPIER

11 Anticipating a flourishing future with tourism experiences 186
CHRISTINA HAGGER AND DUNCAN MURRAY

12 Visitors' restorative experiences in museum and botanic garden environments 202
JAN PACKER

13 A blueprint for tourist experience and fulfilment research 223
SEBASTIAN FILEP AND PHILIP PEARCE

Index 233

Illustrations

Figures

2.1	Comparison of researcher's ratings with the mean ratings of the judging panel	25
4.1	The happiness-inducing role of life events and situations in Hungary, 2008	58
4.2	Carefreeness	62
4.3	Venice is the dream destination for many travellers	66
7.1	Dimensions of the spiritual experience of flamenco	122
8.1	Transformative effects of long-distance walking	142
9.1	A diagrammatic representation of Engagement Theory in volunteer tourism	153
10.1	Mean levels of health and well-being across four types of vacations	174
12.1	Environments, restorative attributes and restorative effects	205

Tables

2.1	Select instances of humour provided for tourists	23
5.1	The flow experience – spa activity vs other physical activities	81
7.1	Respondents' spiritual experiences	112
9.1	Summary: the percentage of time we would expect to obtain these results	151
10.1	Partial correlations of health and well-being during (*Inter*) and after vacation (*Post 1, Post 2, Post 3, Post 4*) with vacation activities and experiences controlled for health and well-being before vacation (*Pre*)	175
12.1	Semi-structured interview questions	204

Contributors

Zoë Alexander, PhD candidate, Faculty of Design, Media and Management, School of Travel and Aviation, Buckinghamshire New University, United Kingdom.

Ali Bakir, PhD, Principal Lecturer (Research), Sport, Leisure, Tourism and Music, Buckinghamshire New University, United Kingdom.

Mihaly Csikszentmihalyi, PhD, Distinguished Professor of Psychology and Management, Claremont Graduate University, United States of America.

Jessica de Bloom, PhD, Department of Work and Organisational Psychology, Radboud University in Nijmegen, the Netherlands; current affiliation: University of Tampere, Finland.

Sebastian Filep, PhD, Lecturer, Department of Tourism, University of Otago, New Zealand; Honorary Research Fellow, Victoria University, Australia.

Sabine Geurts, PhD, Professor, Work and Organisational Psychology, Radboud University, Nijmegen, the Netherlands.

Christina Hagger, PhD, Research Fellow, Joanna Briggs Institute, Faculty of Health Sciences, University of Adelaide, Australia.

Michiel Kompier, PhD, Head of the Department of Work and Organisational Psychology, Radboud University, Nijmegen, the Netherlands.

Jennifer Laing, PhD, Senior Lecturer, Department of Marketing and Tourism and Hospitality, La Trobe University, Australia.

Xavier Matteucci, PhD, External Researcher and Lecturer, Department of Tourism and Hospitality Management, MODUL University, Vienna, Austria.

Gábor Michalkó, PhD, DSc, Professor of Tourism, Kodolányi János University of Applied Sciences, Hungary.

Duncan Murray, PhD, Senior Lecturer, School of Management, University of South Australia, Australia.

Anja Pabel, PhD candidate, School of Business, James Cook University, Australia.

Jan Packer, PhD, Senior Research Fellow, School of Tourism, University of Queensland, Australia.

Jenny Panchal, PhD, School of Business, James Cook University, Australia.

Philip Pearce, PhD, Foundation Professor, School of Business, James Cook University, Australia.

Tamara Rátz, PhD, Professor of Tourism, Head of Tourism Department, Kodolányi János University of Applied Sciences, Hungary.

Glenn Ross, PhD, Adjunct Professor of Tourism, James Cook University, Australia.

Rob Saunders, PhD candidate, Monash University, Australia.

Betty Weiler, PhD, Professor, School of Tourism and Hospitality Management, Southern Cross University, Australia.

Mieke Witsel, PhD, Lecturer, School of Tourism and Hospitality Management, Southern Cross University, Australia.

Foreword

Mihaly Csikszentmihalyi

Psychologists who study what makes life worthwhile are lucky: they are exposed to some of the most exciting and invigorating aspects of existence. Among them, those who study tourism are among the most fortunate: the various activities that comprise what we call 'tourism' are unusually rewarding. And not only is tourism a rich and enriching part of life, but it is also one that can be changed and improved with relative ease; thus it lends itself to a variety of 'interventions' that might add a great deal to the overall quality of life.

It is therefore difficult to understand why we do not have a stronger presence of tourism research in the field of positive psychology. Or more precisely, why we did not have one. Because now Sebastian Filep and Philip Pearce, who have contributed a great deal to what we know about tourism from a positive psychological perspective, have brought together a volume that will become an invaluable benchmark for many years to come.

Tourism, in one form or another, has been a way to enrich life for as long as humans have left a record of their actions. Herodotus used his travels to learn about the various strange people and unknown lands that surrounded Greece, and wrote down what he saw and experienced. Others have travelled to relax from stress, to recover from illness, to complete their education, to gain points for a pleasant eternal life by visiting shrines, and many, many other reasons. And they still do.

Despite the availability of information that electronics has put at our disposal, visiting the alleys of an Arab city with its unique sights, sounds, smells; and to look the inhabitants in the eye, see their frowns and their smiles, is an experience that no book, movie or video can begin to duplicate. A food market in China, the view of the Alps at sunrise, mingling with the neighbourhood families gossiping in the marble splendour of a Venetian square – are some of the thousands of memories that at the end of life one might return to with a feeling of gratitude for the privilege of having been alive.

Now that travelling is no longer a luxury for the few, it is important that we learn more about how tourism – which like everything else, can be a trivial waste of time if it is not done well – can help people to open up their lives to all sorts of new dimensions. For all of us, this volume can lead to richer and more meaningful experiences.

Claremont, CA, 2012

Acknowledgements

We would like to acknowledge professional assistance of several people who have helped us finalise this volume. We are particularly appreciative for assistance provided by Trudie Walters, advanced level PhD Candidate at the University of Otago. Trudie has been instrumental in bringing this book project to completion. Trudie provided us with the following technical assistance: detailed corrections of grammar, spelling and English language expression throughout the volume, completion of list of contents, reference checks (in-text citation checks, reference list corrections and Harvard style formatting), formatting of tables and figures, headings and subheadings, and collation of abstracts into a single document as per Routledge guidelines. She has also graced us with her genuinely kind and courteous demeanour and in times of stress, diligently helped us move the book project forward. For their encouragement of this edited book initiative, we would also like to thank friends and colleagues at the Department of Tourism, University of Otago and at the Centre for Tourism and Services Research of Victoria University in Melbourne. Colleagues and postgraduate students at James Cook University, Queensland, Australia, have interests and ongoing studies in this area and their support is also warmly acknowledged.

We owe special thanks to Distinguished Professor Mihaly Csikszentmihalyi, a leading international scholar and senior researcher, best known for his research of flow experiences and for seminal, introductory, positive psychology works. Professor Csikszentmihalyi has written a foreword to this book; our research community is grateful for his words of encouragement and support and for his contributions to this volume. Finally the support of our immediate families has been critical to the completion of the book. We thank them for their patience and understanding.

1 Introducing tourist experience and fulfilment research

Sebastian Filep and Philip Pearce

Our research problem

Towards the end of 2012 the United Nations World Tourism Organisation provided a press release signifying that one billion tourists had crossed international borders during the year (UNWTO, 2012). Undoubtedly this figure will be quoted and re-quoted by tourism students and scholars as they use it to justify, albeit indirectly, the significance of their work. The attention to the statistic of one billion tourists at the start of this book is much more circumspect. It is difficult to provide coherent generalisations about even one million tourists, let alone one billion, even when they are from the same demographic segments and from the same country. It is therefore appropriate to identify our interests in the topic of tourist experience and fulfilment as consistently localised and specific. Our broad intention in this book is to highlight the way well-defined groups of tourists travelling in particular ways to specific kinds of tourist places develop their sense of well-being.

This sense of purpose is not apologetic or necessarily limiting for the scope of the work. A persistent and mindful appreciation however that each chapter describes a component part of the total tourism jigsaw is important. A prevailing awareness that each study and treatment of tourist experience and fulfilment is specific might prevent the problem of researchers seeing contradictions across studies where none really exist. A focus on the context and an awareness of tourism as a variegated phenomenon is also a healthy reminder that many tourist groups remain to be studied as we apply the concepts of positive psychology to tourists' personal growth and well-being. Couch surfing tourists and those who volunteer their time for altruistic purposes are a part of the jigsaw of fulfilment opportunities but so too and in different ways are the package tourists emerging from the growth tourism markets of India and China.

In the following chapters the multiple personal benefits which people may realise through tourism are considered. Insights from the theories and methods of positive psychology help define the special contribution of the work (Seligman and Csikszentmihalyi, 2000). The book seeks to complement the vast body of knowledge on health and wellness in tourism (Voigt and Pforr, 2013). The work reported in the following chapters also complements emerging traditions of research on transformative travel (Reisinger, 2013) and experience economy perspectives on personally enriching consumption processes (Gilmore and Pine, 2002; Morgan et al., 2010). In these contributions, however, authors often do not access the core literature in psychology that underpins this volume (Pearce and Packer, 2012). As such, we aim to enrich investigations of quality of life and tourist behaviour from psychological standpoints such as those offered by Neal et al. (2007) and contemporary work in leisure studies on accentuating the positive value of leisure behaviour (Stebbins, 2011; Freire, 2013). Drawing on insights and theories from the research field of positive psychology, this edited volume presents 12 original research chapters investigating fulfilling tourist experiences. The work has a positive, optimistic and potentially personally rewarding tone. It forms a contrast to the more extensive research into so-called 'dark tourist' experiences, such as those involving visits to battlegrounds and places of genocide (Dann, 1998; Stone and Sharpley, 2008; Institute for Dark Tourism Research, 2013).

According to the Oxford dictionary, fulfilment is 'the achievement of something desired, promised, or predicted' or a 'satisfaction or happiness as a result of fully developing one's potential'. It is further defined as the meeting of a requirement, condition or need (Oxford Dictionaries, 2013). Fulfilment is therefore a broad term that encompasses diverse aspects of well-being and this broad definition fits the labels of the part titles in this book. The happiness and humour, and meaning and self-actualisation parts respectively resemble the hedonic and the eudaimonic conception of well-being, suggesting that tourist experiences are clearly not just about hedonism, but a sense of achievement, meaning and purpose in life. The health and restoration parts fit the physical well-being dimension of fulfilment. Before we outline the book structure in more detail, we address research challenges which need to be considered in empirical examinations of tourist experience and fulfilment through the lenses of positive psychology.

Our research challenges

First, there is the challenge of defining key terms, such as happiness – a subject of one of the part headings in our volume. Holt (2006) in his review of McMahon's book, *Happiness: A History*, argues in jest that the history of the idea of happiness could be thought of in terms of a series of bumper stickers: happiness – luck (Homeric era), happiness – virtue (Classical era), happiness – heaven (Medieval era), happiness – pleasure (Enlightenment era) and happiness – warm puppy (Contemporary era). He argues that in each era societies have had their own interpretation of happiness. The reality of clearly defining happiness is a far more intricate process than the bumper stickers would suggest and the nature of happiness has puzzled Western and non-Western philosophers for more than two millennia (Tatarkiewicz, 1976).

Kesebir and Diener (2008) suggest, however, that while modern psychologists cannot hope to define happiness to everyone's satisfaction, they have uncovered coherent and separate components of subjective well-being. These components include life satisfaction (global judgements of one's life), satisfaction with important life domains (satisfaction with one's work, health, marriage, etc.), positive affect (prevalence of positive emotions and moods) and low levels of negative affect (prevalence of unpleasant emotions and moods). There are also more prescriptive and less subjective theories that specify certain needs that have to be fulfilled (such as self-acceptance and mastery) as a prerequisite of happiness. These theories, such as Ryff and Singer's (1996) concept of psychological well-being, and Ryan and Deci's (2001) self-determination theory are more akin to the eudaemonist flourishing theories of happiness of the classical era, like those of Aristotle (Tiberius, 2006). Both conceptions of happiness – the subjective well-being conception and the eudaemonist conception – have been utilised by researchers to help define happiness of tourists (Nawijn, 2011; Filep, 2012). Any academic attempts at defining happiness in the context of tourist experiences, hence must take into account these theories of happiness. Therefore while a formulaic definition of happiness may not exist and while we recognise the complexity of the term, we rest on the shoulders of the subjective well-being and the eudaemonist theories (e.g. Ryan and Deci, 2001; Seligman, 2011). Happiness is mostly, if not entirely, a conscious state of mind (Veenhoven, 2000). A consistent approach in this volume from the authors has been to address research challenge of defining happiness by referring to the theories of happiness from modern psychology.

The second challenge we faced in this empirical examination related to the variability of tourist experiences. Sharpley and Stone (2012, p. 7) argue:

> the tourism-happiness equation is infinitely variable; people consume tourism in numerous different ways and for a multitude of different reasons, whilst the source of happiness or contentedness undoubtedly varies significantly from one person to another. Therefore, there is no simple answer to the question: is to experience tourism to experience happiness?

We have addressed this second research challenge of variability by recognising that tourist experiences are diverse but also by recognising that we are able to imperfectly bring together our empirical contributions under a single umbrella of tourist experience and fulfilment. Much of tourist behaviour is indeed complex and variable, yet our colleagues have over the years developed many conceptual schemes and theoretical models to study the tourist experience (Ryan, 2002; Morgan *et al.*, 2010). Research on the complex state of flow (optimal state of meeting a challenge) has received much empirical focus in tourism and leisure (Ryan, 1995; Han *et al.*, 2005), yet we know flow is a deeply subjective state, comprising immediate conscious dimensions such as time transformation or unambiguous feedback (Csikszentmihalyi, 1975). So while the experience of happiness might include a strong degree of subjectivity which would make it variable and hard to study empirically, the tourism research problem is not very different to that characterising the studies on leisure and flow. Sharpley and

Stone (2012) highlight the perspective that people consume tourism for a multitude of different reasons and in numerous ways. Their argument effectively implies that we cannot study such variable systems. It is our argument that it is possible to respect diversity and to study diversity. Some guidance here for studies of fulfilment reside in the study of motivation. Certainly tourists vary in their motives but there are patterns of motives which can be identified for coherent clusters of tourists (Pearce, 2005, 2011). Certainly we have persevered with the study of tourist motivation for decades despite the challenges (Harrill and Potts, 2002; Hsu and Huang, 2008). The infinite variability argument need not be a permanent impediment to the study of human experiences. Social scientists have studied the complexities of variable human behaviour for centuries and have been able to develop insights in many complex topic areas. It is the contention of this volume that contexts do matter and variability must be recognised but tourist experience and happiness or fulfilment studies can be assembled in ways which provide some coherent overviews of the forces involved. An overview of key themes the editors see as emerging from the research chapters will be presented in the concluding chapter.

A third research challenge also shapes the style of work in this volume. A persistent challenge lies in reconciling the relationship between tourism as a commercial phenomenon and greater well-being of those who travel. Some would argue tourist experiences are about consumption and consumption has been linked to depression – not happiness or greater fulfilment (DeLeire and Kalil, 2010). While we agree that consumption is an often inescapable part of tourism (as reported in *Tourists, Tourism and the Good Life*; Pearce et al., 2011) we are hesitant to suggest the totality of tourism leads to depression because materialism is linked to depression (Kasser, 2002). It will be noted in several of the research chapters that the tourist experience often leads to higher subjective well-being levels compared to non-tourist experiences. Occasionally holidays result in enhanced levels of eudaimonic well-being. It is useful here to distinguish tourism from other forms of consumption and perhaps part of the reason for this paradox about tourism is that while most people may trade in an old vehicle for a better vehicle, many may be hesitant to trade in their holiday memories. Tourist experiences are simply not commercial commodities like bars of soap or old vehicles even though many tourist experiences may involve shopping for tangible goods.

The fourth research challenge is sometimes raised by critical tourism scholars (Higgins-Desbiolles and Whyte, 2013). The argument is that tourism is an activity that is simply outside the reach of many people, so why should we worry about the well-being of those privileged few who can afford to travel? There are, in research terms, always other problems and topics which might be seen as more valuable or ethical areas of endeavour that are seen to matter more than others (Becher and Trowler, 2001; Thouless, 1938). We can however report that there can be direct and indirect benefits to studying the well-being of tourists. A better understanding of what makes certain groups of tourists value their experiences may lead to a more complete understanding of the inadequacies as well as the strengths of current tourism practices. There are then consequences here not just for tourists but for communities, business and the very heart of positive health and sustainability. As editors we have addressed one component of this challenge by asking contributors to report on a diverse set of tourist experiences in this volume. We do not advocate expensive, environmentally destructive or indulgent long-haul travel. Packer's research chapter for example reports on benefits of tourist experiences in parks and gardens – experiences that are arguably affordable and accessible to a diverse cohort of individuals. Positive psychology is not a psychology of luxury whose benefits accrue to the rich and the untroubled but is for everyone (Seligman, 2011). We have also recently commenced a research initiative that examines well-being derived from tourist experiences by underprivileged minority groups (Filep and Bereded-Samuel, 2012). In fact Sharpley and Stone (2012) highlight that the cost of holiday may not be related to the level of happiness it generates; subsequently, a cheap holiday may in fact lead to considerable happiness.

Sharpley and Stone (2012) also suggest people may travel out of habit and they question if habit can be equated to happiness. For us a more important question here is what kind of behaviours do people engage in when they habitually travel? Clearly some tourist habits are destructive as they are personally addictive and bad for the environment – for example 'binge flying' or travelling frequently and to many different destinations (Cohen *et al.*, 2011). There are, however, many potentially beneficial tourist habits which have received limited empirical focus, such as the use of humour with travel companions (Mitas *et al.*, 2012) or acts of kindness, generosity and gratitude in numerous cross cultural tourist–host situations (Duckworth *et al.*, 2005). The view that tourists can learn to cultivate positive habits should not be dismissed as necessarily naïve optimism or a defence of the commercial tourism business. Some 'habits' that characterise some of the positive tourist experiences have changed in recent years, consumer consciousness towards pro-environment actions are an example, and some are documented in this volume. A biochemist turned Buddhist monk, Matthieu Ricard, argues we can train our minds in habits of well-being to generate a sense of fulfilment (TED, 2012); we therefore reiterate the comments made by Csikszentmihalyi in the foreword, that tourism lends itself to a variety of interventions that might add a great deal to the overall quality of life.

Our research team

Our team includes a growing international team of scholars who study tourist experiences from a positive psychology perspective. As editors we have tried to incorporate contributions by senior as well as emerging scholars, male and female researchers and from various countries. Our friends and colleagues – authors of this volume are: Dr Mieke Witsel, Ms Zoë Alexander, Dr Ali Bakir, Ms Anja Pabel, Dr Jenny Panchal, Dr Jan Packer, Dr Xavier Matteucci, Dr Christina Hagger, Dr Duncan Murray, Mr Rob Saunders, Dr Jennifer Laing, Professor Betty Weiler, Dr Jessica de Bloom, Professor Sabine Geurts, Professor

Michael Kompier, Professor Gábor Michalkó, Professor Tamara Rátz and Professor Glenn Ross. The following outlines biographical statements of each author to better introduce the contributors to the readers.

Dr Mieke Witsel, PhD (SCU), MA (University of Amsterdam) is an academic with the School of Tourism and Hospitality Management at Southern Cross University in Australia. With an international background in sociology, language and culture and social psychology, she has been teaching and lecturing in intercultural, interpersonal and business communication, and tourism and leisure for more than 20 years. She has worked in Australia and Europe, at various levels of education, ranging from undergraduate to postgraduate and corporate levels. Mieke's research focuses on tourism education, intercultural communication, sustainability and interpersonal competence. Mieke is a member of Centre for Tourism Leisure and Work (CTLW), the International Positive Psychology Association (IPPA), the Council for Australasian University Tourism and Hospitality Educators (CAUTHE) and the Academy of Hope.

Zoë Alexander is a PhD student at the Faculty of Design, Media and Management, School of Travel and Aviation, Buckinghamshire New University, UK. Her research interest is in 'the self' (the tourist) and the impact that tourism has on the individual. Recent publications on this subject include: an investigation into the impact of vacation travel on the tourist in the *International Journal of Tourism Research* and a chapter titled 'Understanding voluntourism: a Glaserian grounded theory study', in *Volunteer Tourism: Theoretical Framework to Practical Applications*, edited by Angela M. Benson. Her research is undertaken at Buckinghamshire New University, UK, under the guidance of Dr Ali Bakir and Dr Eugenia Wickens. Her academic background is psychology, a subject she taught in Adult Education. In 2007, she completed her MSc in Tourism Management and Development to support her tourism business in Cape Town and Scotland. Her commercial background is Project Management and she has worked for a large retailer in the UK. Her interests lie in the development of self, horses and hiking.

Dr Ali Bakir, PhD, lectures on Strategy and Marketing in Sport, Leisure, Tourism and Music at Buckinghamshire New University, UK. He also leads the School's sports management postgraduate programme. Ali's research interests lie in interpretive studies in strategy and the creative and cultural industries. He is Editor-in-Chief of the Journal of Crowd Safety and Security Management (JCSSM); member of the Editorial Board of The London Journal of Tourism, Sport and Creative Industries (LJTSCI); and creative industries expert reviewer to Emerald Group Publishing. He is a regular reviewer of a number of academic journals in Tourism and Management, and is frequently called upon to serve as member of scientific committees of tourism conferences. Ali graduated from the University of Newcastle-Upon-Tyne with BSc (Hons) in Geology and Chemistry and MSc in Rock Mechanics and Engineering Geology; obtained the PGCE from the Institute of Education, University of London; and was awarded an MBA and a PhD in Strategy from the University of Essex.

Anja Pabel is currently a PhD student at the School of Business, James Cook University in Australia. She holds a Bachelor of Business with Honours majoring in tourism management. Her Honours research project examined how certified scuba divers perceive their Great Barrier Reef experience compared to other reef destinations. Her PhD investigates the role of humour in the tourism setting. As part of this research project humour is considered from the perspective of positive psychology where it is regarded as one of the virtues or character strengths that can lead to life satisfaction. The research project will assess whether humour can be used to create more enjoyable tourism experiences.

Jenny H. Panchal completed her Masters in Tourism Management at the Victoria University of Wellington (VUW) in New Zealand. She was a PhD student at the School of Business, James Cook University in Townsville, Australia, at the time of writing the book chapter. Her doctoral thesis focused on Asian spa experiences, tourist behaviour and positive psychology. She investigated spa-going motivations of tourists while travelling in Asia. She incorporated positive psychology concepts in her project by identifying flow experiences resulting from spa activities. She explored the extent to which spa experiences contribute to holistic wellness.

Dr Jan Packer, PhD, has a BA with Honours in Psychology (University of Queensland, 1976) and a PhD in Education (QUT, 2004). Her research in the area of positive psychology and tourism has focused on visitors' perceptions of the nature, value and benefits of museum experiences (Packer, 2008), museums as restorative environments (Packer and Bond, 2010) and the impact of music festival attendance on young people's psychological and social well-being (Packer and Ballantyne, 2011). This research has contributed to theoretical understandings in the field and introduced new ways of conceptualising the nature and outcomes of visitor experiences. Her most recent study has focused on 'capturing' the visitor experience at cultural attractions, activities and events using an innovative adjective checklist approach. Since 2005, Dr Packer has been the Chief Editor of the international academic journal *Visitor Studies*, which is published by Routledge in the United States.

Dr Xavier Matteucci is an external academic at the Department of Tourism and Hospitality Management at MODUL University, Vienna, Austria. His main research interests lie in the areas of travel experiences, transformative travel, cultural tourism and sustainability. Xavier's doctoral research examined external and personal factors that influence the tourist experience of intangible heritage with a particular view to understand the role that the body and senses play in that experience. Xavier's work has been published in both French and English in the form of conference and refereed journal articles.

Dr Christina Hagger, PhD, is a Research Fellow in the Joanna Briggs Institute in the Faculty of Health Sciences at the University of Adelaide where she focuses on the synthesis of qualitative research. She has a professional background in both health and tourism policy and this underpins her research which is situated within a context of positive ageing. Her research focuses on understanding the psychological benefits of tourism for a healthy retired population who have lost the sense of meaning associated with their former employment role. Christina is interested in the translation of evidence into advice for policymakers and, in particular, the potential to more broadly introduce an adapted version of the Social Tourism model for retirees.

Dr Duncan Murray, PhD, is a Senior Lecturer in Sport and Recreation Management, in the School of Management at the University of South Australia. He is founding member of the Centre for Tourism and Leisure Management. His research focuses on understanding the psychology behind volitional behaviour, including participation and involvement in fitness, sport and tourism, service quality in sport and tourism settings, physical appearance and consumer behaviour, and issues of life satisfaction and personality. He has published over 20 journal articles as well as numerous refereed conference papers and is internationally recognised for his work in consumer behaviour research. Duncan's recent work has included a focus on reconceptualising the future and how leisure and tourism patterns may be seen as reflective of wider generational and social cycles. He is particularly interested in how leisure and tourism will face the next 20 years of generational change.

Rob Saunders is a PhD candidate at Monash University. Before beginning his PhD journey, Rob worked in national park management in Victoria and Tasmania for 30 years. His responsibilities included visitor interpretation and communication, park policy and planning, visitor research, and risk management. A life-long passion for walking as a means of exploring natural and cultural values in a variety of countries stimulated Rob's interest in the cultural history and meanings of walking, and led to his research on the psychological benefits of long-distance walking. His qualifications include a Master of Environmental Science from Monash University.

Dr Jennifer Laing, PhD, is a Senior Lecturer in the Department of Marketing and Tourism and Hospitality, La Trobe University, and has a law and marketing background. Her research interests include travel narratives, the role of myth in tourism and extraordinary tourist experiences. Her PhD focused on motivations for travelling to frontier regions. Jennifer has published in journals such as *Annals of Tourism Research*, *Tourism Analysis* and *Journal of Sustainable Tourism*. She was the recipient of the 2010 Council for Australian Tourism and Hospitality Education (CAUTHE) Fellows Award for Tourism and Hospitality Research, and was recently appointed a convenor of the International Tourism and Media Conference.

Professor Betty Weiler, PhD, is Professor in the School of Tourism and Hospitality Management at Southern Cross University. Her research has focused on ecotourism, nature and heritage interpretation, tour guiding, persuasive communication with tourists, and the tourist experience and has published widely in these areas. She has also managed numerous national and international research projects, many focused on enhancing the quality of the tourist experience. Known for her collaborative approach to research, Betty has worked to produce practical research products and tools in partnership with industry.

Dr Jessica de Bloom was a PhD student at the Department of Work and Organisational Psychology at the Radboud University in Nijmegen, the Netherlands, at the time of writing the book chapter. Jessica studied psychology at the

University of Twente in the Netherlands. She specialised in Safety and Health Psychology in her Bachelor degree and Work and Organisational Psychology in her Masters degree. During the four years Jessica was working in Nijmegen, she conducted a meta-analysis and several longitudinal field studies on the effects of vacations on health, well-being, work performance and creativity. She focused on the impact of vacation activities and experiences on health and well-being changes during and after vacation. She communicated the results of these studies in several empirical papers published in academic journals in the field of occupational health psychology.

Professor Sabine Geurts, PhD, is a Professor in Work and Organisational Psychology. Since 2000 Sabine has worked as an Associate Professor at the Department of Work and Organisational Psychology at the Radboud University in Nijmegen, the Netherlands. In 2000 she earned an Aspasia grant from the Netherlands Organisation for Scientific Research (NWO) for her research qualifications. Her expertise as a senior researcher and lecturer is in the field of occupational health psychology. Her scientific work covers a broad area with special interests in effort, stress and recovery, work–home interaction, workplace absenteeism and work disability. Sabine has published over 70 papers and book chapters in these areas, serves as a reviewer for various national and international scientific journals, and works as a Consulting Editor for the journal *Work and Stress*. She participates as a full member in the KNAW acknowledged Behavioral Science Institute (BSI), and is a member of the BSI Scientific Committee.

Professor Michiel Kompier, PhD, is head of the Department of Work and Organisational Psychology at the Radboud University Nijmegen, the Netherlands. His research concentrates on the research field of work, stress and health. He has published many (inter)national articles, books and book chapters on topics such as work stress, the psychosocial work environment, work motivation, job design, mental work load, sickness absenteeism, work disability, work and health, productivity, overtime work, work–home interaction and working conditions policies. In his studies the emphasis is on the psychological and behavioural mechanisms between work characteristics and health and performance, prevention and intervention studies in organisations and applied research methodology. Michiel is Associate-Editor of the *Scandinavian Journal of Work, Environment and Health*, member of the international advisory board of the *Journal of Occupational Health Psychology* and member of the editorial boards of *Work and Stress* and the *International Journal of Stress and Health*.

Dr Tamara Rátz, PhD, is a Professor of Tourism and Head of the Tourism Department at the Kodolányi János University of Applied Sciences in Hungary. She is also a Visiting Lecturer at HAMK University of Applied Sciences in Finland. She is the author or co-author of seven books and more than 120 book chapters or journal papers. Her current research interests include the complex relationship between tourism and quality of life, and cultural and heritage tourism development. Her latest major research projects include tourism as a catalyst in the European integration process (2006–2009, supported by the

Bolyai Research Scholarship of the Hungarian Academy of Sciences) and health tourism and quality of life (2007–2011, supported by the Hungarian National Scientific Fund, with Gábor Michalkó).

Dr Glenn Ross, PhD, is Adjunct Professor of Tourism at James Cook University. He is a Fellow of the International Academy for the Study of Tourism, a Member of the Australian Psychological Society (MAPS), a Member of the Division of Research and Teaching within the Australian Psychological Society, an Associate Fellow of the British Psychological Society (AFBPsS), a Member of the Divisions of Teachers and Researchers in Psychology within the British Psychological Society, a Member of the Association of Psychological Science (formerly the American Psychological Society) and he has a Chartered Status within the British Psychological Society (CPsychol). His research interests are primarily tourism ethics, tourist behaviour and senior tourism. Dr Ross's recent award includes the winner of the 2005 Elsevier/International Journal of Hospitality Management Prize for the Best Paper in 2004.

Dr Gábor Michalkó, PhD, DSc, is Scientific Advisor at the Geographical Research Institute of the Hungarian Academy of Sciences and Professor of Tourism at the Kodolányi János University of Applied Sciences, Hungary. He graduated from the University of Debrecen, Hungary, in 1993 with a Master degree in Geography and History. He also received a BA in Tourism from the Budapest Business School in 2000. He was awarded a PhD in Geography by the University of Debrecen in 1998, and a DSc in Geography by the Hungarian Academy of Sciences in 2009. He has published five books and more than 100 scientific articles in different languages. His recent research interests include urban tourism, shopping tourism, human ecology of tourism and the relationship between tourism and quality of life. His latest major research projects include the happiness-inducing role of tourism (2006–2009, supported by the Bolyai Research Scholarship of the Hungarian Academy of Sciences) and health tourism and quality of life (2007–2011, supported by the Hungarian National Scientific Fund, with Tamara Rátz).

Our book structure

The chapters by the contributors are grouped under three broad areas or parts: (1) happiness and humour; (2) meaning and self-actualisation, and (3) health and restoration. The part headings reflect a range of positive psychological outcomes that personal holiday experiences can produce.

The first part broadly covers the topic of happiness and humour. First, Pearce and Pabel explore the role of humour in tourism. They provide a framework depicting the links between humour and tourism, both as an integrating device linking key facets of the topic and as a guide to stimulating further inquiry. Witsel then analyses a subset of business travellers and provides a qualitative analysis of teaching in multicultural and transnational contexts leading to happiness outcomes. Rátz and Michalkó's chapter follows. In their Hungarian based study, happiness inducing benefits of tourism are explored. The analysis of the

Introducing tourist experience and fulfilment 11

interviews describing the respondents' travel-related happiness experiences showed that most of the experiences reflect the presence of both cognitive benefits (e.g. mindfulness, total concentration) and affective benefits (e.g. relaxation, tranquillity). Finally, Jenny Panchal's chapter ends this part on happiness and humour. She examines flow experiences of spa tourists to highlight the personal benefits achieved through these experiences in tourism. The findings presented in this chapter were extracted from an on-site survey of tourist spa goers in India, Thailand and the Philippines. The research study shows that while the changing phases of tourist behaviour can be truly stimulating, exciting, puzzling and perplexing at the same time, spa experiences can increase tourists' happiness.

A part on meaning and self-actualisation follows and explores the eudaimonic dimensions of fulfilment. This part opens with a chapter by Ross who provides an overview of the research area of religious travel, highlighting the various contributions that draw an association between religious expression and well-being. Matteucci then follows in this part with a chapter that is concerned with how tourists in Spain experience intangible heritage, taking the example of flamenco as an art form. The data revealed a number of themes which represent the tourist experience as a spiritual journey. An essential aspect of the spiritual experience is the active involvement of individuals in intrinsically motivated activities. This study also suggests that the multi-sensory and kinaesthetic experience of music leads to spiritual, eudaimonic, fulfilment. Saunders, Laing and Weiler's chapter then investigates how long-distance walking can help people make positive changes in their lives. In-depth interviews with 20 long-distance walkers were completed. The interviewees reported many personally significant benefits of long-distance walking. Among other findings, results from in-depth interviews highlight that long-distance walking provides an environment conducive to eudaimonia. In the final chapter of this part, Alexander and Bakir employ in-depth interviews to gain insight into the volunteering tourist experiences in South Africa and any resulting changes in the volunteers' day-to-day lives. The findings point to significant positive changes in seven traits, including some eudaimonic outcomes, such as increases in adventurousness, trust and artistic interests.

The third and the final part of the book covers health and restoration benefits of tourist experiences in two chapters. The part addresses the physical health aspects of fulfilment from a positive psychology perspective. De Bloom, Geurts and Kompier's chapter reports on an investigation that shows that health and well-being (H&W) improved during various types of vacations they studied. The increase in H&W during vacation supports the idea that the absence of work demands during vacation enables psychobiological systems to return to baseline, reduces work-load effects and replenishes depleted resources, which in turn enhances basic H&W (McEwen, 1998; Hobfoll, 1989). Consequently, a holiday from work constitutes a powerful opportunity to recover from work demands. The evidence from their research however also suggests that positive vacation effects on basic H&W are generally short-lived: they fade out within the first week after resuming work, independent from the type and duration of the holiday. De Bloom, Geurts and Kompier's chapter is followed by a chapter on healthy ageing and life satisfaction by Hagger and Murray. Hagger and Murray's study aimed to investigate whether multiple tourism experiences by Australian retirees lead to greater life satisfaction. Findings demonstrate that tourism facilitates healthy ageing by increasing overall life satisfaction. The authors argue that there are implications for health and tourism government policies based on their results. Last, Packer's chapter on health and restoration explores tourist experiences in museums and botanic gardens. The aim of her study was to explore, from the perspective of visitors, the circumstances that facilitate and enhance restorative experiences in tourism and leisure contexts, and the ways in which visitors experience the restorative processes. Visitors' comments illustrate the ways in which the unique environments encountered at museums and botanic gardens facilitate restorative processes. Visitors experienced fascination by being engaged in cognitive experiences (especially at the museum) and sensory experiences (especially at the gardens).

A conclusion by the editors offers a synthesis of the key contributions. As readers can notice, this is a research intensive edited book. We required each chapter to report on at least one research study that contributes to a better understanding of tourist experience and fulfilment. We hope that readers will enjoy this volume as much as we enjoyed reviewing the submissions.

References

Becher, T. and Trowler, P. (2001) *Academic Tribes and Territories: Intellectual Enquiry and the Cultures of Disciplines* (2nd edition). Buckingham: Open University Press/SRHE.

Cohen, S.A., Higham, J.E.S. and Cavaliere, C.T. (2011) 'Binge flying: behavioural addiction and climate change', *Annals of Tourism Research*, 38 (3): 1070–1089.

Csikszentmihalyi, M. (1975) *Beyond Boredom and Anxiety*. San Francisco: Jossey Bass.

Dann, G. (1998) 'The dark side of tourism', *Etudes et Rapports, Se'rie L*. Aix-en-Provence: Centre International de Recherches et d'Etudes Touristiques.

DeLeire, T. and Kalil, A. (2010) 'Does consumption buy happiness? Evidence from the United States', *International Review of Economics*, 57 (2): 163–176.

Duckworth, L.A., Steen, T.A. and Seligman, M.E.P. (2005) 'Positive psychology in clinical practice', *Annual Review of Clinical Psychology*, 1: 629–651.

Filep, S. (2012) 'Moving beyond subjective well-being: a tourism critique', *Journal of Hospitality & Tourism Research*, DOI: 10.1177/1096348012436609.

Filep, S. and Bereded-Samuel, E. (2012) 'Holidays against depression? An Ethiopian Australian initiative', *Current Issues in Tourism*, 15 (3): 281–285.

Freire, T. (2013) *Positive Leisure Science: From Subjective Experience to Social Contexts*. New York: Springer.

Gilmore, J. and Pine, B. (2002) 'Customer experience places: the new offering frontier', *Strategy and Leadership*, 30 (4): 4–11.

Han, S.Y., Um, S. and Mills, A. (2005) 'The development of on-site Experience Measurement Scale', *The 11th APTA Conference-New Tourism for Asia-Pacific*. Busan, Korea: Dong-A University, 14–22.

Harrill, R. and Potts, T. (2002) 'Social psychological theories of tourism motivation: exploration, debate and transition', *Tourism Analysis*, 7 (2): 105–114.

Higgins-Desbiolles, F. and Whyte, K.P. (2013) 'No high hopes for hopeful tourism: a critical comment', *Annals of Tourism Research*, 40: 428–433.

Hobfoll, S.E. (1989) 'Conservation of resources: a new attempt at conceptualizing stress', *American Psychologist*, 44 (3): 513–524.

Holt, J. (2006, 12 February). 'Oh, joy' [Review of the book *Happiness: A History*]. *New York Times*, p. 20.

Hsu, C.H.C. and Huang, S. (2008) 'Travel motivation: a critical review of the concept's development', in Woodside, A. and Martin, D. (eds), *Tourism Management Analysis, Behaviour and Strategy*. Wallingford, UK: CABI, pp. 14–27.

Institute for Dark Tourism Research (2013) www.dark-tourism.org.uk/ [Accessed 10 January 2013].

Kasser, T. (2002) *The High Price of Materialism*. Cambridge, MA: MIT Press.

Kesebir, P. and Diener, E. (2008) 'In pursuit of happiness: empirical answers to philosophical questions', *Perspectives on Psychological Science*, 3 (2): 117–125.

McEwen, B.S. (1998) 'Stress, adaptation, and disease: allostasis and allostatic load', *Annals of the New York Academy of Sciences*, 840 (1): 33–44.

Mitas, O., Yarnal, C. and Chick, G. (2012) 'Jokes build community: mature tourists' positive emotions', *Annals of Tourism Research*, 39 (4): 1884–1905.

Morgan, M., Lugosi, P. and Ritchie, J.R.B. (2010) *The Tourism and Leisure Experience: Consumer and Managerial Perspectives*. Bristol, UK: Channel View.

Nawijn, J. (2011) 'Happiness through vacationing: just a temporary boost or long-term benefits?' *Journal of Happiness Studies*, 12 (4): 651–665.

Neal, J., Uysal, M. and Sirgy, J. (2007) 'The effect of tourism services on travellers' quality of life', *Journal of Travel Research*, 46 (2): 154–163.

Oxford Dictionaries (2013) http://oxforddictionaries.com/ [Accessed 10 January 2013].

Packer, J. (2008) 'Beyond learning: exploring visitors' perceptions of the value and benefits of museum experiences', *Curator: The Museum Journal*, 51 (1): 33–54.

Packer, J. and Ballantyne, J. (2011) 'The impact of music festival attendance on young people's psychological and social well-being', *Psychology of Music*, 39 (2): 164–181.

Packer, J. and Bond, N. (2010) 'Museums as restorative environments', *Curator: The Museum Journal*, 53 (4): 421–456.

Pearce, P.L. (2005) *Tourist Behaviour: Themes and Conceptual Schemes*. Clevedon, UK: Channel View Publications.

Pearce, P.L. (2011) *Tourist Behaviour and the Contemporary World*. Bristol, UK: Channel View.

Pearce, P.L. and Packer, J. (2012) 'Minds on the move: refreshing the links from psychology to tourism studies', *Annals of Tourism Research*, DOI:101016/j.annals.2012.10.002.

Pearce, P.L., Filep, S. and Ross, G. (2011) *Tourists, Tourism and the Good Life*. New York, NY: Routledge.

Reisinger, Y. (2013) *Transformational Tourism: Tourist Perspectives*. Wallingford, UK: CABI.

Ryan, C. (1995) *Researching Tourist Satisfaction: Issues, Concepts, Problems*. New York, NY: Routledge.

Ryan, C. (2002) *The Tourist Experience*. London: Continuum.

Ryan, R.M. and Deci, E.L. (2001) 'On happiness and human potentials: a review of research on hedonic and eudaimonic well-being', *Annual Review of Psychology*, 52: 141–166.

Ryff, C.D. and Singer, B. (1996) 'Psychological well-being: meaning, measurement and implications for psychotherapy research', *Psychotherapy and Psychosomatics*, 6 (1): 14–23.

Seligman, M.E.P. (2011) *Flourish*. Sydney, Australia: Random House.
Seligman, M.E.P. and Csikszentmihalyi, M. (2000) 'Positive psychology: an introduction', *American Psychologist*, 55 (1): 5–14.
Sharpley, R. and Stone, P. (2012) 'Introduction: experiencing tourism, experiencing happiness?' in Sharpley, R. and Stone, P. (eds), *Contemporary Tourist Experience: Concepts and Consequences*. New York, NY: Routledge, pp. 1–8.
Stebbins, R. (2011) 'Leisure studies: the road ahead', *World Leisure Journal*, 53 (1): 3–10.
Stone, P. and Sharpley, R. (2008) 'Consuming dark tourism: a thanatological perspective', *Annals of Tourism Research*, 35 (2): 574–595.
Tatarkiewicz, W. (1976) *Analysis of Happiness*. Warsaw: Polish Scientific Publishers.
TED (2012) *Matthieu Ricard: The Habits of Happiness*; video on TED.com. www.ted.com/talks/matthieu_ricard_on_the_habits_of_happiness.html [Accessed 8 January 2013].
Thouless, R. (1938) *Straight and Crooked Thinking*. London: Pan.
Tiberius, V. (2006) 'Well-being: psychological research for philosophers', *Philosophy Compass*, 1 (5): 493–505.
UNWTO (2012, 12 December). *International Tourism Hits One Billion*. http://media.unwto.org/en/press-release/2012-12-12/international-tourism-hits-one-billion [Accessed 7 January 2013].
Veenhoven, R. (2000) 'The four qualities of life', *Journal of Happiness Studies*, 1: 1–39.
Voigt, C. and Pforr, C. (2013) *Wellness Tourism*. New York, NY: Routledge.

Part I
Happiness and humour

2 Humour, tourism and positive psychology

Philip Pearce and Anja Pabel

Introduction

Peter Collett, a prominent British commentator on social behaviour, argues that humour and laughter are central to our well-being and social judgements. In particular, he observes that those who respond to our humour and jokes are seen as attractive to us. Those who fail to laugh with us are seen much less favourably (Collett, 2004). In earlier analyses other social psychologists argued that appreciating and responding to humour can generate positive health outcomes by reducing stress and enhancing personal control (Argyle, 1987; Solomon, 1996). Positive psychologists have identified having a sense of humour as a core character strength. In this view humour is effectively a virtue which helps individuals forge connections to the larger universe and provides them with meaning (Peterson and Seligman, 2004; Park *et al.*, 2005).

Following these multiple perspectives, it can be suggested that, at least in contemporary Western society, having a good sense of humour is widely regarded as a positive trait. The temptation to suggest that a good sense of humour is a positive universal trait is appealing, although the ways in which humour is displayed and appreciated across cultures may be quite different and not easily understood by external observers (Dann, 1996). In tourism studies the role of humour has been specifically identified as first, helping tourists concentrate, second, assisting them to relax and feel comfortable in novel settings, and finally as being useful in enhancing their connections with others (Pearce, 2009).

In this chapter two kinds of evidence will be used to add to our understanding of the humour–tourism connection. The first kind of material to be considered will be humour produced for tourists; that is communication designed to appeal to tourists' sense of humour. Instances of this kind of humour will be drawn from tourism businesses and awareness campaigns. A second source of information to build our understanding of the tourism humour connection consists of humour produced by tourists. In particular humorous blogs written by tourists will be considered. This dual approach is consistent with the view that researching a sense of humour must consider the ability to comprehend humorous situations and a different and independent ability to produce humour (Köhler and Ruch, 1996).

As an additional consideration the concept of optimism can usefully be included in these introductory observations. The suggestion here is that being able to laugh about a situation may be a part of a style which creates a positive and optimistic problem solving approach to daily life which in turn promotes well-being (Diener and Biswas-Diener, 2008). The potential to add to the positive psychology literature itself arises due to the novelty and challenges of the many situations which confront tourists. For example, instances of culture confusion represent interesting opportunities to study both optimism and humour beyond that which exists in everyday working and social worlds (Hottola, 2004). In summary, this chapter seeks to build the further understanding of humour in tourism contexts through linking the work to positive psychology approaches (including optimism). The discussion specifically addresses two kinds of humour – that offered to tourists in select settings and that produced by tourists when recording their experiences.

Literature review

Defining a sense of humour

Scholars have spent considerable effort in characterising the two meanings (appreciation and production) of a sense of humour. Martin (2007), for example, suggests that the perception of humour may involve habitual behaviour (such as people who laugh easily), temperament differences (such as ongoing cheerfulness), cognitive abilities (being able to comprehend subtleties and incongruities), select attitudes (a positive view of humour) and a world view which embraces a non-serious outlook on life. By way of contrast, the production of humour is dependent on individuals being good self-monitors (that is sensing how others are reacting to them) as well as having the memory, creativity and divergent thinking skills to spot the comic components of situations (Feingold and Mazzella, 1991; Köhler and Ruch, 1996). This production component may be readily related to tourists' on-site experiences where identifying and joking about the odd, the bizarre and the unusual may ease social tensions in groups and provide social harmony (cf. Pearce, 2005, p. 115). One familiar interpretation of these two different meanings of a sense of humour resides in everyday statements where people assert that they enjoy humour (appreciation) but are unable to remember jokes or effectively tell funny stories (production).

Humour and individual differences

One immediate response to a discussion of humour is that it is often seen as depending on an individual's personal style. The detailed studies of the links between personality types and humour appreciation have revealed a number of enduring and consistent relationships (Ruch, 1994; Martin, 2007). Factor analytic studies suggest that most of the variation in humour appreciation is accounted for not so much by content but by the structure of the humour. The dominant categories involved in humour appreciation are first incongruity, and second, nonsense or zany humour. The third consistent category which appears in the factor analysis studies of jokes and humour types is the one content based dimension which recurs across studies: it is humour built on sexual themes (Ruch, 1993). In assessing the links between personality and these types of humorous material, researchers in this field measure the humour responses in two ways. First, there is the obvious dimension of the extent to which the material is judged as amusing or funny. The second dimension is one of how unpleasant or aversive the humour is seen to be.

Typical studies by Ruch (1994, 1997) and Ruch and Hehl (1998) have produced an array of findings which broadly indicate that extroverts enjoy all kinds of humour a little more; that perceived aversiveness is weakly correlated with neuroticism; that religious fundamentalism is negatively correlated with seeing jokes as funny; that sensation seekers enjoy all humour types more, that conservative and authoritarian personalities appreciate the incongruity of jokes much more than the bizarre or zany jokes and that those known as tough-minded, that is low on empathy, appreciate the sexual humour more. These kinds of individual differences are broadly useful for interpreting humour receptiveness and production at the individual and personality level of analysis. Nevertheless, a wider view is also required to understand how humour might function in tourism contexts and how tourism audiences including those coming from different countries might respond to the types of humour.

Nationality issues

One of these wider contexts is that of the nationality differences in humour. A relatively obvious dimension about humour which is of interest to tourism researchers is the challenging question of humour appreciation differences amongst different nationalities. This is a rich area for stereotypes and national prejudices. The work of Wiseman (2007) who collected 40,000 jokes and had them rated by 350,000 people from 70 countries provides information beyond the stereotypes. Working at this macro-scale of analysis, Wiseman reported few differences in the joke appreciation across the multiple countries in his sample. It is important to remember that this finding is centred on the appreciation of provided jokes and so does not consider other ways of expressing humour nor does it deal with the spontaneous production of humour or seeing humour in a situation. The only slight differences reported were that overall the Canadians rated the jokes as less amusing and the Germans scored them as slightly more amusing. Wiseman did exclude the sexual jokes from the mammoth repertoire of jokes used in the rating process so any nationality differences, limited as they are, depend only on responses to incongruity and the zany or bizarre humour types identified by Ruch (1993).

Other studies indicate some incipient links between the outcomes of the humour and nationality characteristics. Kazarian and Martin (2004) suggest that cultures which are strong in collectivism as opposed to cultures high in scores of individualism appreciate jokes which have different affiliative outcomes. Aggressive humour including sexual humour may be better appreciated by individualistic cultures and integrative humour styles more aligned to the cultural traits of collectivist cultures. It is apparent that both in researching the situational contexts and investigating national differences to humour, tourism researchers can play a role in these lightly explored topics. It remains important however to limit the generalisability of any specific humorous material considered to an immediate nationality context. In this chapter the researchers are working in Australia, a community where arguably humour is valued and is often seen as having a certain irreverence and ironic tone (Knightley, 2000; Bryson, 2000).

Connecting humour and positive psychology

Several approaches being emphasised in positive psychology underpin the study of humour. The three linked areas of particular interest are the value of positive emotions, the role of mindfulness and the value of social support and interpersonal bonds. It can be argued that laughing and responding to humour has the potential to improve our moods and the resulting positive emotions assist our health (Fredrickson, 1998). The act of laughing is rich in physiological and physiognomic micro-responses, many of which have hormonal and chemical releasing effects which serve to reduce our body tension and assist relaxation (Ruch and Ekman, 2001). There are also powerful psychological effects. Positive emotions, associated with responding to many types of humour (but not all) include feeling joyful, amused and content. These kinds of responses have a particular capacity to enlarge our perspectives and approaches to the world. This perspective, supported by solid experimental evidence, has been termed the 'broaden and build' theory of positive emotions (Fredrickson, 1998, 2001). The approach can be seen as particularly relevant to thinking about the benefits of humour in a tourism context. Fredrickson argues that positive emotions

> share the ability to broaden people's momentary thought action repertoires and build their personal resources, ranging from physical and intellectual resources to social and psychological resources.
>
> (2001, p. 219)

In this view perceiving the amusing side of situations results in being joyful and enthusiastic which are not only hedonistic states valued in themselves but also enriching conditions which predispose people to seek more information, reach out to others, better understand the world and foster resilience to difficult times. Having an amusing, laughter enriched time, prompts further positive human experiences. Results from a number of experimental studies where people in positive, joyful emotional states behaved in these broadening, resilience building ways effectively support Fredrickson's model (Folkman, 1997; Folkman and Moskowitz, 2000; Fredrickson and Levenson, 1998).

Additionally, there is potentially an ascending spiral of positive influences in these explanations. Building positive relationships through sharing humour emotions can reduce stress and promote health. Being healthy and having positive emotions expands travellers' views of the possibilities of their holiday experiences and predisposes them to investigate new relationship opportunities and networks. In some ways there has been a broad, even glib, suggestion for a long time that these processes exist. Nevertheless it is the recent detailed medical and experimental psychology work which has thoroughly identified some of the links. The detailed work includes recent clinical and experimental studies demonstrating how quality relationships and positive optimistic views of the world 'inoculate' individuals against common forms of ill-health (Cohen et al., 2000; Cohen, 2005, p. 130)

As argued in previous work, the construct of humour ties in with the literature on positive psychology because it has the potential to 'establish visitor comfort levels, to assist visitor concentration and to establish connections to tourism presenters' (Pearce, 2009, p. 639). For the purpose of this chapter and in line with previous work these three outcomes can be defined as follows:

Comfort – humour used to enhance the comfort of the people involved in a situation. This includes humour which helps to create a pleasant atmosphere and reduces stressful, awkward or frustrating travel situations. Such humour makes people feel that they have gained a certain level of control.

Concentration – humour used to broaden people's attention and capture their level of interest. This helps keep people mindful and mentally engaged with what is going on since they need to actively listen to what is being said to 'get the joke'.

Connection – humour used to bring people together. Such humour fosters interpersonal relationships and causes feelings of liking and rapport. This category also includes humour which is used to bring ideas and situations together in an unexpected way.

The further analysis and application of these three ideas help structure the empirical work in this chapter.

Humour research and methodology

Researchers studying humour are subject to some unique pressures. There is an obvious expectation that the work will have a certain entertainment value given the apparently light-hearted nature of the topic (cf. Martin, 2007, pp. 1–2). A small effort to meet this expectation will be offered in this chapter by providing select instances of tourism related humour. More importantly, there are further pressures to ensure that what is studied is agreed on as representing humour. Following the points already discussed concerning individual and nationality differences in humour appreciation, the selection of what is amusing can be seen as a subjective appreciation of materials and texts, thus making the researcher pivotal in the selection and assessment of cases. As with other efforts at interpretive research or views of everyday life built on social constructionist views (Jennings, 2010), the justification for the personal perspectives can be understood and to some extent supported by thorough and open documentation of the cases cited. In brief, by using detailed examples and quotations the researchers' perspectives can be shared with the relevant community of interest (Phillimore and Goodson, 2004). These illustrative and documentary practices are pursued in this chapter.

A further and supporting humour validating process is to have other researchers or colleagues consider any selected material and rate them for their humorous value. Such ratings can be the basis for rejecting episodes or items which only the researcher or the research team find distinctively amusing. As noted earlier, two dimensions are typically collected in these assessments of humour: how funny the material is and the extent to which the material is unpleasant or aversive (Ruch and Hehl, 1998). This kind of rating approach has been employed in studies of jokes and reviews of humorous material (Wiseman, 2007). In the study of the blogs this issue of the reliability of the humour assessment will be specifically addressed.

1 The study of provided humour

This study seeks to introduce some examples of humour from tourism businesses and sources which link to the three functions of humour – comfort, concentration and connection already reviewed. In Table 2.1 some instances of humour provided for tourists are highlighted. The selected examples encompass humour provided to promote destinations as well as humour to assist the delivery of safety messages and humour to add excitement at tourism attractions and activities. Researchers and readers who visit the identified websites or YouTube videos can explore the situations in rich visual detail. The examples cited in this section represent a small selection of the multiple uses of humour by tourism businesses. The selection is justified by the public attention to the social media sites, awards to the businesses for their humour and the longevity of the humour approaches in commercial settings.

There are several commonalities in these instances of humour provided for tourists. Aspects of this kind of presentation have been discussed in Pearce (2009) but the examples cited in Table 2.1 reinforce a particular observation made in the earlier study. Much of the success of the humour (and the instances cited have been widely praised and have been sustained as humorous styles for tourists over some time) reside in the self-deprecating humour employed. In particular the presenters seek to mock themselves rather than their audience or other groups. The popular YouTube presenter Natalie Tran, for example, reflects on her inadequacies and the contradiction of being single in destinations specially designed for honeymooners and romantic couples. The rugby team adopts roles

Table 2.1 Select instances of humour provided for tourists

Situation	Description	Reference source
Promotion and commenting on tourism destinations	Natalia Tran, a prominent national and international social media presenter in conjunction with Lonely Planet provides amusing and wry observations on multiple destinations	www.lonelyplanet.com/blog/natalietran/
On board safety messages	Air New Zealand uses New Zealand's world famous rugby team to demonstrate tourist safety messages	www.youtube.com/watch?v=_r9rIrRt-sk&feature=related
Meeting local people	Switzerland Tourism provides characters to promote the destination and reduce stereotypes	www.youtube.com/watch?v=UD0qCPAY2oU
Enhancing a family attraction	Disney's presenters in the Jungle Cruise provide an array of puns and comic quips to boost family fun	www.youtube.com/watch?v=XERflsPaLPs&feature=related
Presenting a cultural experience	Presenters at the Polynesian Cultural Centre, Hawaii engage diverse audiences through role plays and parodies	www.youtube.com/watch?v=3U6hIQmuCFg

and provides advice quite out of character with their strong man image while the Swiss farmers reveal a disarming but appealing humorous naivety when visiting the sophisticated offerings of city environments. Similarly the Disney presenters mock their own role as 'adventure guides' in a theme park while the Samoan cultural presenter plays out his role as a 'primitive man' but intersperses the acting with quips about post-modern life. Successful humour in the tourism context may well rely on humour directed at one's own foibles and situation rather than aggressive jokes and jibes targeted at others.

The specified roles of comfort, concentration and connection can be discerned in these presentations. In terms of comfort, the jokes surrounding both airline safety and the Disney family attraction reassure audiences that the threats to their well-being and any demands on their skills are likely to be minimal. For the Samoan cultural experience the humour connecting traditional life and the contemporary world converts a potentially pedagogic piece into a sympathetic and amusing portrayal of an individual and country versed in the nuances of alternate worlds. Safety messages require those who are new to settings to concentrate but the obligatory presentation of procedures and warnings on airlines becomes highly familiar to most experienced travellers. In this context gaining tourists' attention and jolting them out of a mindless appraisal of the situation is effectively achieved through humour.

Of course humour may not always work and its failure to achieve the kinds of goals indicated in this section is worthy of much further empirical attention. Ideas to stimulate this further research include attending to presenter timing, humour content and the nationality differences of tourism audiences.

2 The travel blog study

A second and more detailed approach to reviewing the tourism–humour link was developed by exploring the production of humour by tourists. Travel blogs represent an accessible and multi-national body of data which can be investigated to assess humour production and reactions. The study reported here has two aims. First it seeks to provide examples of tourist humour by presenting a classification driven by the data in the travellers' blogs. Second, the study explores the reach and the applicability of the conceptual scheme – the comfort, concentration and connection approach – to the written archives of travel stories.

Selection of blog entries

Travellers' blogs were selected using the key search tool 'Google blog search' (www.google.com/blogsearch). The selection of suitable websites was based on an initial scan of the content of these websites for humorous and funny material. Websites were only chosen if they were publically available, that is if the researcher had direct access to the content of the blogs without having to register as a member or subscriber. Four travel blog websites were selected for further analysis – travelblog.org, travelpod.com, travbuddy.com and mytripjournal.com. All these websites are virtual travel communities which provide travellers with free web space which can be used as online travel diaries to publish their travel stories. Carson (2008) notes that having clear objectives as to what is to be investigated in blogs can help to reduce the 'noise' returned by the search engines. Five keywords were chosen to ensure a wide range of blogs were captured by different bloggers. The online thesaurus Thesaurus.com was used to obtain synonyms for 'humorous'. The five keywords used to search for humorous episodes in the four pre-selected travel blog websites were humorous, funny, comical, hilarious and amusing.

Ten blogs were selected per keyword and per travel blog website using systematic sampling. A total of 200 blogs were chosen during June and July 2011. The first two blogs on every webpage were selected until the required number of ten per keyword was achieved. The researcher read the 200 blogs and extracted the humorous episodes of every blog. These humorous episodes were then rated for their funniness on a scale from 0 (not at all humorous) to 5 (very humorous). As a checking procedure, a judging panel was used to rate the funniness of 20 randomly selected blogs from the blog dataset. The 19 members of the judging panel consisted of males and females of various age groups and different nationalities. The judges' scores were averaged to yield an overall perceived humour score. Funniness ratings between the researcher and the judging panel differed slightly in the degree of funniness as can be seen in Figure 2.1.

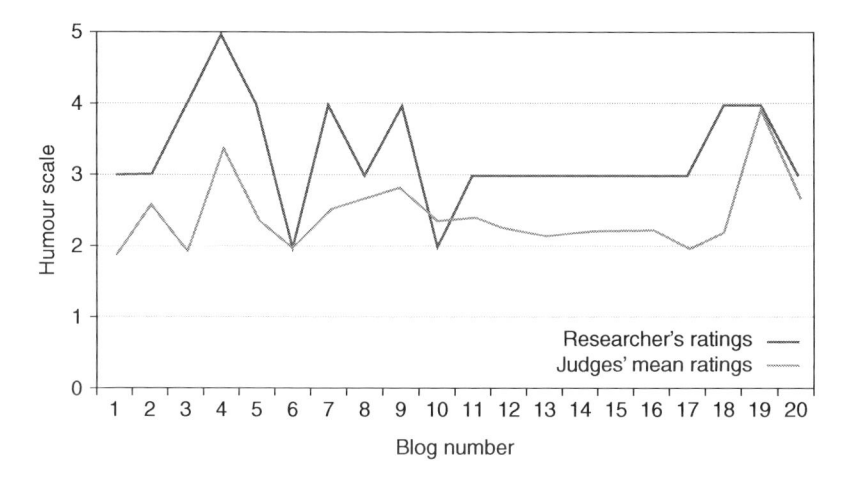

Figure 2.1 Comparison of researcher's ratings with the mean ratings of the judging panel.

The judges were also asked to code the humorous blog episodes as to what they believed were humorous outcomes in the blog. They were given clear instructions as to how to code the blog episodes and the same definitions of the humour outcomes that were used by the researcher. Cohen's kappa was calculated to check for interrater agreement between the researcher's rating and the ratings of the individual judges. The kappa value for the humour outcomes was 0.22 and according to Landis and Koch (1977) this represents a 'fair' strength of agreement. Some of the judges commented that they found it quite difficult to choose between humour outcomes. This can be clarified by reviewing one of the kappa assumptions which state that categories need to be mutually exclusive and exhaustive (Cohen, 1960). This however cannot be fully assured with the humour outcomes since they are almost interrelated. If someone feels connected to another person because something humorous they said made them laugh, then inevitably this person would also feel an increased level of comfort. Likewise, one's overall level of comfort could be enhanced even though a specific humorous comment was meant to be attention grabbing.

Using blogs as a data source does not come without some limitations. In general, bloggers only represent a subgroup of tourists (Volo, 2010). Blog content should not be assumed as representative of the general population since bloggers are 'self-designated authorities' (Gelb and Sundaram, 2002, p. 22). For this reason care should be taken when any generalisations are made beyond the study population.

Findings

Content of humorous travel experiences

The first aim of the blog study was to identify the humorous travel experiences tourists report in their blogs. Thematic content analysis was used to look for aggregated themes within the datasets (Gibson and Brown, 2009). Cyclical reading of the stories resulted in the development of codes or themes which became more focused after every re-examination. Gibbs (2007) refers to this process of reading a text and determining its meanings as data-driven coding. These codes emerged through the analysis and were not pre-defined by material in the literature. Whilst reading the humorous episodes, notes were taken about content and who participated in each episode.

Following the advice of Gibbs (2007), to keep the coding process as consistent and systematic as possible, short descriptions of the defining features of each evolving category were recorded. During the coding process, it was these descriptions of the defining features of the thematic categories that also helped in achieving data saturation. According to Bowen (2008), data saturation takes place when the same categories repeatedly arise within the data and no more new information is added. Four broad themes could be identified: (1) travel essentials, (2) humorous episodes that can happen to everyone, (3) social influence and control of humour, and (4) the observant tourist.

Travel essentials

This category included humorous experiences which occurred in relation to core tourism activities such as shopping, visiting attractions, eating at restaurants, staying in hotels, undertaking border crossings or dealing with different cultures. An example of a humorous episode which occurred while shopping includes laughing at furry bikinis while window shopping in Alaska. Humour experienced at attractions mainly occurred in museums or cultural centres. Examples include perceiving displays and stories as funny which were encountered in museums. At a cultural centre in Polynesia, one of the bloggers posed with the tiki god of fertility which resulted in much laughter for by-standing tourists as they gave their congratulations to the 'expecting couple'. Humorous examples during dining experiences were based on eating with chopsticks using the rather Western technique of poking food to pick it up or being entertained by waiters as they put on a special act. Within an accommodation setting, humour included laughing at the micro-bathroom in a hotel room in Paris. Going to the toilet in a foreign country can also be a source of humour. One example includes a tourist who sets off an alarm when pressing a button on a Japanese toilet which was thought to be the button for the flush.

Fun was also to be had with lengthy and overly complicated border crossings. In Vietnam, bus drivers collect all passengers' passports and hand them to an immigration official who then shouts out names on the passports or something that sounds similar to the names on the passport thereby indicating that the tourists should approach the immigration counters. The mispronunciation of names offered a sustained source of amusement to tourists. Another example included the blogging tourist having to climb through a hole in the border fence after being instructed to do so by an immigration official since he did not have a key to the gate at the time.

Humour based on being exposed to a different culture contains examples such as Korean children laughing at one of the blogger's inability to bow in the correct way; sitting 25 passengers in a mini van which in fact only allowed for a maximum of 15 passengers while playing loud music in Barbados; having a first encounter with lady boys in a cabaret in Thailand; and experiencing the wife-carrying championships in Finland.

Humorous episodes that can happen to everyone

This theme was based on humorous episodes which do not necessarily need to occur within a travel or tourism context. Humour in this category for example includes embarrassing situations and late night behaviour which are likely to happen in circumstances beyond tourism. Examples of the embarrassing but funny category included a friend of a blogger getting stuck in a Cu Chi tunnel in Vietnam. Another blogger's swimming shorts tore while cave climbing in Laos. Humorous episodes which seemed funny but bizarre include a blogger watching a woman getting almost completely undressed while waiting at a bus stop. Yet another example includes seeing 'Superman' strutting past in full costume while sitting at a restaurant in Italy.

Humorous episodes based on clumsy behaviour where people lack physical skill include examples such as falling over when leaving the Colosseum. This resulted in much laughter by the nearby locals. Similarly, humour was seen in a situation where a waiter spilled two pints of beer over a tourist. The funny mishaps category reaches beyond physical coordination. This category included humour that involves situations which might be perceived unfortunate at the time but turn out to be funny later when writing a blog such as walking along a road on a rainy day and being splashed from head to toe with water by a bus driving past. The category of a wild night out or drunken behaviour includes examples such as having one of the blogger's friends passing out after drinking too much and getting his head stuck in an automatic doorway that kept trying to close on his head. Another blogger found amusement in a situation where she got so drunk that she fell off a table while dancing.

Social influence and control of humour

Much of the humour in this category is based on the interactions with other people, that is, fellow travellers and locals. The category of fun with communication involved humour caused by lost in translation moments, unusual accents or miscommunication of any kind. One blogger notes in her blog that her Swahili is still not improving after she asked for 'wealth' instead of 'rice' at dinner. The category of making fun of others includes a blogger making fun of the many obese people on a cruise ship stating that the ballast calculations for the ship would need careful recalculation. The same category also included making fun of objects, such as some bloggers making funny comments about the infrastructure or local traffic conditions in some countries.

The humour category defined as appearance and body parts focuses on people's physical appearances and how people dress. Examples include a blind masseuse in Cambodia who was trying to find a blogger's feet while massaging him and could not believe how long his limbs were or another blogger reporting on a humorous experience which entailed cross-dressing before going on a Zambezi river cruise. The pranks and jokes category includes playing tricks on others, for example one of the bloggers believed to be in possession of a never-ending jar of peanut butter but eventually found out that a fellow traveller refilled the jar every night.

The observant tourist

Humour episodes in this category reflect instances of tourists being observant of their immediate travel surroundings. The category of unintentionally funny situations include, for example, one blogger trying to refill her friends' empty glasses with a bottle of wine but forgetting to take out the cork. Fun was also to be had with humorous signs, prints or names which were highlighted by several tourists and were usually supported by photos in the blogs. Examples of humorous signs include a 'dial a cow' sign on a road in South Africa. Many examples of humorous t-shirt prints were mentioned which seemed to be based on either 'Chinglish' (Chinese English) or 'Konglish' (Hong Kong English). The names of some places were also perceived as humorous such as going to eat at 'Poo restaurant' in Thailand or finding the name of 'Lake Titicaca' quite amusing.

Wildlife was also a source of humour. One tourist wrote about a humorous episode where a monkey stole the camera of another traveller. Another tourist's blog referred to the funny behaviours and noises that the hippos made while camping in Africa. Last, the category of creepy crawlies included exaggerated comparison between Dutch and Canadian mosquitoes. Encounters with cockroaches either under mattresses or in showers were also sources of amusement.

Humour outcomes

Concept-driven coding, which is distinct from the previously mentioned data-driven coding, was used to address the more conceptual aims of the empirical work. Concept-driven coding entails the development of a list of key thematic ideas before reading a narrative (Gibbs, 2007). Categories are therefore predefined by theories already published in the research literature (Gibbs, 2007; Lieblich *et al.*, 1998). The categories used to classify the humorous episodes in this case included the outcomes of humour scheme (comfort, connection and concentration) proposed by Pearce (2009).

Comfort

Results show that the majority of humour reported in the travel blogs was based on comfort (64.2 per cent). As previously mentioned, the comfort category includes humour used to create a pleasant atmosphere. The bloggers did indeed write about incidences that were carried out 'just for the fun of it' and consequently enhanced the comfort of a given situation, for example by amusing themselves in a boring museum by trying to imitate the poses of statues or by tricking fellow travellers into believing that they were in possession of a never-ending jar of peanut butter.

Other comfort enhancing circumstances include seeing the funny side of things even if these circumstances might have been quite uncomfortable when they occurred. Several bloggers noted rather frustrating travel situations such as lengthy, overly complicated border crossings when entering Vietnam or Uzbekistan but they were able to point out humorous things to amuse themselves and their fellow travellers. Likewise, having encounters with cockroaches in India and in Indonesia which were described as 'being bigger, meaner and faster' made for fine entertainment. Humour also helped the blogging tourists to cope with awkward situations. One blogger writes about his money exchange experience in Uzbekistan where the money seemed to be worth so little that some people were walking around with plastic bags full of money. The safety of this practice was seen as less than perfect. Travel situations of the embarrassing kind were also presented, such as bloggers accidentally locking themselves out of their caravan and then, dressed only in their nightwear, having to ask for another camper's phone to be able to call for help. Another tourist wrote about her experience with a group of nudists while swimming with her friends. Mary described the funniness of the situation on travelblog.org like this:

> We were cracking ourselves up. It was hard not to look, I mean, come on. I really wanted a picture, just for proof this actually happened, but thought that might be a bit much. At one point, they started going over the top ... lol ... the hot water comes from this small waterfall type thing and they were standing in it and saying 'June' – a guy would strike a pose ... they were acting out calendar poses and we about died of laughter. But it was that kind of classroom laughter where you know you're not supposed to laugh, so it makes it even worse! Finally, they all left and it was back to just us.

Connection

A further humour outcome can be used to foster interpersonal relationships and rapport with other people. This outcome was present in 26.5 per cent of the blog dataset. One blogger wrote about a friend and herself taking a taxi in Calcutta where the taxi driver suddenly shouted 'Bandega' which the two passengers repeated several times. This caused the taxi driver to laugh and it ended up being the ice-breaker for further conversation. Another example includes a humorous episode where a waitress made paper hats with hilarious sayings because the blogger and her friends had missed some of the night's entertainment. This resulted in increased liking of the waitress but also caused a lot of laughter between the friends. Tour guides seem to play an important role in establishing rapport between people. Several examples mentioned tour guides and their humorous ways. One such tour guide in Venice is cited for saying that Venetian people do not get fat because of the 420 bridges found in Venice.

The connections category also entails bringing ideas and situations together in a surprising or unexpected way which causes people to perceive humour. Two bloggers travelling through Egypt were frequently asked where they were from. When they replied Canada, they were given answers such as 'Canada Dry', 'Canada Dry or Canada Wet?' or 'Canada Dry, No Woman No Cry'. The two bloggers seemed to find this surprising since no single can of Canada Dry was found in all of Egypt. One further example includes two bloggers making fun of the information requirements by accommodation providers in Peru. Barnaby saw the humour in this situation and wrote in his blog on travelpod.com:

> One thing that I find amusing in Peru is the preoccupation of all hotels and guest houses with your occupation when you check in. By law, each accommodation stop has to record details of all the guests that stay there, including name, passport number and occupation. If you are an international spy, someone who craves privacy or just an idiot you can end up writing all manner of things in this space over the course of a 3-month trip. Pierpaolo and I have so far been logged as astronauts, hand models and jockeys depending on our mood at the time of check in. But perhaps the finest one I heard was a British lad who was going around South America, his trip funded by his excellent work as a cigarette lighter repairman.

Concentration

This category was defined as humour that was used to capture people's level of interest and their attention and make them more mindful of the present situation. In the blog dataset this category was represented 9 per cent. An example of a humorous episode includes one of the bloggers attending a CPR course where she writes about the two instructors making sure that everyone's attention level was maintained by wiggling their behinds while performing compressions or pretending to make out with the mannequin in a corner.

In this blog on travbuddy.com, Jerry described how his Vietnamese tour guide's humour caught his attention:

> His English was excellent and he was very funny. He explained the difference between things which are 'free' or 'included' in tour packages. 'Meals during the today's tour will be provided for you. They are not "free". Note. They are "included", that's "included" as you have already paid us for your meals. Beware people, nothing is "free" in Vietnam!'

While this episode clearly shows that the blogger was listening with interest to what his Vietnamese tour guide had to say, it can also be used as an example to illustrate how relationships can be fostered through the use of humour.

Another blogger went to the wife-carrying championships in Finland where most of this competition was carried out between Finland and Estonia. Even though the blogger did not speak either of the two languages, she understood enough to work out that the two nationalities were talking one another down which she found very amusing. Furthermore, several bloggers report about signs or t-shirt prints which they perceived as funny. For them to spot these signs and prints they had to be mindful of their surroundings in order to share these sightings with others in their blogs. One road sign in India cautions drivers to reduce their speed. The blogger who wrote about the sign in his blog found this funny since the roads in India are actually so bad that speeding would not even be possible.

Discussion

This chapter offers insights about the various humorous experiences that tourists encounter during their travels. The first study shows that humour is used by tourism businesses to make tourist attractions more entertaining, to promote destinations and to assist with the delivery of safety messages. The second study identified what kinds of humorous travel experiences tourists report in their stories. Content analysis revealed that various themes and categories could be identified and these were followed up using examples from the humorous blog episodes. The result of this study can be linked to the existing literature on positive psychology.

In the Values in Action Inventory of Strengths (VIA-IS) classification, humour is stated as one of 24 character strengths and is categorised under the heading of transcendence which is associated with a hopeful and optimistic perspective on life (Peterson and Seligman, 2004). In this classification scheme, humour is described as enjoying non-serious communication, maintaining a good mood, being composed and cheerful even when adversity strikes and using wit to affect emotional states in others (Ruch, 2002). In the context of tourism, Frew (2006) applied Stebbin's social comic relief theory to see if humour can in fact be used to help reduce awkward, frustrating or embarrassing travel situations which allow tourists to gain control of situations and make them appear as less embarrassing or threatening (Solomon, 1996). This relates to the humour outcome of comfort identified in this study. The humorous episodes found in the blogs did in fact show that humour was used to alleviate frustrating travel situations such as lengthy border crossings or transit situations. Humour also helped tourists cope with travel situations of the awkward or embarrassing kind such as coping with insects or dealing with torn swimming costumes. Many blog episodes also described humour used to amuse themselves in boring situations or to play tricks on fellow travellers just for the fun of it. This is consistent with the literature where humour is used to provide fun and entertainment (Ball and Johnson, 2000; Martin, 2007).

The connections outcome observed that humour was used to entertain and amuse others which lead to positive feelings that could then build further connections with people. Fredrickson (1998; 2001) explains in her 'broaden and build theory' that positive emotions enhance one's momentary thought-action repertoire. Positive emotions do not only broaden a person's attention but they also build a person's social resources. The blog episodes in this study showed that humour was in fact used as an ice-breaker in various situations to connect with other people more easily. Other humorous blog examples mention tour guides as sources of humour. This is in accord with the literature where apart from roles such as leader and communicator, a tour guide also needs to be an entertainer aiming to produce positive feelings and a supportive enabling atmosphere for the tourists (Black and Weiler, 2005; Heung, 2008).

Humour also affects cognitive functioning by making key points more memorable (Ruch, 2002). One blogger describes the numerous attempts of her CPR instructors to gain and hold the interest of the entire class. Events which are emotionally arousing are excellent attention-grabbers and also tend to be better remembered than natural events (Medina, 2008). Such emotionally arousing events can stem from positive emotions such as joy and happiness which are triggered by the use of humour. The rationale behind this idea is that humorous stories are linked to more or less strong positive emotions which can be imprinted in people's memories (Meeus and Mahieu, 2009). Another perspective is offered by Takahashi and Inoue (2009) who suggest that it may be the bizarreness of humour which leads to better memory performance. Bloggers perceived numerous signs, prints and names as funny which indicates that they were actively engaged with the immediacy of the situation. This finding fits well with the mindfulness enhancing properties of humour. The use of humour in certain situations can create increased mindfulness by 'forcing people to see a new and unexpected side to a given situation' (Carson and Langer, 2006, p. 41).

The outcomes of humour scheme also relates to the humour style model developed by Martin *et al.* (2003) which includes four unique humour styles. Affiliative humour focuses on saying funny things to amuse others and reducing interpersonal tensions and is therefore used to enhance relationships with others. Self-enhancing humour is based on the notion that when individuals have a humorous outlook on life, they are able to use humour to enhance the self and adjust their emotions to particular situations. Aggressive humour uses humour to enhance one's own feelings at the expense of others. Examples include racist and sexist humour and individuals using this kind of humour usually do not think about the effects that this can have on others. Self-defeating humour is described as a form of defensive denial where funny things are said to amuse others at one's own expense in order to gain the approval of others. By its own definition it can be argued that self-defeating humour could also be used to facilitate liking and relationships with others.

Three of these four humour styles have the potential to be used in tourism settings to make tourist experience more enjoyable. Affiliative and self-defeating kinds of humour produced by either the tour guides or the tourists can contribute to the outcome of connections between these groups of people. Self-enhancing humour, in appreciation as well as production relates to the outcome of comfort since it could be used to co-create the experiences that tourists are involved in. The dimension of concentration requires tourists to be mentally alert to recognise affiliative, self-enhancing and self-defeating kinds of humour. Since tourism businesses are attempting to create financial value from the presence of tourists, it is perhaps obvious to note that aggressive kinds of humour should not be used because this can have a rather negative impact on people's feelings and satisfaction with tourism experiences.

Conclusion and implications

In this chapter it was postulated that humour may induce increased comfort levels in tourists, better social connections between tourists and enhanced concentration outcomes for tourists. The two studies presented in this chapter gave examples of humour which was created for tourists or was reported by tourists themselves. It is the playful nature of humour that can contribute to tourists having positive experiences during their travels. Proyer and Ruch (2011) indicate that humour is the single best predictor of playfulness which can lead to the 'good life' since it impacts on a person's subjective and psychological well-being.

The two studies and particularly the blog analysis study revealed that there is a rich base for the investigation of humour in the tourism setting. In particular blogs have been described as 'research-uncontaminated' data (Volo, 2010, p. 31). They offer researchers an opportunity to collect much emic-derived interpretive material (Martin et al., 2006; Volo, 2010). The same kind of observation about studying humour through naturally occurring data can be made about the humour produced for tourists online or at public tourism attraction settings. Future analysis of humorous and funny travel experiences could also focus on online forums. Online forums that have titles such as 'funny travel experiences' give travellers the opportunity to express their experiences in a much more concise way. Therefore these forums are more to the point and might also be less time-consuming for the researcher.

Being mindful of the humour used in tourist settings may assist researchers in further exploring the roles of those who amuse, entertain and provide comic relief for millions of the world's global travellers. These roles include the intentional humour provided by tourist guides, service personnel and sometimes the members of the host community. Additionally, further questions could be directed quite specifically to the perceived benefits tourists report from either appreciating or producing humour. In this way the operation of a sense of humour in the broad field of tourism and travel may extend the findings of more constrained psychology work on what it means to have and use this specific character strength.

References

Argyle, M. (1987) *The Psychology of Happiness*. London: Methuen.

Ball, S. and Johnson, K. (2000) 'Humour in commercial hospitality settings', in Lashley, C. and Morrison, A. (eds), *In Search of Hospitality: Theoretical Perspectives and Debates*. Oxford: Butterworth Heinemann, pp. 199–216.

Black, R. and Weiler, B. (2005) 'Quality assurance and regulatory mechanisms in the tour guiding industry: a systematic review', *The Journal of Tourism Studies*, 16 (1): 24–37.

Bowen, G.A. (2008) 'Naturalistic inquiry and the saturation concept: a research note', *Qualitative Research*, 8: 137–152.

Bryson, B. (2000) *Down Under*. London: Doubleday.

Carson, D. (2008) 'The "blogosphere" as a market research tool for tourism destinations: a case study of Australia's Northern Territory', *Journal of Vacation Marketing*, 14 (2): 111–119.

Carson, S.H. and Langer, E.J. (2006) 'Mindfulness and self-acceptance', *Journal of Rational-Emotive & Cognitive-Behavior Therapy*, 24 (1): 29–43.

Cohen, J. (1960) 'A coefficient of agreement for nominal scales', *Educational and Psychological Measurement*, 20 (1): 37–46.

Cohen, S. (2005) 'The Pittsburgh common cold studies: psychosocial predictors of susceptibility to respiratory infectious illness', *International Journal of Behavioural Medicine*, 112 (3): 123–131.

Cohen, S., Gottlieb, B. and Underwood, L. (2000) 'Social relationships and health', in Cohen, S., Underwood, L. and Gottlieb, B. (eds), *Measuring and Intervening in Social Support*. New York: Oxford University Press.

Collett, P. (2004) *The Book of Tells*. London: Bantam.

Dann, G.M.S. (1996) *The Language of Tourism: A Sociolinguistic Perspective*. Oxon: CAB International.

Diener, E. and Biswas-Diener, R. (2008) *Happiness: Unlocking the Mysteries of Psychological Wealth*. Oxford: Blackwell.

Feingold, A. and Mazzella, R. (1991) 'Psychometric intelligence and verbal humor ability', *Personality and Individual Differences*, 12: 427–435.

Folkman, S. (1997) 'Positive psychological states and coping with severe stress', *Social Science Medicine*, 45: 1207–1221.

Folkman, S.W. and Moskowitz, J.T. (2000) 'Positive affect and the other side of coping', *American Psychologist*, 55: 647–654.

Fredrickson, B.L. (1998) 'What good are positive emotions?' *Review of General Psychology*, 2 (3): 300–319.

Fredrickson, B.L. (2001) 'The role of positive emotions in positive psychology: the broaden-and-build theory of positive emotions', *American Psychologist*, 56 (3): 218–226.

Fredrickson, B.L. and Levenson, R.W. (1998) 'Positive emotions speed recovery from the cardiovascular sequelae of negative emotions', *Cognition and Emotion*, 12: 191–220.

Frew, E. (2006) 'The humour tourist: a conceptualisation', *Journal of Business Research*, 59: 643–646.

Gelb, B.D. and Sundaram, S. (2002) 'Adapting to "word of mouse"', *Business Horizons*, 45 (4): 21–25.

Gibbs, G.R. (2007) *Analyzing Qualitative Data*. London: SAGE Publications Ltd.

Gibson, W.J. and Brown, A. (2009) *Working with Qualitative Data*. London: SAGE Publications Ltd.

Heung, V.C.S. (2008) 'Effects of tour leader's service quality on agency's reputation and customers' word-of-mouth', *Journal of Vacation Marketing*, 14 (4): 305–315.

Hottola, P. (2004) 'Culture confusion: intercultural adaptation in tourism', *Annals of Tourism Research*, 31 (2): 447–466.

Jennings, G. (2010) 'Research processes for evaluating quality experiences: reflections from the "experiences" field(s)', in Morgan, M., Lugosi, P. and Ritchie, J.R.B. (eds), *The Tourism and Leisure Experience: Consumer and Managerial Perspectives*. Bristol: Channel View, pp. 81–98.

Kazarian, S.S. and Martin, R.A. (2004) 'Humour styles, personality, and well-being among Lebanese university students', *European Journal of Personality*, 18: 209–219.

Knightley, P. (2000) *Australia: A Biography of a Nation*. London: Jonathan Cape.

Köhler, G. and Ruch, W. (1996) 'Sources of variance in current sense of humor inventories: how much substance, how much method variance?' *Humor: International Journal of Humor Research*, 9: 363–397.

Landis, J.R. and Koch, G.G. (1977) 'The measurement of observer agreement for categorical data', *Biometrics*, 33 (1): 159–174.

Lieblich, A., Tuval-Mashiach, R. and Zilber, T. (1998) *Narrative Research: Reading, Analysis, and Interpretation*, vol. 47. Thousand Oaks, CA: Sage Publications.

Martin, D., Woodside, A.G. and Dehuang, N. (2006) 'Etic interpreting of naive subjective personal introspections of tourism behaviour: analyzing visitors' stories about experiencing Mumbai, Seoul, Singapore, and Tokyo', *Journal of Culture, Tourism and Hospitality Research*, 1 (1): 14–44.

Martin, R.A. (2007) *The Psychology of Humor: An Integrative Approach*. Burlington, MA: Elsevier Academic Press.

Martin, R.A., Puhlik-Doris, P., Larsen, G., Gray, J. and Weir, K. (2003) 'Individual differences in uses of humor and their relation to psychological well-being: development of the Humor Styles Questionnaire', *Journal of Research in Personality*, 37: 48–75.

Medina, J. (2008) *Brain Rules*. Brunswick: Scribe Publications Pty Ltd.

Meeus, W. and Mahieu, P. (2009) 'You can see the funny side, can't you? Pupil humour with the teacher as target', *Educational Studies*, 35 (5): 553–560.

Park, N., Peterson, C. and Seligman, M.E.P. (2005) *Character Strengths in Forty Nations and Fifty States*. Unpublished manuscript. University of Rhode Island.

Pearce, P.L. (2005) *Tourist Behaviour: Themes and Conceptual Schemes*. Clevedon, UK: Channel View.

Pearce, P.L. (2009) 'Now that is funny: humour in tourism settings', *Annals of Tourism Research*, 36 (4): 627–644.

Peterson, C. and Seligman, M.E.P. (2004) *Character Strengths and Virtues: A Handbook and Classification*. Washington, DC: American Psychological Association.

Phillimore, J. and Goodson, L. (2004) *Qualitative Research in Tourism: Ontologies, Epistemologies and Methodologies*. London: Routledge.

Proyer, R.T. and Ruch, W. (2011) 'The virtuousness of adult playfulness: the relation of playfulness with strengths of character', *Psychology and Well-Being: Theory, Research and Practice*, 1 (1): 1–12.

Ruch, W. (1993) 'Exhilaration and humor', in Lewis, M. and Haviland, J.M. (eds), *The Handbook of Emotions*. New York: Guilford Publications, pp. 605–616.

Ruch, W. (1994) 'Temperament, Eysenck's PEN system, and humor-related traits', *Humor: International Journal of Humor Research*, 7: 209–244.

Ruch, W. (1997) 'State and trait cheerfulness and the induction of exhilaration: a FACS study', *European Psychologist*, 2: 328–341.

Ruch, W. (2002) 'Humor', in Peterson, C. and Seligman, M.E.P. (eds), *The Values in Action (VIA) Classification of Strengths*. Cincinnati, OH: Values in Action Institute.

Ruch, W. and Ekman, P. (2001) 'The expressive pattern of laughter', in Kaszniak, A. (ed.), *Emotion, Qualia and Consciousness*. Tokyo: Word Scientific Publisher, pp. 426–443.

Ruch, W. and Hehl, F.-J. (1998) 'A two-mode model of humor appreciation: its relation to aesthetic appreciation and simplicity–complexity of personality', in Ruch, W. (ed.), *The Sense of Humor: Explorations of a Personality Characteristic*. Berlin: Mouton de Gruyter, pp. 109–142.

Solomon, J.C. (1996) 'Humor and aging well: a laughing matter or a matter of laughing?' *American Behavioral Scientist*, 39: 249–271.

Takahashi, M. and Inoue, T. (2009) 'The effects of humor on memory for non-sensical pictures', *Acta Psychologia*, 132: 80–84.

Volo, S. (2010) 'Bloggers' reported tourist experiences: their utility as a tourism data source and their effect on prospective tourists', *Journal of Vacation Marketing*, 16 (4): 297–311.

Wiseman, R. (2007) *Quirkology: The Curious Science of Everyday Lives*. London: Pan Books.

3 Walking the talk

Positive effects of work-related travel on tourism academics

Mieke Witsel

Introduction: travelling tourism educators

Tourism as a subject is taught as an undergraduate and postgraduate degree in Australia, as well as at the vocational level in the Technical and Further Education (TAFE) system. At present (2013) there are 44 Australian universities (both private and publicly funded) and a large number of TAFEs (more than 1,100 in Victoria alone). Many of these offer tourism and tourism related degrees and diplomas. Many universities have joint articulation agreements with offshore education providers, and thus academics from Australian universities are occasionally required to travel abroad to teach their subject at partner universities. In the subjective experience of the academic, the practice of teaching abroad may entail additional workload and occasional stress which can at times be considerable (Witsel, 2006). Sharpley and Stone (2012) point out that travel and tourism can be stressful and consumption of goods and services can in some instances be linked to a decrease in well-being.

This chapter presents and discusses findings based on an interpretive study geared to explore whether and in what manner tourism academics travelling for work related reasons (i.e. transnational education) experienced *positive* benefits from their travels and work.

The travelling tourism academics involved in this study are a subset of occupational and business travellers. As has been successfully argued in previous publications, in almost all business travel there is an element of leisure (Leiper *et al.*, 2008). Most tourism academics would by nature of their field of study place a strong emphasis on the travel experiences component. The participants in this research can be described as tourism academics travelling for work purposes, and in so doing are practising what they are about to preach, walking the talk (as it were). The tenet of the research is to explore the social and psychological benefit they derive from this.

A synopsis of salient literature on positive psychology, work, travel and education

Happiness is more than simple pleasure. Some researchers use the term 'happiness' interchangeably with 'subjective well-being' (Graham, 2001). Others

(Layard, 2005; McGowan, 2006; Noddings, 2003) distinguish quite clearly between the two, and acknowledge that happiness is more profound than subjective or emotional well-being and satisfaction. According to Layard (2005, p. 12), happiness can be defined as a 'state of feeling good', and can fluctuate from day to day, and hour to hour, and can most certainly depend on the activity being carried out at any particular time. Obviously, then, our state of happiness is subject to various influences, both from our external world, as well as our internal world of perception and mood. Having said that, solid arguments exist which counter the idea that happiness is or can be a definable state which can be liberally applied on a universal scale. Christopher and Hickinbottom (2008) argue that the very notion of positive psychology does not necessarily transcend cultural and temporal boundaries and that in fact the notion may be narrow and ethnocentric with decidedly Western bias. While there is validity in their assertions, this does not mean that the notion of happiness, well-being and satisfaction are not universal human characteristics, even though the root causes may be culturally defined.

According to Lutterbie (2011), it is worthwhile to distinguish between three main types of happiness. There is *emotional happiness*, which is relatively short-term, a 'burst' of positive affect. Then there is *mindset happiness* which is more stable than the former, but is sensitive to change and can be influenced in positive and negative ways. Finally there is *trait happiness*, which tends to be stable across one's lifetime and is to a certain extent dependent on character traits and genetic disposition. This chapter will focus on mindset happiness and how work-related travel can influence this in tourism academics.

In order of importance, the 'big seven' factors affecting mindset happiness are family relationships, financial situation (up to a point: overall happiness has not risen despite increases in wealth), work, community and friends, health, personal freedom, and personal values (Layard, 2005, p. 62). The contribution of work in overall happiness is important not only because of its generation of income, but the fact that it gives extra meaning to life as we feel we contribute to a wider society, which has an impact on not only social relationships, but also self-respect. Studies have shown that fulfilling work can and does lead to higher levels of emotional well-being (Helliwell, 2003; Layard, 2005). However, due to a psychological process known as 'adaptation', new experiences and new stimuli are required to raise your well-being. Challenges, thus, can be quite beneficial in maintaining emotional well-being and happiness.

Although some people are biologically more predisposed to being cheerful and happy than others (Lisanby, 2003), research has also shown that those who care about others are, on average, happier than those who are more preoccupied with themselves (Lyubomirsky *et al.*, 2003). One's philosophy of life has an influence on happiness (Layard, 2005), as does the development of attainable goals and immersion in rewarding tasks. Boredom, it appears, has an immensely negative effect on happiness. Csikszentmihalyi (1990) described 'flow' as the experience when you are so absorbed in what you are doing that you 'lose yourself'. However this does not suggest that a pursuit of pleasure will guarantee a good life. Rather, psychologists suggest a broader definition of 'the good life' which blends 'deep satisfaction and a profound connection to others through empathy' (McGowan, 2006). In addition, Ryff and Singer (2003) found that people who achieve a sense of meaning in their lives are happier than those who do not.

So, in summary thus far, the following factors assist in achieving a deeper sense of happiness in life: engaging in fulfilling work which remains challenging, contributing to wider society, caring about others, developing attainable goals, immersing oneself in rewarding tasks and developing a sense of meaning in life (in part) through a profound connection to others through empathy.

Furthermore, research into positive psychology suggests that it is not only the activity of working itself which is very important for individuals. In order for the working environment to contribute positively to the emotional well-being of the individual, the context of the person's work should be challenging (Layard, 2005), meaningful (Ryff and Singer, 2003), and contain not only the potential for socialisation (Helliwell, 2003; Layard, 2005) but also the potential for profound connection and empathy with participants in the work environment (Lyubomirsky *et al.*, 2003; McGowan, 2006). For academics, thus, the context of their work is most positive if it contains these four elements.

Travel and positive psychology is yet to be the focus of much empirical research, but some significant studies have shown a correlation between travel and its effect on both immediate and longer term happiness. Filep (2009) studied 20 university student travellers who spent a year studying abroad. Filep found that despite experiencing culture shock, including loneliness and language barriers, the students' experiences involved love, interest, joy, contentment, engagement and meaning. Couper (2001) explored the experiences of 126 college graduates five years after graduation, comparing the life outcomes between those who had, and had not, attended a study abroad programme. Among her findings were that those who had studied abroad more readily accepted new challenges and environments, were more flexible and less scheduled in terms of time allocation, and found it easier to adjust to corporate culture.

Travel, as suggested by Sheldon (2005) and corroborated by findings from several studies conducted by the Institute for International Education (IIE, 2005), has a positive impact at a personal level, an academic level, intercultural level and career level. However, simply pursuing hedonistic pleasure trips may not have a lasting effect on emotional well-being. Nawijn (2011) found that the effect of holiday trips on vacationers' happiness was for the most part short-lived. It appears that longer term well-being and the deeper mindset happiness (as discussed by Lutterbie, 2011) can be a result of pursuing eudemonia, which incorporates virtue, rather than the more limited hedonism (Kler and Tribe, 2012). Seligman (2011) uses the PERMA model to describe positive psychology's research finding that humans seem happiest when they have access to (or achieve) pleasure, engagement, satisfying relationships, meaning and accomplishments.

Happiness or joy in education is not a topic that is commonly researched. Rather, many educational researchers tend instead to look at the negative aspects or difficulties in education, focusing on problems and offering potential solutions. Education itself is sometimes seen as a source or cause of great unhappiness (see, for example, Steven's (1978) book *Education and the Death of Love*). The cultural historian and educationalist Jacques Barzun (1959) argues comprehensively that intellect is eroded by intellectuals and educators, as schools are the product of our politics, business and public opinion (as fully as these are the product of our schools), as they are run by adults to suit other adults in political, intellectual and business life. And thus, argues Barzun, there can be no such thing as a perfect school, working as they do with spoiled materials, with 'teachers marred by the ugly world and children already stamped with the defects that their parents condone by habit or foster on principle' (Barzun, 1959, p. 88).

Nonetheless, the educationalists Neill (1960), Makiguchi (for English translations see Bethel, 1994) and Barrow (1980) have researched the topic of happiness in education quite extensively. Interestingly, Makiguchi (Bethel, 1994) identified happiness with the creation of value, and argues strongly for happiness as a prime aim of education. Barrow (1980) analyses happiness and presents the implications of the analysis for schooling, but in a very theoretical manner. More recently, Noddings (2003) explored happiness and its intimate relation to education. As is often the case, the focus of the book is students rather than the teachers, but the prime tenet of the book – happiness as an aim in education – is as valid for teachers as it is for students. It goes without saying that without teachers who are capable of experiencing joy in education, education cannot be a source of happiness for the students. This is not to say that an unhappy teacher is necessarily a poor teacher, but a joyful teacher is more able to evoke motivation, even joy, in students. In fact, Noddings remarks in her conclusion, 'Clearly, if children are to be happy in schools, their teachers should also be happy. Too often we forget this obvious connection.' (Noddings, 2003, p. 261).

The current study seeks to further explore the benefits and impacts of work-related travel on the mindset happiness of tourism academics required to teach transnationally. Findings are discussed in the context of positive psychology, focusing on the impacts of work, travel and education. In particular, this chapter seeks to explore and elucidate why and in what manner the travelling tourism academics found benefit from 'walking the talk'.

Accessing the travelling educators' views

Forty academics from two Australian universities teaching tourism in multicultural and transnational contexts were interviewed in depth and two focus groups were held. The study identified a potential positive perspective to internationalisation of education and travel for academics. This closer examination of travelling tourism educators and their travel experience uncovered the potentially transformative nature of work-related travel, and the concomitant benefits for positive personal development and increased well-being.

A phenomenological analysis of the interviews using mind-mapping techniques (Witsel, 2006) yielded a picture of the academics' own experiences of joy and benefit, found in journeying and teaching in multicultural and transnational contexts. The sense of journeying was experienced physically as well as metaphorically, and in a personal as well as a professional sense, and had positive impacts on the academics' happiness, and on the subject area as a whole.

Major themes emerging from the research

The interviews and focus groups were analysed using mind-mapping techniques which generated two major themes, each with several underlying themes. The first major theme concerned travel and journeying as an essential and beneficial activity. The sub-themes covered the following:

- the benefit of cultural exposure (fresh exposure as a result of travelling, as well as previous exposure due to cultural background);
- the benefit of 'cognitive journeys of self-knowledge', which resulted in enrichment for self and for the subject area as a whole.

The second major theme concerned happiness, enjoyment and joy. This was experienced in a personal sense as well as an interpersonal sense:

- personal happiness engendered by discovery and cognitive journeys;
- enjoyment and joy engendered by the development of an interpersonal relationship of mutual care between academic and international students.

The remainder of this chapter discusses and elaborates on these two themes drawing on quotes from the research findings. Discussion and reflection on the potentially transformative nature of work-related travel, and the concomitant benefits for positive personal development and well-being are interwoven in this section. All names used are pseudonyms.

Travel and journeying as an essential and beneficial activity

Travel was seen as an essential component for the professional development of tourism academics by many participants. The following was mentioned by an associate professor in considering which tourism academics would be good at overseas teaching:

> ...A lot of staff are not able to connect if they have not travelled much, with the global contact that this entails
>
> (Charles)

A good educator was seen as someone who combines the right sort of personality with good educational practice and travel experience:

> I think that is something that relates to both people's personality, their experiences of education, and their experiences of travelling, so I think for me that would be the biggest number one factor, and what makes a good lecturer, versus say, a not so good lecturer.
>
> (Charles)

It was not so much the length of time travelling and teaching abroad that was seen as of great importance but rather the experience of an 'other' culture, as a benefit which 'stays with you'. The experience of another culture creates sensitivity, which may not be achieved to the same degree if the academic does not travel:

> ... So, it's just a general feeling that I think stays with you, and I think the more that you go overseas, the more that is with you. I think that lecturers here that have not travelled at all, may be aware of it, but may be a bit less sensitive for those sorts of things.
>
> (James)

In addition, the experience of the other culture was seen as most beneficial if it happens overseas, rather than experiencing the 'other' in one's own country. The following academic, a highly experienced academic of Confucian background, explained that there is a real need to understand students (rather than rely on stereotypes); and being really interested and really wanting to know more about them is the most important factor in becoming a more effective teacher:

> I also think it's one thing to give lip service to something, and it is another thing to say 'oh I really am interested and I really want to know, if those students that I teach are from a different background'. I need to understand a bit more about them, so that I can be more effective in my teaching, rather than come with this stereotype thinking, such as 'Confucian heritage students learn by rote'. You know if you do that you're not going to get through at all.
>
> (Kim)

In the experience of this academic, travel is seen as an integral part of this, as he goes on to explain:

> Travel is the other thing that I think helps a lot. If you travel to other countries ... I think an exchange project is very helpful.... Even just one semester: a person who has lived in the country for a few months, will have learned a lot, and that is an invaluable learning experience.
>
> (Kim)

So it is a matter of getting to know the students, rather than relying on stereotypical knowledge, which makes an academic more effective, and thereby increasing competence and confidence, which in turn increases well-being. Also, in the eyes of the academic above, travel transforms the teacher into a learner, able to experience an 'invaluable learning experience', which is the very same experience teachers hope their students will undergo. This point is supported by the following comments from Bill and Jennifer; a British and Australian senior lecturers with extensive offshore teaching experience. Again, travel is seen as a learning experience for themselves as a teacher, and the lesson learned is that making judgements or decisions based on cultural knowledge is not valid or useful, however easy they may be:

> But of course when you come back to the situation here where you usually have a mixture of people, I find some difficulty. I've never been to India for example. I don't really have much of a feel for those people relative to say to the Thai or Chinese: I guess I feel I have a degree of comfort with Chinese culture now, and places that you have also been to as a tourist, I've been to South-America, I've been to parts of Europe and so on that all helps. Being a traveller does help the relationship. Even if your knowledge of Brazil is pretty superficial, they do appreciate it, it does seem to mean something. At that level I almost have to go to India to improve my teaching in a sense.
>
> (Bill)

> Some of the other things that I have certainly learned, is to not base any decisions on the basis of culture, you can't predict anything, any more than you can predict on men and women on the basis of their sex. And it can be very easy to think of certain cultures in stereotypical terms.
>
> (Jennifer)

The above supports the argument put forward by Gannon (2000) and Witsel (2006), that it is not so much an understanding of the cultural stereotypes (accurate or not) that helps create cultural sensitivity and awareness, but a more subtle, personalised understanding, which is developed through personal contact and travel, and helps create a pedagogy of intercultural experience, such as proposed by Alred et al. (2003), where the teacher becomes the learner. As mentioned above, Lyubomirsky et al. (2003) illustrated that those who care about others are on average happier. This sense of appreciation of others and sense of connection has a positive effect on the academics' emotional well-being.

Travelling overseas and teaching in a multicultural environment was not seen as the only source of cultural exposure that had a beneficial impact on the academic, however. The cultural background (such as their birthplace) of the academic can have a profound impact on teaching, and on the academic's approach to the tourism and hospitality curriculum. The following academic, Ellie, is a migrant to Australia and finds that the experience of migrating has had a decided impact on her relationship with people; both on a personal level as well as on a professional level:

> I actually came to Australia when I was eight, as a person from another country and that has had impact on my whole life and how I related to people and my students.
>
> (Ellie)

On a professional level, the cultural background which is brought with these migrants to Australia – the different set of norms, values and attitudes – can have a distinct effect on the academic's choice of interest area. Kim's Confucian heritage background, with its focus on politeness, face and hospitality, had a strong influence on his keen interest in service and service delivery. It was mainly for this reason that upon arrival in Australia he stepped into the restaurant industry. It was only later, once he had become an established academic and researcher, that he recognised that his focus on hospitality and service stemmed from this background; and found that the research supported his interest. There is a distinct sense of the past resonating in the present in Kim's words as he enthusiastically relates his story:

> During that time when I was in the restaurant business I was keenly interested in service and service delivery. That stems from my Chinese background. For Asian Chinese, hospitality is an important aspect of one's life and one's dealings. I would have been practising a lot of the things that I now know theoretically. I already knew in terms of practice what to do, but years later when I read some books, some research findings, these are the things that I've been doing!
>
> (Kim)

Whether the cultural exposure to 'otherness' is a result of travel for business, holidays or education, or whether it is a result of birthplace and upbringing, there is a strong sense among the academics interviewed that exposure to other cultures increases interpersonal, even intercultural sensitivity. This is reassuring and of benefit when teaching overseas as it 'helps you appreciate the differences more':

> I am more tolerant of the cultures, more observant of differences, because I also teach in Malaysia and in Hong Kong, and in Singapore; and I've been teaching there a number of times, so when you go to these other countries I think that actually helps you to appreciate the differences more than when you're just seeing the students here in this environment.
>
> (James)

This reassurance and benefit is important to academics, as is simply 'being aware of what's happening' in other countries. When possible, immersion in the culture is seen as beneficial and important. In the next excerpt, the academic reiterates 'going into' as a way of describing how he immerses himself into the culture:

Well certainly being aware of what's happening in the other countries has been very important to me, so when I'm there I read a lot of their newspapers, so I go into the shops I go into the supermarkets and I read the newspapers, I collect local examples and so on.

(James)

For the following academic, both birthplace as well as professional exposure to other countries (in this case Africa) has increased his appreciation of the students' backgrounds and lives:

So I lived in Africa for the first half of my life and I came to Australia for the second half, so I've sort of had, you know, exposure to Asia is what I'm getting now, and I've had exposure to Africa, so when I have students from Ghana, in Burundi and Ethiopia,... I can appreciate their backgrounds and their lives as, as much as I can appreciate the Chinese and the Malaysians, and the Singaporeans and the rest of it.

(James)

This sense of appreciation is extremely important. Consider the strength of the word 'appreciate' in the context of tertiary education: appreciating difference, appreciating background, appreciating life, as in the case of the academic above. Appreciation of one's workplace and the people in it is a significant motivating factor in life. According to Robbins *et al.* (2003), appreciation is one of the most powerful, yet overlooked aspects of successfully motivating and empowering people and groups. In this case, rather than the students appreciating their teacher (although it is likely that they do), it is the academic who is appreciating the students' backgrounds and lives, and this is partly what motivates the academic. This reflects and enforces the findings of Seligman (2011) who noted that developing relationships and meaning, part of the PERMA model, contributes more to lasting well-being than the pursuit of hedonism.

On a very practical level, the experience of travelling and meeting other people creates a wealth of knowledge which is seen as very pertinent to tourism education, and in fact, in the experience of the following academic, actually 'forms the basis' of their tourism education, and is seen as a 'strength'. This is put to great practical use when teaching tourism and tourism related subjects, for the experiences and knowledge are indeed so closely related to tourism. In addition, anecdotes which are so pertinent to teaching (as they sketch pictures for the students as they show how theory and practice are related), come readily to hand. In the words of this academic, it all 'pays off in spades'.

I think from my perspective, one of my strengths is that I've travelled a lot, and so often I've got some knowledge of where the students are from, and when it's not from where they are from its from somewhere near there, or so [...] I've got a lot of experiences, a lot of places; I met a lot of people and that forms the basis of my tourism education in many ways I think, and the five years on Hamilton Island before I came here, so I think that pays off in spades now, 'cos it means that I've got a lot of anecdotes I can talk about and, and, can relate to the different cultures in some way.

(Gary)

The above quotes illustrate that travel and overseas teaching creates knowledge, skills and attitudes which are seen as pertinent; the experience creates awareness and sensitivity, and gives strength. The skills required to teach the subject area of tourism are seen as being harder if the academic has not travelled: 'So it's a hard skill to ask, if they haven't done their travel'. (Charles)

Pure exposure to other cultures alone, it has been suggested, is not necessarily sufficient (although it may be necessary) to create a condition for interculturality (Alred *et al.*, 2003). An awareness of one's own culture-specific norms, values and practices (Pinto, 1990) is a key element in improving cultural competence, according to many theoreticians which deal with intercultural business communication. According to Trompenaars and Hampden-Turner (2001, p. 196), 'Genuine self-awareness accepts that we follow a particular mental cultural program and that members of other cultures have different programs. We may find out more about ourselves by exploring those differences'. Scollon and Scollon (1995, p. 15) also believe that 'effective communication requires a study of cultural and discourse differences on the one hand, but also requires a recognition of one's own limitations'. This is borne out by the following quote from Gary, a tourism academic who travelled quite extensively and who feels that travel, and meeting people have formed the basis of his tourism education in many ways. The sense that it is when travelling that one learns the most about oneself is seen as very beneficial:

When you travel you learn a lot about different cultures, different ways of living, different economic systems, so many different ways of living a life, but ultimately you're going to learn a lot about yourself: and you know I think that is probably the benefit of the travel.

(Gary)

However, this 'self' need not only be an individual self. The 'self' can refer to tourism as a subject area too. The focus is on learning, only this time it is not the single individual academic who learns, but the subject area as a whole:

I do think it's a good thing, particularly with this subject area, because I'm in tourism, and it is so international, and I think the more we learn from each other, the better the subject will become; so for me to teach from a purely Australian perspective is very narrow. I can involve the students' end, their experience, it really broadens the subject area, and I think the students also learn from each other, so, you know, they give their examples, their experiences. I can then put them into a theoretical framework, but the others have learned from people, and often I think we tend to learn more from our colleagues than from somebody that is out there giving the talk. So I think it's a really good thing.

(Gary)

The feeling that the subject area of tourism and hospitality as a whole benefits from a multicultural teaching environment is quite prevalent among the participants, and there is a sense that this benefit is reciprocated, that there is a mutual link between, especially, tourism and internationalisation. The academic below feels that internationalisation is a very positive factor and that *because* they teach tourism, they are, *ipso facto*, pro-internationalisation:

> Well I'm a tourism academic, I teach tourism, so I am pro internationalisation. Very much so.
>
> (Patrick)

Although internationalisation is seen as a global phenomenon, it does not preclude a focus on the individual. Here, the academic attempts to explain that in an ideal future, a school of tourism and hospitality management would have a large proportion of its students from various cultural groups, while at the same time being able to deal with students on an individual level rather than through a cultural stereotype:

> I would like to see us, in five years, having half the cohort from overseas; and of the 50% that is domestic, a big chunk of that from different cultural backgrounds as well. And I know that sounds contradictory, but earlier I said, we've got to cut though culture and focus on the individual, but I think there is still a richness in sort of cultural background.
>
> (Wayne)

Interestingly, Wayne emphasises the 'richness' in the potentiality of diversity. The concept of multicultural education generating richness or enrichment in affective terms is quite prevalent among the participants in this study. Kim stated that teaching in a multicultural context 'enriches my life', and suggested that the enrichment came partly through an increase in confidence with respect to interpersonal relationships: '... and I am able to relate to all sorts of people, without being worried' (Kim).

This state of 'enrichment' does not always come about immediately upon travelling and teaching multicultural cohorts. Quite often the academic undertakes a journey of their own as they develop as an educator. The transnational teaching particularly becomes an important tool for self-development, even though initially there is a lot of effort required on the part of the academic and a certain amount of emotional discomfort:

> It was hard work,... a lot of effort to get to where I got to, but over the three years or so,... I feel fairly well satisfied that I now do that far better than I

did at the start ... I really came to grips with Thai culture, which you could do with a homogeneous group like that.

(Bill)

Travel is therefore significant in developing intercultural competence in the academic, increasing happiness and well-being. This does not necessarily mean that it all has to be 'fun'. Travel and journeys create a personalised understanding of culture and of otherness, which means that one's own culture is placed in a frame of reference. This can be quite unsettling as intercultural understanding refutes the notion that one's own culture is naturally superior to others: we question our beliefs and values and can no longer take them for granted. 'Cultural frame of reference' implies that the teacher has undergone a journey of learning. It can be developed through physical journeys involving work or play and can be ongoing, as with those academics whose birthplace is elsewhere. The journeys and the understanding are of great value to the tourism academic, both in terms of the epistemology of teaching and of the subject matter, as well as ontology – 'being' a teacher.

In all, the journeys and the travel aspect of international education were seen by the tourism academics as enriching, and valuable, as these journeys increased intercultural awareness, and eventually increased intercultural competence. In addition, the journeys were generally viewed in a positive light, were experienced as pleasurable and increased the participants' emotional well-being and levels of happiness. This raises the question then of where, more precisely, this happiness was found, and what aspects of international education the participants found enjoyable, and when they experienced joy.

Happiness, enjoyment and joy

Given that the transnational teaching experience is not necessarily enjoyable per se, and can entail significant amounts of 'hard work' and possible emotional discomfort before the academic feels that they have 'come to grips' with the culture and the teaching, there are nonetheless significant elements of joy in teaching in a multicultural context. Some of this joy is a result of the rewarding sense of personal and academic development, but some is on a much simpler level.

Outside the possible sense of hard work and emotional discomfort due to inexperience as outlined above, first time travel as a transnational academic is seen by some as a very positive and enjoyable experience. The following academic, Rowan, describes his first experience of teaching transnationally, working with a local tutor:

The teacher was terrific, she was great; the experience was extremely positive, I really enjoyed it, the students were always very polite, keen to learn, apply themselves.

(Rowan)

The interaction with students in transnational teaching is of course only a part of the entire international experience of the participant. The academic can also have the opportunity to experience the overseas location as a tourist and experience leisure. This can certainly enhance the well-being of the participant. In the next excerpt, notice, on a discourse level, how this academic slips from using the past and perfect tenses when recalling the offshore teaching, into the present tense as the experience is re-lived with enthusiasm:

> I just think the reality of going to another place was terrific, I like Malaysian food anyway, and the lecturers were very hospitable, and take me out to lunch, and ask me to go to the market area and have some authentic cuisine. I took myself off for a couple of days to the city, to have a look, so you explore the place a bit, so it's an adventure, and the result is absolutely ... you've finished work, you go back to the hotel, you go down to the hall, sit down with a can of beer, or whatever they had, a bottle of ... fantastic way to end the day, it's great.
>
> (Rowan)

We move now to a different aspect of travel, namely cognitive journeys: those non-physical journeys we are led along in an academic sense but which also have the effect of broadening our horizons and leading us to new experiences. The following academic, a highly experienced associate professor in tourism, explains the phenomenon in the light of their multicultural class of onshore Master's degree students, which contained 17 different nationalities. This academic relates with much confidence and satisfaction, how the students bring their experiences to the classroom, and share their experiences and knowledge, and thus take the academic on marvellous journeys:

> They [the international students] take me to parts of the world, that I have never thought about, or worked in, or that I've been in.
>
> (Tehani)

Tehani might never have been in a particular student's country of origin, but the experience of teaching the student and listening empathetically to their experiences and descriptions gave her the sense that she could vicariously experience that other country through her imagination and understanding.

As mentioned in the introduction, emotional well-being and happiness derived from the workplace are of great importance to the overall happiness of people. Several of the academics interviewed actually expressed the opinion that teaching the multicultural classroom was in fact preferable to any other activity they were engaged in in their work:

> From the here and now, my main enjoyment comes from my overseas post grad classes.
>
> (Rowan)

Perhaps the best journey the academic is taken on is the interpersonal journey of mutual care. This seems to be the salient issue that redresses much of the stress inherent in multicultural teaching. The following excerpt is from Jennifer, a professor with many years teaching experience, both onshore and transnationally:

> I would prefer my post graduate probably to any other group, they are the nicest group to teach, and that is partly one of the most interesting things, teaching other cultures is that most of the overseas students that I teach, the relationship is very important.
>
> (Jennifer)

The relationships of care that are built are mutual and generate genuine fondness:

> When I had to cancel a class of the post graduate [international students], I was really sick, and practically everyone in the class sent me an email, saying 'we are really worried about you', 'are you ok?', 'we're praying for you',... whereas with the local students it would never enter their heads: 'oh well, no class, that's great', 'what do we do? Go home, that's good'. They would not think to be concerned about the member of the staff, that's not a Western thing,... Certainly if I think of the people I am genuinely fond of, the majority would be overseas students: (a) they tell me more about themselves, and (b) because they are more interested in you as a person, and so this relationship does develop.
>
> (Jennifer)

Jennifer, despite considerable research and administrative commitments commensurate with her position as Head of School, portrays a passion about and motivation for multicultural and transnational teaching. To Jennifer, it is an intensely valuable part of her academic work, in part because of the sense that she feels valued in the context of the student–teacher relationship. To come back, then, to Helliwell (2003), Layard (2005) and Seligman (2011), it is this socialisation and relational aspect that generated happiness in Jennifer's work environment. Furthermore, this level of socialisation and interaction potentially enables the academic to empathise with and create profound connection with participants in the work environment. These are factors which according to Lyubomirsky *et al.* (2003) and McGowan (2006), can have profound implications for enhancing happiness.

Conclusions and implications

Travel and teaching in a multicultural context not only aids the tourism academic in developing the skills, attitudes and knowledge required to successfully (and happily) teach multicultural cohorts, but has a deeper effect of increasing self-knowledge and an enhanced awareness of oneself as a cultural being. The academic is transformed to learner as they negotiate the sometimes disquieting contradictions imposed by being immersed in a different culture, and broaden their perceptions of education, of culture and of societies.

Learning – and the ability for lifelong learning – is a significant trait of a successful interculturalist, and the flexibility inherent in this ability is a significant factor in increasing mindset happiness. As has been pointed out above, experience of other cultures alone is not a sufficient condition for interculturality: the successful interculturalist requires 'reflection, analysis and action' (Alred *et al.*, 2003, p. 5). This is where the experience of learning becomes so important for the tourism academic: not purely in an epistemological sense where the subject knowledge is enhanced, but in an ontological sense where there is a degree of learning about the self. The increased understanding of self happens in two areas. It happens on the level of the individual 'self' as the participant develops in a personal sense. Furthermore, as the participant learns about their own culture because they have seen their own culture from a different, possibly refreshed, angle, the participant develops a cultural frame of reference. This increased self-knowledge is, as we have seen, put to good use in enhancing the teaching experience. However little of the current research into travel, tourism and happiness reflects the importance of increased self-knowledge gained through work-related travel and touristic experience.

As we have seen, however, teaching in a multicultural context does become rewarding, and increases the emotional well-being and happiness of the academic. As it is and continues to be a learning experience, teaching international students involves challenge, and as Layard (2005) points out, the innate human ability to adapt necessitates changing environments to enhance continued emotional well-being. A successful negotiation of these changing environments brings satisfaction to the academic, and increases knowledge of the subject matter and enhances the ability to teach successfully.

The learning component whereby the teacher becomes a cultural student is only one of the factors in which teaching in the multicultural classroom can enhance the happiness of the participant. As has been seen above, meaningful interactions and social relationships improve well-being as we feel we contribute to wider society: self-respect improves, and the journey of 'mutual care', as described by the participants above, is seen as particularly rewarding. The element of joy in 'enjoyment' is in these cases generated by the mutual social empathy developed by the interaction of the academic and the international students. Ryff and Singer (2003) pointed out that this sense of meaningful interaction has positive outcomes for overall happiness. As Lyubomirsky *et al.* (2003) and McGowan (2006) have illustrated, empathy is a key factor in human happiness, because it breaks down the barriers of the individual and allows for the potential for profound connection and empathising with participants in the work environment.

Here, two considerations must be made. First, an academic who is successfully negotiating the intercultural journey of teaching and is happier as a result is not, ipso facto, necessarily a good teacher or a knowledgeable academic. It seems highly likely that a happier academic with an accurate level of self-knowledge, enhanced self-awareness as a cultural being and increased levels of intercultural competence will be more successful at their teaching and in the eyes and experiences of the students, but this is not a guarantee. Second, as Christopher and Hickinbottom (2008) have suggested, it is important to keep in mind that concern with inner states of mind such as happiness, emotional well-being and a search for self-understanding and knowledge may in all likelihood be a predominantly Western pursuit. It is for these reasons that further research into the principles and practices of tourism academics who have been proven to be successful international teachers would be a valuable enterprise. Nonetheless, the experiences of the academics participating in this study indicate the significance of travel for the tourism academic teaching in a multicultural context. The potential joy that can be generated by the rewarding aspects of the teaching in a multicultural classroom contributes not only to the subject knowledge but also to the participants' sense of 'being' a successful teacher.

References

Alred, G., Byram, M. and Fleming, M. (eds) (2003) *Intercultural Experience and Education*, Languages for Intercultural Communication and Education 2. Clevedon: Multilingual Matters Ltd.
Barrow, R. (1980) *Happiness and Schooling*. New York: St. Martin's Press.
Barzun, J. (1959) *The House of Intellect*. London: Mercury Books.
Bethel, D.M. (1994) *Makiguchi the Value Creator*. New York: Weatherhill.
Christopher, J.C. and Hickinbottom, S. (2008) 'Positive psychology, ethnocentrism, and the disguised ideology of individualism', *Theory & Psychology*, 18: 563–589.
Couper, G.E. (2001) 'The psychology of travel: a theoretical analysis of how study abroad and positive regression affect personal growth and career choice', PhD thesis, Northcentral University.
Csikszentmihalyi, M. (1990) *Flow: The Psychology of Optimal Experience*. New York: Harper and Row.
Filep, S. (2009) 'Tourists' happiness through the lens of positive psychology', PhD thesis, James Cook University.
Gannon, M. (2000) *Understanding Global Cultures: Metaphorical Journeys Through 23 Nations*. Thousand Oaks, CA: Sage.
Graham, C. (2001) *Happiness and Hardship: Opportunity and Insecurity in New Market Economies*. Washington, DC: Brookings Institution Press.
Helliwell, J. (2003) 'How's life? Combining individual and national variables to explain subjective well-being', *Economic Modelling*, 20: 331–360.
Institute for International Education (2005) www.iie.org [Accessed 14 January 2013].
Kler, B. and Tribe, J. (2012) 'Flourishing through SCUBA: understanding the pursuit of dive experiences', *Tourism in Marine Environments*, 8 (1/2): 19–32.
Layard, R. (2005) *Happiness: Lessons from a New Science*. New York: The Penguin Press.
Leiper, N., Witsel, M. and Hobson, P. (2008) 'Leisure travel and business travel: a comparative analysis', *Asian Journal of Tourism and Hospitality Research*, 2 (1): 1–10.
Lisanby, S. (2003) 'Focal brain stimulation with repetitive transcranial magnetic stimulation (rTMS): implications for the neural circuitry of depression', *Psychological Medicine*, 33: 7–13.

Lutterbie, S.J. (2011) 'The research and practice of building happiness at work', paper presented to The Second World Congress on Positive Psychology, Philadelphia, 23 July.

Lyubomirsky, S., King, L. and Diener, E. (2003) *Happiness as a Strength: A Theory of the Benefits of Positive Affect*, University of California.

McGowan, K. (2006) 'The hidden side of happiness', *Psychology Today*, 39 (2): 68–78.

Nawijn, J. (2011) 'Happiness through vacationing: just a temporary boost or long-term benefits?' *Journal of Happiness Studies*, 12: 651–665.

Neill, A.S. (1960) *Summerhill*. New York: Hart.

Noddings, N. (2003) *Happiness and Education*. Cambridge: Cambridge University Press.

Pinto, D. (1990) *Interculturele communicatie: drie-stappenmethode voor het doeltreffend overbruggen en managen van cultuurverschillen*. Houten: Bohn Stafleu Van Loghum.

Robbins, S., Bergman, R., Stago, I. and Coulter, M. (2003) *Foundations of Management*. Frenchs Forest Australia: Prentice Hall.

Ryff, C. and Singer, B. (2003) 'The role of emotion on pathways to positive health', in Davidson, R., Sherer, K. and Goldsmith, H. (eds), *Handbook of Affective Science*. New York: Oxford University Press, pp. 1083–1104.

Scollon, R. and Scollon, S.W. (1995) *Intercultural Communication: A Discourse Approach*. Oxford: Blackwell.

Seligman, M. (2011) *Flourish: A Visionary New Understanding of Happiness and Well-Being*. New York: Simon & Schuster.

Sharpley, R. and Stone, P. (eds) (2012) *Contemporary Tourist Experience: Concepts and Consequences*. Abington, Oxon: Routledge.

Sheldon, P. (2005) 'Importance of international experiences for tourism students', paper presented to International Panel of Experts, Brisbane, November 2005.

Stevens, R. (1978) *Education and the Death of Love*. London: Epworth Press.

Trompenaars, F. and Hampden-Turner, C. (2001) *Riding the Waves of Culture* (2nd edition). London: Nicholas Brealey Publishing.

Witsel, M. (2006) 'Concerns and constraints of teaching tourism and hospitality in a multicultural context', in Whitelaw, P. (ed.), *To the City and Beyond*. Melbourne: Council of Australian Universities in Tourism and Hospitality Education (CAUTHE).

4 Travel as a factor of happiness in Hungary

Tamara Rátz and Gábor Michalkó

Introduction

Tourism – particularly leisure travel, but some aspects of business-related travel too – has a major influence on people's well-being around the world. Although the residents of host communities may perceive the socio-cultural impacts of tourism development both favourably and unfavourably (Rátz and Puczkó, 2002), there is a general consensus among many tourism researchers that holiday-taking as a leisure activity can enhance one's sense of happiness (Gilbert and Abdullah, 2004; Pearce and Foster, 2007). In addition to short-term, temporary pleasures, travel also holds the possibility of change and personal growth, and opens up learning opportunities, both in the formal and the informal sense of the word (Mayo and Jarvis, 1981; Noy, 2004; Bowen and Clarke, 2009).

In Hungary, during the socialist period, although domestic tourism was significantly subsidised by the state in order to provide relaxation opportunities to the working classes, international travel, particularly to the West, was considerably limited (Hall, 1991). Following the political changes of 1989–1990, the world 'opened up' for Hungarians, trips abroad suddenly became possible for almost anyone due to such changes as the introduction of the 'global passport', visa waiver agreements and the convertibility of the Hungarian currency. However, the unfavourable consequences of the economic transformation such as growing unemployment and inflation, and decreasing real income levels had a negative impact on Hungarians' actual travel propensity during the 1990s (Puczkó and Rátz, 2006). Consequently, travelling abroad, especially travelling to 'exotic' faraway destinations, was long seen as a privilege – and although today's young generations have only heard about the earlier political constraints of travelling from their parents and grandparents, the economic realities of many families make leisure tourism a special, infrequent experience for certain segments of the Hungarian society.

In order to better understand the complexity of the tourism and quality of life relationship in contemporary Hungarian reality, two major research projects were carried out by the authors between 2006 and 2011. The 'Health tourism and quality of life in Hungary: a geographical synthesis of social, economic and environmental factors of health-oriented mobility' project supported by the Hungarian Scientific Research Fund (2007–2011) aimed to assess the impacts of spa and health tourism development on the affected social groups' – visitors and residents of spa destinations – objective and subjective quality of life (Rátz and Michalkó, 2011). The objective of the 'Spatial characteristics of the relationship of tourism and quality of life' project supported by the Bolyai János Research Scholarship of the Hungarian Academy of Sciences (2006–2010) was to explore the significance of tourism among the factors that influence one's quality of life and to understand how different social factors affect the happiness-generating role of travel (Michalkó, 2010).

Happiness and tourism

During the five years of studying the relationship of tourism and quality of life, it has become clear for us that subjective well-being research has certain difficulties in defining both the concept of quality of life and its relationship with tourism. Although subjective well-being, happiness and life satisfaction are often treated as synonymous categories, certain distinctions can be made between these concepts. Following definitions of the concepts introduced by Lengyel and Janky (2002), differences may best be understood if we accept the notion that people associate personal happiness rather with their personal microsurroundings (family, children or social relationships), while life satisfaction is seen as something of a broader concept, related to work, institutions and life history. Other than the clarification of concepts, the subjective assessment of well-being has another cornerstone: its a priori experience. When examining the relationship between objective and subjective well-being one may find it convenient to extend these concepts in such a way that the former is associated with material prosperity, and the latter is paired to individual happiness; for this reason the majority of studies on subjective well-being have focused on the relationship between these two phenomena (e.g. Molnár and Kapitány, 2006).

Happiness is a complex and elusive concept (Kesebir and Diener, 2009) that has been approached from many different angles in tourism research (Smith, 2005; Filep, 2009). Most studies using the concept are based upon the subjective dimension of happiness, conceptualised in terms of pleasant emotions and feeling good (Veenhoven, 2003), linking the notion of happiness to that of subjective well-being perceived by the individual whose feelings are investigated (Diener, 1984). However, there are researchers who believe that a purely hedonistic concept is not adequate (Kahneman, 2003), and it is possible to assess a person's happiness objectively through the measurements of objective happiness factors over time (Krueger and Schkade, 2008). According to Marks and Shah (2004), to a certain extent happiness is determined by genetic predisposition, but it is also affected by life conditions (such as material possessions, income, social and interpersonal relationships, living conditions) and by intentional activities (e.g. sports, socialising, meaningful work, a positive attitude to life). Tourism may have an influence on one's objective happiness level in various ways. In the case of residents of tourist destinations, their life circumstances – for example, job or income – may be directly determined by tourism development, while the experiences of travellers may increase sense of satisfaction with their lives (Neal and Sirgy, 2004; Filep, 2009).

The normative dimension of happiness is rooted in the *eudaimonia* notion of Aristotle and his followers who believed that the object of human life was a 'type of happiness associated with virtuous conduct and philosophical reflection' (Layard, 2005, p. 22). The word 'happy' – 'boldog' – in Hungarian reflects the latter conceptualisation, since the same word also means 'blessed' or 'beatified', referring to virtuous behaviour or advanced spiritual knowledge as the preconditions of 'being happy'.

Most interpretations of happiness, including those constructed by the representatives of positive psychology (e.g. Csikszentmihalyi and Csikszentmihalyi, 2006; Filep, 2009, 2012; Snyder and Lopez, 2009), are based on hedonic as well as cognitive elements. According to Christopher and Hickinbottom (2008), currently two major approaches can be identified in the research of happiness and life satisfaction: the subjective well-being theory and the authentic happiness theory. The same two core research directions are also applied to the investigation of tourist happiness (Filep, 2012): the subjective well-being theory conceptualises tourist happiness in terms of positive, pleasant feelings, while the authentic happiness theory is based on Seligman's (2002) complex notion of the pleasant life, the good life and the meaningful life. In this understanding, the 'pleasant life' refers to pleasurable experiences and positive emotions about the past, the present and the future. The concept of 'good life' is connected to the notion of engagement (Filep, 2009) and consists of people developing their strengths and virtues in activities that are important in their lives, using positive individual traits and talents. The domain of 'meaningful life' develops when individuals use their strengths in activities that contribute to the greater good. The three domains are unequally represented among the major motivations of tourists – whereas searching for pleasant, positive experiences is the key motivational factor in leisure travel (Pearce, 2005), the need to derive meaning from life through tourism has only recently started to emerge to greater extent (Bowen and Clarke, 2009; Kler and Tribe, 2012). However, the currently growing popularity of volunteer tourism, for example, may be explained by travellers' quest for authentic happiness beyond the usual hedonic experiences to increase their feelings of self-respect and expand their sense of personal character strengths (Wearing, 2001; Stoddart and Rogerson, 2004). Filep (2009), in his study of Australian study-abroad students in Spain also found that the students' reflections on their tourist experiences created powerful post-trip meanings, and similar transformational effects/meanings have been found by other researchers among backpackers (e.g. Noy, 2004; O'Reilly, 2006). Nevertheless, all these studies explored atypical travel experiences with longer length of stay and higher than average levels of involvement in the host destinations' reality.

The relationship of tourism and happiness in Hungary

According to a previous study on the Hungarian society's perception of happiness (KSH, 2010, cited in Michalkó, 2010, pp. 34–35), respondents proved to be moderately satisfied with their own life (3.32 on a scale of 1–5, with 1 being 'not happy at all' and 5 being 'very happy'). Their perception was significantly influenced by age, education level, financial situation, family size and travel frequency, with younger, more educated, wealthier persons being happier. Family size only seemed to have a positive influence on life satisfaction to a certain extent: the happiest respondents were those who lived in families of four persons, while those with more or less family members expressed less satisfaction with life. The relationship between travel frequency and happiness proved to be obvious: the happiness indicator of those respondents who participated in four or more trips in the year of the survey was 3.73, as opposed to 3.05 among those who did not participate in any trip during the year. However, the available data do not make it possible to ascertain the cause-effect relationship of the two factors, leaving it open to whether happiness is increased as a result of higher travel frequency or if the combined effect of life-satisfaction-increasing factors (such as better financial situation, higher education level, younger age, etc.) leads to better opportunities to actively participate in tourism. In addition, respondents perceived the contribution of travel to their own happiness as very moderate (2.53 on a scale 1–5), with the highest value (3.63) within the wealthiest segment of the sample (Michalkó et al., 2010), underlining the assumption that the Hungarian society still considers tourism a somewhat luxurious activity as opposed to the gradually emerging Western belief that everybody needs and deserves a holiday (McCabe, 2009).

Taking into consideration the perceived positive impacts of travelling, a quantitative national survey performed by the Hungarian Central Statistical Office in 2007 demonstrated that 'developing and maintaining stronger relationships with family and friends' was seen as the main benefit of participating in leisure tourism among adult Hungarian residents (achieving a mean value of 3.84 on a 1–5 Likert-scale with 1 being 'not important at all' and 5 being 'very important'). The second-ranked benefit proved to be 'recreation and renewing energies needed for everyday activities' (3.68), while 'a thirst for more travel' came third. The adult Hungarian population valued tourism's ability to generate desire for further travelling higher (3.44) than its favourable influence on health improvement (2.83). Travelling proved to have the lowest influence on one's sense of being successful (2.67) (Michalkó et al., 2009).

Life events may have a significant influence on individuals' mental state (Zautra and Reich, 1983). Several life events are closely connected to travel (e.g. wedding and honeymoon), and several journeys in themselves can be considered as life events (e.g. proposing in a romantic location, an exchange semester abroad, the first foreign journey to a country outside the Iron Curtain). Although negative life events may also be related to travelling (e.g. serious accidents, death), it may be assumed that most of the journeys considered as life events generate positive thoughts leading to a perception of happiness (Michalkó, 2010). In an attempt to connect leisure travel with the concepts of quality of life and life events, respondents of a subsequent survey in 2008 were asked to select those life events and more trivial life situations on a pre-determined list

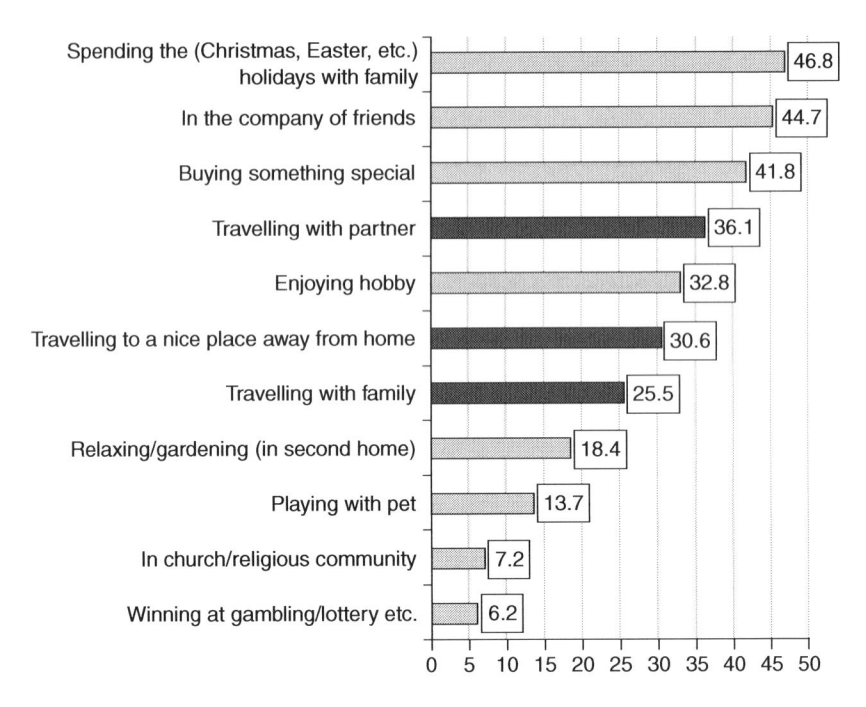

Life event/situation	%
Spending the (Christmas, Easter, etc.) holidays with family	46.8
In the company of friends	44.7
Buying something special	41.8
Travelling with partner	36.1
Enjoying hobby	32.8
Travelling to a nice place away from home	30.6
Travelling with family	25.5
Relaxing/gardening (in second home)	18.4
Playing with pet	13.7
In church/religious community	7.2
Winning at gambling/lottery etc.	6.2

Figure 4.1 The happiness-inducing role of life events and situations in Hungary, 2008 (source: Michalkó, 2010).

(a maximum of 7 events from a list of 21 variables) that gave them the highest sense of happiness (Michalkó *et al.*, 2010) (Figure 4.1).

Among the listed events, holidays such as Christmas or Easter spent in the family circle (46.8 per cent) seemed to be the events which generated the most happiness, whilst successful gambling (6.2 per cent) generated the least. Travel altogether occupies a relatively important place in the order of happiness-generating events (highlighted by darker coloured bars): travelling with partner (36.1 per cent), travelling to a 'nice place' away from home (30.6 per cent) and travelling with family (25.5 per cent) are found among the first seven happiness-generating factors. Overall, events connected to travel seemed to be able to generate a memorable perception of happiness, particularly travelling as a couple, which might be explained by romantic implications or by giving an opportunity for those with families to leave their daily routine behind.

Research methods

As discussed above, the study presented in this chapter was carried out within the framework of a five-year-long investigation based on two major projects examining the relationship between tourism and quality of life in Hungary

(Michalkó, 2010; Michalkó and Rátz, 2011; Rátz and Michalkó, 2011). The aim of the study was to explore the contribution of leisure travel to individuals' perceived happiness. A qualitative approach was used through 200 structured interviews with Hungarians – in the memory and reflection phase of the tourist experience (Larsen, 2007) – who needed to meet the following criteria in order to qualify for participation:

- Experienced traveller (who travels regularly for leisure and/or business purposes in Hungary and abroad, and whose quality of life is generally more affected by their travel opportunities than on average)
- At least 18 years old

In addition to enquiring about the general characteristics of respondents' travel behaviour, the research aimed to explore participants' desires in terms of 'dream destinations' and their most memorable experiences, by asking them the following questions (translated from Hungarian):

- 'If you could travel anywhere in the world tomorrow, wherever you wish, where would you go?'
- 'During your travels have there been actual places or situations where/in which you felt happy, felt a real satisfaction with your life?' 'Can you recall your exact thoughts and emotions in those places and/or situations?'

The narratives were analysed using qualitative content analysis (Stepchenkova *et al.*, 2009). Both authors coded the responses, searching for recurrent themes; any overlapping themes and coding differences were then discussed and the resulting dimensions were further refined until consensus was reached. In addition to investigating the happiness-inducing capability of geographical spaces, we aimed to explore the conscious perception of the 'tourist moment', a special, highly satisfactory, heightened experience during which tourists connect to the 'other' and feelings of difference are inverted into feelings of sameness (Hom Cary, 2004).

The travel experiences recalled by the respondents reflected a great variety of destinations, situations, dates and types of interactions, but were generally related to trips of relatively short lengths of stay, as opposed to Filep's (2009) research of study abroad students or Noy's (2004) investigation of Israeli backpackers.

Research results

The spatial aspects of travel-related happiness

Eric Weiner, an American journalist who explored the characteristics of the happiest and the unhappiest countries of the world, travelled a long way only to finally understand that the sources of happiness do not differ significantly:

Places are the same. It's not the elements that matter so much as how they're arranged and in which proportions. Arrange them one way and you have Switzerland. Arrange them another way, and you have Moldova. Getting the balance right is important.

(Weiner, 2008, p. 322)

The extent to which certain geographical places are likely or able to increase one's sense of happiness depends on a variety of factors such as travel propensity and previous travel experiences, attitudes towards travel, religion and personality. When it comes to the selection of destinations, the majority of travellers wish to choose places that 'have got the balance right'. Although the perfect combination varies, as our research also demonstrated, there seems to be a consensus that certain constructions of geographical spaces are more able to increase happiness than others (Egedy, 2009). The geographical and tourist milieu of a destination affect the visitors, although their post-trip recollections seem to be slightly more influenced by the well-known sights than by the atmospheric characteristics of the visited destinations (Michalkó and Rátz, 2006). Since seaside destinations, for example, have been among the most visited tourist areas around the world for decades, it may be assumed that countries with long stretches of warm, pleasant beaches provide a higher chance of experiencing happiness than landlocked countries or very cold and windy destinations: the number of tourist arrivals is a direct reflection of the given place's happiness-inducing capacity.

According to Weiner (2008), happiness seems to have a subconscious geographical connotation: we search for happiness the same way as we are trying to find locations on a map, and many places carry a promise of happiness to visitors. When selecting their travel destination, people are looking for 'nice places', as evidenced by one of our respondents who said, 'we travel to be at a better place than the one where we are now'. These memorable places, the spatial components of the leisure travel-induced happiness, are perceived and evaluated by potential visitors through many layers of associations – factual knowledge, media messages, subjective information from our environment, personal experiences or emotional attachment (Michalkó, 2010).

Although the great majority of Hungarians travelling abroad stay within Europe (Magyar Turizmus Zrt., 2012), when naming their dream destinations our respondents were slightly more inclined to leave the old continent. Without being limited in their choices by financial and temporal constraints, Europe would only attract 34.5 per cent of the respondents, the Americas would come second (23.2 per cent), Asia third (18.6 per cent), and Africa and Australia/Oceania would tie at fourth place (10.7 per cent each) (2.3 per cent of the interviewees gave geographically irrelevant answers). In terms of countries or specific regions/places within countries, this study also confirmed the United States' status as the most admired country globally (GfK Custom Research North America, 2011) (14.7 per cent). Although the great variety of responses suggests that happiness may be embodied in many different geographical locations, it was interesting to see that the US state of Hawaii was perceived as more attractive than India, China or Australia. The happiness-inducing tropical paradise image of the Pacific islands (Goss, 1993) seems to remain strong even in Central-Eastern Europe. Among the countries that at least 3 per cent of the interview participants mentioned as their most desired destinations were also Italy, Greece, France, India, China, Australia, Spain and Peru, suggesting a relatively restrained travel imagination which might be attributed to a variety of social, political, economic and personal factors.

The conscious perception of travel-related happiness

While happiness may be associated with places, it may also be increased or generated by certain travel situations, encounters and events. The content analysis of the 200 interviews focusing on the conscious perception of such happiness-generating experiences resulted in 12 separate dimensions that are discussed below with the help of illustrative quotes.

1   Carefreeness (number of components=27): key components of this dimension are escaping the daily hassles in a tourist milieu that has a favourable impact on one's general mood, and the recognition of the fact that it is possible to focus only on relaxing and having fun, usually in the pleasant company of friends or partner, being engaged in a favourite leisure activity (Figure 4.2).

    I felt relaxed, I didn't have to think about my work all day, I could take a rest and I could do what I love most: riding my motorbike.
    (male, 25–44 years old)

2   Change of environment (27): simply escaping temporarily from one's permanent environment may improve physical and mental well-being. In addition, the pre-trip preparations, the new and unusual activities, the complex adaptation to the differences of a temporary residence, the challenges associated with a new environment, all contribute to personal development and may improve one's self-image.

    I feel happiness every time I travel, because a new environment always puts me in a good mood. I realise every time that I would need such experiences more often.
    (male, 73 years old)

    Although the perception of happiness is generally associated with the experiences and encounters found in the final destination, the activity of travelling may also be happiness-inducing in itself.

Figure 4.2 Carefreeness (photograph by Tamara Rátz).

> I feel happy when normal people don't: like sitting on a 36-hour train trip with already 10 hours delay ... but such things always happen at these end-of-the-world places and that's why I feel it's so damn great being there.
> (female, 41 years old)

3 Family (25): spending the holidays with one's family usually gives an opportunity for family members to focus on each other, share experiences and even discover each others' personal characteristics or abilities that remained hidden in their everyday life. Although the data in Figure 4.1 suggested that travelling with partner has a higher probability of increasing happiness than family trips that also include the kids, this may also be explained by the greater likelihood of conflicts among different generations; relatively peaceful family holidays however may result in truly memorable experiences and may contribute to children's long-term travel socialisation.

Every summer, when the family is together in the cottage ... when we have breakfast together or take a walk along the shore together in the evening ... I can't describe this feeling, but I never feel happier.

(female, 47 years old)

4 The sea (24): although the first meeting with the sea often has a particularly deep impact on individuals (especially coming from a landlocked country such as Hungary where the notion of 'seaside' is associated with romantic feelings), the appreciation of the coastal landscape has been a common theme in the arts, in literature or even in cinematography, thus popularising the seaside experience and creating expectations. The aesthetic features of the sea and the leisure activities available at seaside resorts can contribute to travellers' sense of happiness, so gazing over the endless water may generate enjoyment just as much as sailing, sunbathing or diving.

We went by car, it was an incredible feeling to see the sea for the first time ... I was looking at the sea and wished that this holiday would last forever.

(female, 23 years old)

5 Sense of belonging (22): since humans are social creatures, those experiences that are able to generate a sense of community among travellers may play an important part in the conscious perception of happiness. The community's role in one's well-being is related to shared experiences, dependence on each other, helping each other, collective creative activities, verbal and nonverbal communication or even in the discovery of personal similarities and differences. Although this sense of belonging to a new community is generally associated with youth travel, partying during holidays and participation in festivals, age is not necessarily a limiting factor, and this kind of personal benefit is often unrelated to typical tourist attractions or activities.

In a compact-sized town I was involved in an activity that I liked ... already the first week I felt that things were happening at my pace, according to my biorhythm ... I had this happy feeling in the shared kitchen that 13 of us used together, it was a very pleasant evening, we were cooking and eating together.

(male, 26 years old)

In the following illustration, the interviewee's happiness was less related to the enjoyment of an event than to the sense of community felt by the, most probably, all-Hungarian audience in a foreign (neighbouring) country.

> We spent New Year's Eve in Transylvania [Romania] with our friends from there, and before the evening party we went to the first Transylvania–Hungary ice hockey game. It was a great feeling when everybody was singing the Transylvanian and the Hungarian hymns together.
>
> (male, 35 years old)

6 Self-actualisation (19): in this context, happiness is brought about by meeting self-determined challenges that test one's cognitive or physical skills, using maximum concentration, and proving one's abilities and perseverance both to oneself and to others. In leisure tourism, such experiences are generally related to extreme sports and other types of physical activities, although they may also be present in creative pursuits or learning (e.g. in learning a foreign language sufficiently well for successful communication).

> I feel happy when I climb a mountain or hike a trail. I set these challenges for myself, and I'm the happiest when I succeed to meet them. When I was on a hunting safari in Africa, I felt I was becoming one with my environment, I didn't only see the animals, I felt them, it was a totally spiritual experience.
>
> (male, 24 years old)

Self-actualisation may also be experienced through work-related challenges, especially in creative professions, but also in other fields; however, this type of perceived benefit is often connected with Maslow's esteem needs as well (Maslow, 2003).

> I was in Amsterdam, I was very happy because I was assigned that job, I felt proud of myself.
>
> (female, 29 years old)

7 Romance (19): since events and situations associated with love such as proposals, weddings, honeymoons, wedding anniversaries or simply romantic moments such as walking on a beach or kissing in the rain are among the most obvious happiness-inducing factors, it was actually slightly surprising that many other dimensions proved to be more influential among the interviewees. This may be explained by the relatively low travel propensity of Hungarians: if less than 40 per cent of the population can afford to participate in leisure travel (Magyar Turizmus Zrt., 2012), then it is less likely that such crucial romantic moments occur during holidays. In addition, although travelling with one's partner proved to contribute to one's subjective happiness (Figure 4.1), romance also seemed to be present in respondents' everyday life as opposed to carefreeness or a change of environment, thus being a less travel-specific factor.

Proposing to her was very memorable and I was truly happy when she said yes. We were standing on the top of Kékes [the highest peak of Hungary] in winter, there was a lot of snow and a beautiful sunset. I felt warmth in my heart ... that I have finally arrived.

(male, 32 years old)

8 Freedom to travel (17): while partly related to the next dimension (first individual trip), a sense of happiness brought about simply by the ability to travel anywhere (within financial and temporal boundaries) was mainly mentioned by those respondents who grew up in the socialist system, i.e. those older than 40. For the younger generations, a life where people's holiday activities are regulated by the state is almost inconceivable. Although today, in principle, travel opportunities are only constrained by one's financial means, the heritage of the socialist system can still be seen in the way that most Hungarians' mental tourist map of the world is limited to the major European seaside and cultural destinations (Germany, Austria, Croatia, Italy) and the neighbouring countries with significant Hungarian minorities.

When I was growing up it was a big deal to go abroad ... just crossing a border of any neighbouring country was an experience because it meant you were abroad ... I could never imagine travelling around the world and feeling at ease anywhere just as I do now.

(female, 41 years old)

9 First individual trip (15): the 'first' life events (e.g. first day at school, first boyfriend/girlfriend, first job) generally remain memorable, even if their impact on one's future life may vary significantly. The first vacation with friends and without parents, the first holiday paid by one's own savings, the first trip abroad were all mentioned by our respondents as happiness-inducing experiences, as was the first time they could test their foreign language skills in an international environment or the first visit to a destination that later proved to be important in their lives.

When I was 17 and decided to see the world on my own, I felt free, happy, adult, like the whole world was mine.

(female, 22 years old)

10 Beautiful place (13): the aesthetic pleasures of scenic landscapes often increase the overall quality of a tourist experience. The beauty of a place may be associated with many features such as its architecture, geographical location, flora and fauna, or such natural phenomena as sunsets, sunrises or rainbows. Since the attractiveness of the natural environment and the cultural richness of destinations are among the major pull factors of tourism,

there is a logical relationship between perceived travel-related happiness and the beauty of places.

> We were in the Mátra [hills] on a coach trip, it was morning, and when the sun was rising, it was such an incredibly beautiful sight as the rays of light were streaming through the trees, it just filled me with happiness.
>
> (female, 68 years old)

11 Dream (9): visiting a certain place may be seen as the realisation of a dream for various reasons. Many dream destinations are associated with the individual's self-actualisation needs, either for simply having been to a particular, often world-famous or legendary place, or for being involved in a certain site-specific activity (e.g. dancing flamenco in Sevilla or riding an elephant in Thailand). In addition, visiting places that are globally acknowledged as dream destinations, such as Paris or Tahiti, may increase one's sense of satisfaction even if the place does not meet all their expectations (Figure 4.3).

> I got to Venice, to the Piazza San Marco, and standing there I felt that a dream had come true.
>
> (female, 25–44 years old)

Figure 4.3 Venice is the dream destination for many travellers (photograph by Tamara Rátz).

12 Local people (7): taking a glimpse into the everyday life of a destination, communicating with the locals, developing temporary acquaintances or long-term friendships may all induce a sense of happiness in travellers. The attitudes and behaviour of the local community (openness, friendliness, *joie de vivre* or aloofness, inhospitality) may have a major impact on the visitors' overall experience, and may also help them re-evaluate their own society and attitudes.

> The main plaza and the terraces have a good impact on me ... I feel that I'm participating in the locals' life, I eat what they eat, I drink like they drink, I sit where they sit, and I try to see the world as they do.
>
> (male, 48 years old)

Discussion and conclusions

The various findings in our research all confirmed the positive influence of travel on respondents' lives, albeit only to a certain extent. While the quantitative surveys were able to compare the long-term impact of tourism on subjective well-being with that of other significant life factors, the qualitative method helped to explore the dimensions of happiness-inducing travel experiences and situations.

The analysis of the interviews describing the respondents' travel-related happiness experiences showed that most of these moments reflected the presence of both cognitive and affective components. As Pearce *et al.* (2011) demonstrated, instead of being contradictory this is the essence of the flow state which is experienced when an individual engages one's highest strengths and talents to meet just-doable challenges (Csikszentmihalyi, 2001). Flow is a state where one is totally involved in a voluntary activity, the experience is highly rewarding in itself and when everything comes together for an individual (Filep, 2009). Most of the nine core features of the state of flow (Csikszentmihalyi, 2001) are present in the identified 12 interview dimensions of travel-induced happiness, although generally in a combination and to different degrees. The state of flow is most clearly represented by a match between one's perceived skills and challenges, clear goals, unambiguous feedback, concentration, sense of control, and the autotelic nature of the experience. The dimensions of 'carefreeness', 'the sea', 'change of the environment' and 'dream' include characteristics of time transformation and loss of self-consciousness, while 'freedom to travel' and especially 'first individual trip' are based on a sense of control and both may be seen as autotelic experiences. The interpersonal dimensions such as 'family', 'sense of belonging', 'romance' and 'local people', however, do not reveal features of the state of flow, since in these cases the happiness-generating capacity is out of the individual's control.

Taking into consideration the authentic happiness theory (Seligman, 2002), many of the identified happiness dimensions symbolise the concept of the pleasant life, i.e. respondents recalled pleasurable experiences and positive emotions about their travels, suggesting that the majority of Hungarians perceive tourism only as an enjoyable, entertaining activity, and are less aware of its potential eudaimonic benefits.

Since only relatively experienced travellers (by Hungarian standards) were involved in the qualitative stage of the research, most of them expressed their willingness to recreate those – or similar – incidents of happiness that they recalled during the interviews. However, their future travel aspirations and their personal strategies to create further travel opportunities were different, depending on the core dimension of their most memorable experience. Those who emphasised impersonal elements such as scenic beauty, the seaside or the freedom to travel generally wished to visit new, preferably faraway, exotic destinations, while those who highlighted interpersonal components such as family or romance were less interested in making sacrifices to visit distant places – their efforts focused on spending time together, almost irrespective of the destination. Their strategies to create more opportunities to travel also differed according to their financial situation, age, availability of time, work or family obligations. Those motivated by 'places' were more likely to adopt their everyday life to their travel aspirations, while those motivated by people were more apt to arrange their trips around their everyday life.

Since Hungarians are typically unhappy (Helliwell et al., 2012), it should be logical that if travelling has any positive impact on individuals' subjective well-being, then it should be supported and encouraged by various means, both at the macro-level and through micro-level initiatives. Although the improvement of quality of life through the benefits of travelling were given primary importance in the recent Hungarian tourism development strategies (Michalkó et al., 2009), the happiness-inducing capacity of tourism and the ways to make the most of this capacity, at a national level, for different segments, merit further research. In addition, in order to increase the role of tourism in the fulfilment of higher individual needs, it is necessary to raise the consciousness and awareness of travellers concerning the potential social benefits of tourism.

The research was supported by the Hungarian Scientific Research Fund (OTKA K67573).

References

Bowen, D. and Clarke, J. (2009) *Contemporary Tourist Behaviour: Yourself and Others as Tourists*. Wallingford: CABI.
Christopher, J.C. and Hickinbottom, S. (2008) 'Positive psychology, ethnocentrism, and the disguised ideology of individualism', *Theory & Psychology*, 18 (5): 563–589.
Csikszentmihalyi, M. (2001) *Flow: az áramlat. A tökéletes élmény pszichológiája*. Budapest: Akadémiai Kiadó.
Csikszentmihalyi, M. and Csikszentmihalyi, I.S. (eds) (2006) *A Life Worth Living: Contributions to Positive Psychology*. Oxford: Oxford University Press.
Diener, E. (1984) 'Subjective well-being', *Psychological Bulletin*, 95 (3): 542–575.
Egedy, T. (2009) *Városrehabilitáció és életminőség*. Budapest: MTA Földrajztudományi Kutatóintézet.

Filep, S. (2009) 'Tourists' happiness through the lens of positive psychology', PhD thesis, James Cook University, http://eprints.jcu.edu.au/10842 [Accessed 20 July 2005].

Filep, S. (2012) 'Positive psychology and tourism', in Uysal, M., Perdue, R.R. and Sirgy, M.J. (eds), *Handbook of Tourism and Quality-of-Life Research: Enhancing the Lives of Tourists and Residents of Host Communities*. Dordrecht: Springer Science+Business Media B.V., pp. 31–50.

GfK Custom Research North America (2011) *America Remains the Most Admired Country Globally in the 2011 Anholt-GfK Roper Nation Brands IndexSM*. www.gfk.com/group/press_information/press_releases/008789/index.en.html [Accessed 22 July 2012].

Gilbert, D. and Abdullah, J. (2004) 'Holidaytaking and the sense of well-being', *Annals of Tourism Research*, 31 (1): 103–121.

Goss, J.D. (1993) 'Placing the market and marketing place: tourist advertising of the Hawaiian islands, 1972–92', *Environment and Planning D: Society and Space*, 11 (6): 663–688.

Hall, D. (1991) *Tourism and Economic Development in Eastern Europe and the Soviet Union*. Chichester: John Wiley & Sons Ltd.

Helliwell, J., Layard, R. and Sachs, J. (eds) (2012) *World Happiness Report*. New York: The Earth Institute, Columbia University – CIFAR – Centre for Economic Performance.

Hom Cary, S. (2004) 'The tourist moment', *Annals of Tourism Research*, 31 (1): 61–77.

Kahneman, D. (2003) 'Objective happiness', in Kahneman, D., Diener, E. and Schwarz, N. (eds), *Well-Being: The Foundations of Hedonic Psychology*. New York: Russell Sage Foundation, pp. 3–25.

Kesebir, P. and Diener, E. (2009) 'In pursuit of happiness: empirical answers to philosophical questions', in Diener, E. (ed.), *The Science of Well-Being: The Collected Works of Ed Diener*. Dordrecht: Springer Science+Business Media B.V., pp. 59–74.

Kler, B.K. and Tribe, J. (2012) 'Flourishing through SCUBA: understanding the pursuit of dive experiences', *Tourism in Marine Environments*, 8 (1–2): 19–32.

Krueger, A. and Schkade, D. (2008) 'The reliability of subjective well-being measures', *Journal of Public Economics*, 92 (8–9): 1833–1845.

Larsen, S. (2007) 'Aspects of a psychology of the tourist experience', *Scandinavian Journal of Hospitality and Tourism*, 7 (1): 7–18.

Layard, R. (2005) *Happiness: Lessons from a New Science*. London: Penguin Press.

Lengyel, Gy. and Janky, B. (2002) 'A szubjektív jólét társadalmi feltételei', in Lengyel, Gy. (ed.), *Indikátorok és elemzések. Műhelytanulmányok a társadalmi jelzőszámok témaköréből*. Budapest: BKÁE, pp. 105–127.

McCabe, S. (2009) 'Who needs a holiday? Evaluating social tourism', *Annals of Tourism Research*, 36 (4): 667–688.

Magyar Turizmus Zrt. (2012) *A magyar lakosság belföldi és külföldi utazásai 2011-ben*. Budapest: Magyar Turizmus Zrt.

Marks, N. and Shah, H. (2004) 'A well-being manifesto for a flourishing society', *Journal of Public Mental Health*, 3 (4): 9–15.

Maslow, A. (2003) *A lét pszichológiája felé*. Budapest: Ursus Libris.

Mayo, E.J. and Jarvis, L.P. (1981) *The Psychology of Leisure Travel: Effective Marketing and Selling of Travel Services*. Boston: CBI Publishing.

Michalkó, G. (2010) *Boldogító utazás. A turizmus és az életminőség kapcsolatának magyarországi vonatkozásai*. Budapest: MTA Földrajztudományi Kutatóintézet.

Michalkó, G. and Rátz, T. (2006) 'The Mediterranean tourist milieu', *Anatolia: An International Journal of Tourism and Hospitality Research*, 17 (1): 93–109.

Michalkó, G. and Rátz, T. (2011) *Egészségturizmus és életminőség Magyarországon: Fejezetek az egészség, az utazás és a jól(l)ét magyarországi összefüggéseiről*. Budapest: MTA Földrajztudományi Kutatóintézet.

Michalkó, G., Rátz, T. and Irimiás, A. (2009) 'Health tourism and quality of life in Hungary: some aspects of a complex relationship', in De Santis, G. (ed.), *Salute e lavoro. Atti del Nono Seminario Internazionale di Geografia Medica*. Perugia: Edizioni RUX, pp. 79–90.

Michalkó, G., Rátz, T. and Bakucz, M. (2010) 'A theoretical journey along the borders between welfare and well-being: economic aspects based on observations in Hungary', *Megatrend Review: The International Review of Applied Economics*, 7 (1): 231–248.

Molnár, Gy. and Kapitány, Zs. (2006) *Mobility, Uncertainty and Subjective Well-being in Hungary*. Institute of Economics, Discussion Paper Series, MTDP-2006/5, Budapest.

Neal, J.D. and Sirgy, M.J. (2004) 'Measuring the effect of tourism services on travelers' quality of life: further validation', *Social Indicators Research*, 69 (3): 243–277.

Noy, C. (2004) 'This trip really changed me: backpackers' narratives of self-change', *Annals of Tourism Research*, 31 (1): 78–102.

O'Reilly, C.C. (2006) 'From drifter to gap year tourist: mainstreaming backpacker travel', *Annals of Tourism Research*, 33 (4): 998–1017.

Pearce, P.L. (2005) *Tourist Behaviour: Themes and Conceptual Schemes*. Clevedon: Channel View Publications.

Pearce, P.L. and Foster, F. (2007) 'A "university of travel": backpacker learning', *Tourism Management*, 28 (5): 1285–1298.

Pearce, P.L., Filep, S. and Ross, G. (2011) *Tourists, Tourism and the Good Life*. New York: Routledge.

Puczkó, L. and Rátz, T. (2006) 'Product development and diversification in Hungary', in Hall, D., Smith, M. and Marciszewska, B. (eds), *Tourism in the New Europe: The Challenges and Opportunities of EU Enlargement*. Wallingford: CABI Publishing, pp. 116–126.

Rátz, T. and Michalkó, G. (2011) 'The contribution of tourism to well-being and welfare: the case of Hungary', *International Journal of Sustainable Development*, 14 (3/4): 332–346.

Rátz, T. and Puczkó, L. (2002) *The Impacts of Tourism*. Hämeenlinna: Häme Polytechnic.

Seligman, M.E.P. (2002) *Authentic Happiness: Using the New Positive Psychology to Realize Your Potential for Lasting Fulfillment*. New York: Free Press.

Smith, M.K. (2005) 'Happiness and education: theory, practice and possibility', *The Encyclopaedia of Informal Education*, www.infed.org/biblio/happiness_and_education.htm [Accessed 25 July 2012].

Snyder, C.R. and Lopez, S.J. (eds) (2009) *Oxford Handbook of Positive Psychology, 2nd ed*. Oxford: Oxford University Press.

Stepchenkova, S., Kirilenko, A.P. and Morrison, A. (2009) 'Facilitating content analysis in tourism research', *Journal of Travel Research*, 47 (4): 454–469.

Stoddart, H. and Rogerson, C.M. (2004) 'Volunteer tourism: the case of habitat for humanity South Africa', *GeoJournal*, 60 (3): 311–318.

Veenhoven, R. (2003) 'Hedonism and happiness', *Journal of Happiness Studies*, 4 (4): 437–457.

Wearing, S. (2001) *Volunteer Tourism: Experiences That Make a Difference*. Oxon: CABI Publishing.
Weiner, E. (2008) *The Geography of Bliss: One Grump's Search for the Happiest Places in the World*. New York: Twelve.
Zautra, A.J. and Reich, J.W. (1983) 'Life events and perceptions of life quality: developments in a two-factor approach', *Journal of Community Psychology*, 11 (2): 121–132.

5 Tourism, wellness and feeling good
Reviewing and studying Asian spa experiences

Jenny Panchal

The 'positive-tourism' connection

Recent developments in assessing human well-being in general provide some new pathways for understanding the Asian spa experience. Much of this work is implicitly covered by the label *positive psychology*, which is recognised as a new field of study that focuses on human thriving. Following Seligman and Csikszentmihalyi (2000), Pearce (2007) defines positive psychology as a 'scientific study of positive emotions, character strengths and positive institutions concerned with human happiness and well-being' (p. 3). This definition suggests that positive psychology is not just about the individual, but also about communities, institutions, organisations and industries. It is therefore surprising that the relationship between tourism and human thriving remains under-researched (Smith and Kelly, 2006; Gilbert and Abdullah, 2002, 2003; Hunter-Jones and Blackburn, 2007).

The concept of wellness is an indispensable concept in the study of both tourism and positive psychology. Wellness is one of the facets of positive psychology that has received attention recently. Although the wellness-tourism interface has a long heritage (e.g. ancient pilgrimages, travels for health and wellness during the ancient Roman and Greek times), recent studies and the arguable pioneering literature on wellness tourism (for example the wellness issue of *Tourism Recreation Research*, 2006) tend to approach the topic as an exposition of an ostensibly brand new form of tourism. This chapter seeks to review and study spa tourism and interpret the scheme for spa-goers through the lens of positive psychology.

The wellness context and the Asian spa industry

There is a consensus among thinkers in many disciplines and specialisms that a wellness industry exists (Smith and Puczko, 2009; Furrer, 2010; GSS Report, 2008, 2010; Pilzer, 2007). In contemporary society, 'wellness' can be viewed as a trite term that is widely used by the general public. While it is commonly used, wellness is also a slippery term that does not have a universal definition; it is a multifaceted concept and clarifying its meaning is a challenge. The complexities of the term and the concept of wellness reflect its history. Miller (2005), who has provided a comprehensive review of the evolution and development of wellness admits 'the problem for the scholar that this malleability of the term wellness presents is that it is extremely difficult to define precisely what is meant by it, and therefore to adequately trace its origins' (p. 98).

The term wellness has been used in different contexts and because definitions vary from one context to another, a single universal definition is problematic. In the literature, however, the definitions of and discussions about wellness in disciplines such as medicine, psychology and economics (e.g. financial wellness) do have key commonalities. The dominant characteristics of wellness that are evident in the literature are:

1   *multidimensional and holistic* (Dunn, 1959; Finnicum and Zeiger, 1996; Myers *et al.*, 2000; Murray and Miller, 2000, cited in Fain and Lewis, 2002; Puczko and Bachvaroz, 2006; Smith and Kelly, 2006; Adams, 2003, cited in Smith and Kelly, 2006)
2   *involves health, well-being and satisfaction* (Finnicum and Zeiger, 1996; Myers *et al.*, 2000; Cowen, 1991, cited in Carruthers and Hood, 2004; Carruthers and Hood, 2004; Adams, 2003, cited in Smith and Kelly, 2006)
3   *simultaneously a state of being and a process* (Dunn, 1959; Finnicum and Zeiger, 1996; Travis, 1984, cited in Mueller and Kaufmann, 2001; Fain and Lewis, 2002)
4   *it is about choice and self-responsibility* (Mueller and Kaufmann, 2001; Cowen, 1991, cited in Carruthers and Hood, 2004; Finnicum and Zeiger, 1996)
5   *it is relative and subjective* (Travis, 1984, cited in Mueller and Kaufmann, 2001; Mueller and Kaufmann, 2001)

The use of the term wellness has become more widespread despite the consumers' vague understanding of the word and the lack of a clearly delineated wellness industry in the fields of economics and business (GSS Report, 2010). Such an industry does, however, exist and is burgeoning (Smith and Puczko, 2009). The Stanford Research International (SRI) which was commissioned by the Global Spa Summit Committee to analyse the global wellness market, conservatively estimates that the current wellness industry represents a global market of nearly US$2 trillion (GSS Report, 2010). The SRI also reports that the rapid growth of the wellness industry is attributed to three key trends: (1) an increasingly older, segment of unhealthy people; (2) failing medical systems; and (3) globalisation and connection.

Indeed, health and wellness are popular tourism products. The health–wellness–tourism interface represents a long standing relationship that dates back to ancient times. Owing to the Greek and Roman discovery of the healing qualities of water, people started travelling to mineral springs and seaside resorts to recuperate, relax and/or escape from the imperial metropolis (Iovine, 2005). In modern tourism, travelling for health and wellness persists as an activity as noted in the previous section of this chapter.

Thinkers in the specialism of tourism (e.g. Mueller and Kaufmann, 2001; Puczko and Bachvarov, 2006) had already argued, even prior to the GSS 2010 report, that although a wellness holiday may be located in an institution that provides a cure, it is important to draw the line between *medical* and *wellness* tourists. More specifically, Mueller and Kaufmann (2001) differentiate the two types of tourists, especially those who go to hotel/resort-based wellness facilities. They say that wellness in these facilities should not be misclassified and should be clearly segmented as either normal cure guests (i.e. those for treatment or curing their illness/es) or health guests (i.e. those for illness prevention or current health maintenance). The demarcation between medical and wellness tourists has been made clear in the wellness industry cluster model where medical tourism (*reactive*) and wellness tourism (*proactive*) are located on the opposite sides of the continuum (Pilzer, 2007; Travis and Ryan, 2004; GSS Report, 2010).

The literature on health and wellness tourism provides two established categories: medical and spa tourism. Connell (2006) describes medical tourism as purposefully linked to direct medical intervention, and that its outcomes are expected to be extensive and long-term. Horowitz and Rosenweig (2007) also suggest that medical tourists must submit themselves for medical check-ups and may undergo health surgeries. More obtrusive aesthetic/cosmetic procedures include but are not limited to cosmetic surgery, cosmetic dentistry/extensive dental construction and body contouring. In more extreme cases, treatment of infertility and sex change operations are also performed. Although medical tourism in this context is acknowledged as being within the rubrics of wellness tourism, it is not a concentration of the present set of studies.

The health and relaxation component that spas offer to supplement the traditional holiday makes health and wellness tourism an area of rising popularity (Didascalou *et al.*, 2007). Although this is a more recent observation, historical accounts on the origins of spa assert otherwise. While medical tourism is a more contemporary form of tourism, the earliest forms of spa tourism were also directly aimed at increased health and well-being (Connell, 2006). Although it was not termed spa tourism as such, the practice of visiting spas for healing was common by the seventeenth to the nineteenth centuries in many parts of Europe (Douglas, 2001; Kaspar, 1990; Laing and Weiler, 2008; Iovine, 2005; Henry, 2005). Spa tourism is a subtler subset of health and wellness tourism in terms of treatments and therapies.

The twenty-first century spas, according to the International Spa Association (ISPA, 2008), are places devoted to the enhancement of one's overall being through professional services that promote mind, body and spirit renewal. The phenomenon is now diverse as almost any service provider with health-oriented services 'can and does call itself a spa' (Puczko and Bachvarov, 2006). Smith and Kelly (2006) describe spa tourism as:

> tourism which focuses on the relaxation or healing of the body using water-based treatments, such as pools, steam rooms and saunas. Emphasis tends to be focused on relaxation and health and beauty treatments rather than the

spiritual aspect of certain exercises such as yoga. Surroundings are usually sumptuous with pricing schemes to match.

Similarly, Hall (2003) defines spa tourism as:

> a component of health tourism that relates to the provision of specific health facilities and destinations which traditionally include the provision of mineral waters which may also be used to refer to tourist resorts that integrate health facilities with accommodation.

Both definitions suggest that water is a significant element in spa tourism, especially in Europe – the home of spa.

While these definitions may be used in the European context, they cannot be used as a universal definition of spa tourism in Asian spas. The inclusion of the term 'water' in these definitions makes it appear that water is the main element used in spa treatments and therapies. Water and its natural sources such as mineral hot springs are also recognised to have therapeutic effects in Asia (e.g. Japan and Korea). Nonetheless, many other Asian spa practices are not just reliant on water. The use of nature-derived mineral and essential oils is a widespread Eastern practice (e.g. massages). Indeed, nature is an integral part of the Asian spa. The Asian spa phenomenon is more than just a massage or a scrub. Importantly, the daily rituals and ceremonies are all part of Asians' way of life which are designed to restore the body and soul (Chapman, 2006). Chapman (2006) argues that the prime focus of most Asian spas is to return the body to a balanced state through ancient botanical recipes and time-honoured rituals. Apart from minerals and oils, herbs, spices, certain root crops (e.g. ginger) and parts of plants and trees are believed to have healing and/or soothing benefits hence used in traditional spa treatments.

Revered as the 'home to the world's richest and most diverse spa culture' (Spa Wellness Council, 2008), the Asia Pacific is the world's third largest spa market in terms of revenues (more than 24 per cent of the global spa revenues) and second largest market in terms of the number of spas. It employs more than 360,000 people. The 2007 Global Spa Economy contains the most complete and most recent data on Asia-Pacific's spa industry profile. Even without the Pacific region (i.e. Australia, New Zealand and the small island states), the Asian spa industry is clearly a large scale phenomenon with an estimated combined revenue of about US$8,642 million in Japan, China and South Korea alone. Additionally, India and Thailand have a combined contribution estimated to US$778 million (GSS Report, 2008).

It can be observed that much of Asia's age-old traditions which have been a way of life for many generations are now being shared with the rest of the world through their practice not only in Asian spas but also in Western societies' spas (Spa Wellness Council, 2008). The Thai massage and the Japanese shiatsu massage, for example, are traditional healing methods that have gained popularity not only in Asia. Similarly, relaxation practices of Eastern origins such as yoga and meditation have also become well-liked worldwide (Mind, Body and Soul, 2009). Each country in Asia has its own spa heritage to offer (Spa Wellness Council, 2008; Chapman, 2006). Even if this was not the case, it can be said that Asian countries share their wealth of traditions and ancient practices with each other, if not the world. Cupping (suction through the skin), for example, is not just a Chinese tradition but it is also practiced in Arab countries (Mind, Body and Soul, 2009). Apart from treatments, the use of indigenous ingredients and materials are now being used in modern-day spas.

In the Indian sub-continent, Ayurveda is the oldest and still widely practised health and wellness system. India remains the leading destination for this type of healing (Kerala Ayurveda Tourism, 2009; Spitzer, 2009). Ayurvedic tourism is also marketed as part of the global growth in health tourism fuelled by widespread trends including ageing populations, high rates of stress and increased interest in health – most specifically amongst affluent individuals (Messerli and Oyama, 2004). The literature on Ayurvedic tourism describes the practice as a gentle system of holistic healing that is rooted in old traditions while evincing a modern and professionalised stance supported by scientific research (Spitzer, 2009). Sahoo (2006, cited in Spitzer, 2009) suggests that this type of tourism in India 'attracts Westerners exploring the ancient art and science of the exotic other as well as citizens of Southeast Asia, West Asia, and members of the global South Asian diaspora of 20 million persons who reside in 70 countries' (p. 139). Apart from international tourists, domestic tourists visit popular Ayurvedic destinations such as the state of Kerala in South India. The treatments in Ayurveda are akin to those of spas' (e.g. massage, facials) which promote relaxation and harmony of mind, body and spirit (Kerala Ayurveda Tourism, 2009). According to ISPA (2008), the Ayurvedic resorts can be classified as destination spas, while day-use Ayurveda centres are categorised as 'other spas'.

In other parts of Asia, traditional/indigenous healing methods are also used in spas. In the Philippines, for instance, 'hilot' is an ancient massage technique that is now in spa menus in the country. Alave (2008) notes that its benefits are comparable to the Chinese acupuncture, aromatherapy and even Western medicine. Apart from 'hilot', some spas in the Philippines also include 'dagdagay' (an indigenous tribal foot massage using bamboo sticks) and the use of the seven-herb concoction (known as 'pito-pito') in bath treatments (Sanctuario Spa, 2009). Also in many parts of Asia, traditional Chinese treatments are common; acupuncture and body smoking are being offered in spas (The Spa Village, 2008) and are also used in Western societies (Mind, Body and Soul, 2009). The products used in Asian spa treatments and therapies may also be indigenous. In spas in the Cordillera region in the Philippines, for instance, local produce such as rice, coffee and strawberries are used as scrubs (North Haven Spa, 2007). In traditional Malay treatments, turmeric, piper betel and pandanus leaves are widely used (The Spa Village, 2008).

The experiences that are being offered in Asian spas are a fusion of indigenous or traditional practices based on ancient Eastern philosophies and sold in modern-day settings. Although unique in this context, Asian spa experiences are less studied, especially those of tourists. In this chapter, flow and the perceived benefits of spa experiences are measured in tourists' spa experiences.

Positive-tourism linkage 1: flow and the tourist experience

Flow, as an optimal psychological state, denotes special times when things seem to come together for the individual in a particular setting; it is often associated with high levels of performance and a very positive experience (Jackson and Eklund, 2004). The concept of *flow* was introduced by Csikszentmihalyi (1975) who defines it as 'an optimal experience that stems from people's perceptions of challenges and skills in given situations' (Ellis *et al.*, 1994, p. 337). Flow occurs when the individual is completely engrossed in a challenging activity that does not necessarily provoke too much stress. The experience per se is highly rewarding, hence flow is a satisfying state (Filep, 2008).

The flow construct is applicable to tourist experiences (Filep, 2008). Beardsley's (1982) concept of aesthetic experience states that a person's object focus, felt freedom (time transformation) and detached affect (the loss of self-consciousness) are used to characterise flow, enabling tourist experience to be appraised the way flow is measured. Likewise, active discovery (challenge-skills balance and sense of control) and wholeness (the clear goals and unambiguous feedback) typify flow (Filep, 2008). The phenomenology of tourists' experience posits that tourist experience range from the search for mere pleasures to the quest for a spiritual self (Cohen, 1996). The five modes of tourist experience, although described individually, are suggested to be in a virtual continuum from a recreational (hedonic) to an existential mode (eudaimonic). The studies of wellness tourism implicitly or explicitly discuss these modes of tourist experience; many of them focus on the existential mode (Pernecky and Johnston, 2006; Smith and Kelly, 2006; Steiner and Reisinger, 2006; Devereux and Carnegie, 2006; Lehto *et al.*, 2006).

Cohen (1996) suggests that the *recreational mode* is characterised by enjoyment because the activity provides tourists with a general sense of well-being as well as a sense of idle pleasure. This mode is also depicted by tourists that thrive on pseudo-events, but are distantly related to and derived from the religious voyage. In the *diversionary mode*, tourists also thrive on pseudo-events, but the experience is not seen as meaningful. The *experiential* and *experimental modes*, however, involve the search for authenticity and for an alternative spiritual centre respectively. In the latter mode, the tourist is unsure of their real desires and needs, thus the quest may potentially become a way of life. Finally, the *existential mode* is where the tourist could be: (a) realistic idealist (one who accepts the social and cultural shortcomings even in the most ideal place); (b) starry-eyed idealist (one who sees perfection in anything but denies the realities of life), or (c) critical idealist (one who is attached to the ideal, but rejects the reality found at it).

It is possible to link Cohen's modes of experiences with the flow concept and the present interest in spa and wellness tourism. It can be suggested that flow may be optimised when tourists are predominantly in the recreational and diversionary modes, that is, when pleasure characteristics of the experiences predominate. These concepts of flow and experience modes help inform the present study linking spa-going and positive psychology.

Measuring flow in tourist experiences

Literature on positive psychology uniformly suggests that the flow concept is an optimal physical state which is connected with high achievement and positive experiences. For this study, the Event Experience Scale (also known as the Flow State Scale or FSS-2) was used. The FSS-2 was designed to assess flow in physical activity settings. Jackson and Eklund (2004) emphasise that the term *physical activity* is used as an inclusive term. That is, the model is appropriate to use in a variety of physical activity settings. Such setting, they argue, was kept in mind when devising the items and instructions for answering the questionnaire. A qualitative database of athletes' descriptions of being in flow was used when developing the original items for the scales (Jackson and Eklund, 2004). Research has been conducted with the FSS-2 in sports and exercise. Its developers, however, noted a considerable interest in understanding flow across various settings (e.g. business, gifted education, music and yoga) and in relation to a range of psychological constructs (e.g. personality type, intrinsic motivation, self-esteem and anxiety). Parallels can be drawn from such interest with Csikszentmihalyi's (1975) works on flow, which included data from different settings such as music, dance, sports and surgery. This suggests that the use of flow scales for assessing experience across various settings needs further empirical studies.

The rationale behind the employment of the FSS-2 in this study lies in the ways in which it can be used in assessing flow. One of the uses of the scale is as an immediate post-event assessment flow. The other is to measure a person's particular peak experience. The questionnaire is a 5-point Likert scale ranging from 1 (strongly disagree) to 5 (strongly agree). The participants were asked to indicate their extent of agreement with each flow item in relation to other completed spa experiences. One of the requirements in administering this questionnaire was to conduct it as close as possible to the completion of the activity being assessed to promote clear recall. More specifically, its developers recommended that responses be collected within one hour of completion of the activity. By doing so, there is an increased likelihood to obtain a more accurate assessment of the state of flow while minimising intrusion on the participants.

The FSS-2 was used in this study in its original form for two main reasons. The first reason lies in the evident linkages between spa experiences and flow experiences. The use of this scale is therefore aimed at measuring and understanding the applicability of the flow model in spa experiences, and to identify the extent of flow that tourists experience in relation to their spa experiences. The second reason the FSS-2 was used lies in fulfilling one of the many directions of the interdisciplinary means of understanding optimal experiences, as implicitly predicted by the developers of the flow scales. Because the scales were originally designed for activities in a physical setting, measuring flow in passive activity setting wherein the experience receiver (i.e. the tourist) rather than the provider (i.e. the spa therapist) of the spa treatment is examined was deemed to provide a different perspective. This also gives the opportunity to compare FSS-2-related data (from an active physical setting) with the current study conducted in a passive (non-active) physical setting.

The respondent profile

The use of the concept of flow in tourist-related experience such as spa-going activity bridges some gaps in the literature in terms of the meshing of tourism and positive psychology as interrelated fields of study. The findings presented in this chapter were extracted from an onsite survey of tourist spa goers between December 2008 and May 2009 in India, Thailand and the Philippines. The survey was designed to collect information on the tourists' travel and spa-going motivations as well as previous travel and spa experience. Demographic information was also collected to profile spa-going tourists in Southeast Asia, most specifically in the three countries mentioned. At the outset of the survey, however, the respondents were asked about their thoughts and feelings regarding the spa treatment that they just received; this section of the survey essentially measures flow in tourists' spa experiences.

A total of 336 questionnaires were collected, with 319 (92.6 per cent) classified as usable. The sample consisted of a slightly greater number of females (59.4 per cent) than males (40.6 per cent). Respondents in their twenties and thirties constituted about 66 per cent of the sample, with those in the age range of 21–30 making up nearly 43 per cent. In terms of occupation, about a quarter of the sample consisted of individuals who were in professional or technical employment. More than half of the sample comprised international tourists (54.9 per cent) to India, Thailand or the Philippines.

Flow dimensions from spa experiences

The FSS-2 was based on Csikszentmihalyi's (1990) nine elements of enjoyment, which Jackson (1996) refers to as the dimensions of flow. These elements and the mean scores l$\bar{x}$ on a 5-point scale (1 = strongly disagree to 5 = strongly agree) for the spa-going sample in this study are as follows:

1 *Challenge-skill balance* (there is a match between perceived skills and challenges, $\bar{x}=3.38$)
2 *Action-awareness merging* (deep involvement leads to automaticity and spontaneity; there is no awareness of self as separate from the actions one is performing, $\bar{x}=3.42$)
3 *Clear goals* (there is a strong sense of what one is going to do, $\bar{x}=3.64$)

4   *Unambiguous feedback* (clear and immediate feedback that the person is doing his/her activity well and is succeeding in his/her goal, $\bar{x}=3.34$)
5   *Concentration on task* (total concentration on the task at hand, $\bar{x}=3.30$)
6   *Sense of control* (sense of exercising control without actively trying to be in control, $\bar{x}=3.36$)
7   *Loss of self-consciousness* (concern for the self disappears and the person becomes one with the activity, $\bar{x}=3.53$)
8   *Time transformation* (time disorientation or a loss of time awareness, $\bar{x}=3.51$)
9   *Autotelic experience* (an intrinsically rewarding experience involving a sense of deep enjoyment, $\bar{x}=4.08$)

The mean score for the overall flow state was 3.45. A slight variation across the scores for each of the nine flow dimensions was observed, which reveals the relative importance of the various dimensions to the spa experience. Overall, the moderate mean scores obtained in each dimension suggests some degree of endorsement for the spa activity as flow experience. Some ambiguity regarding the relevance of some of the items to the person's spa experience do exist, but it is maintained that the scores yielded in this study indicate that tourist spa-goers are somewhat linked to the experience of flow.

The results of this study were compared with the results from previous research by Jackson and Eklund (2004) where participants were involved in an active physical setting such as individual sporting activity, dance, yoga, exercise (focus on health/fitness) and team sport. It was discovered that the spa activity was the lowest on the overall flow score (see Table 5.1). Among the host of activities, yoga practitioners have the greatest propensity to experience flow. Yoga can be seen as reinforcing one's ability to concentrate, to control memory and to limit awareness to specific goals (Csikszentmihalyi and Csikszentmihalyi, 1988). The evidently low mean scores in terms of action-awareness merging can be linked to the nature of the activity per se. The passive feature of the spa experience such as receiving a massage, for example, does not require much action or voluntary active movement compared to the other activities. This lack of action causes an imbalance in the dimension. This result was therefore anticipated even at the outset of the study.

Similarly, the low mean score in the loss of self-consciousness dimension can also be related to the common practices in spas as well as to the respondents' culture. In most spa treatments, especially those that involve most parts of the body such as massages, wraps and scrubs, the customer is required to remove most, if not all pieces of clothing, and must only be covered by a towel or a similar sheet for proper treatment. While some tourists are already accustomed to such situations, there are many who find this practice uncomfortable and often embarrassing. In this case, one's culture may have contributed to this result. It should be noted that most of the respondents live in Southeast Asian societies, which are understood to be more culturally conservative than their Western counterparts.

Table 5.1 The flow experience – spa activity vs other physical activities

Dimension	Spa experience	Individual activity*	Dance	Yoga	Exercise activity**	Sport activity#	Team sport activity
	M	M	M	M	M	M	M
Flow	3.45	3.78	3.58	3.81	3.78	3.78	3.72
Challenge-skill balance	3.38	3.67	3.53	3.58	3.64	3.71	3.75
Action-awareness merging	3.42	3.57	3.12	3.28	3.35	3.66	3.67
Clear goals	3.64	4.08	3.88	3.97	3.94	4.09	3.98
Unambiguous feedback	3.34	3.87	3.79	3.85	3.90	3.88	3.91
Concentration	3.30	3.70	3.84	3.54	3.62	3.73	3.75
Control	3.36	3.74	3.55	3.72	3.81	3.72	3.66
Loss of self-consciousness	3.53	4.02	3.15	4.17	4.08	3.92	3.59
Time transformation	3.51	3.38	3.52	3.88	3.56	3.36	3.46
Autotelic experience	4.08	4.02	3.85	4.27	4.11	3.95	3.73

Notes
* Some individual activities are sporting in nature, but many individual activities also include exercise, and creative and performing arts (including dance and music) activities.
** Activities labelled as exercise; non-competitive physical activities.
# Involved in a diverse number of activities typically regarded as sport activities.
M Mean scores

Positive-tourism linkage 2: perceived benefits of spa experiences

Additional results presented in this chapter are from a larger survey that collected tourists' travel and spa-going motivations in their most recent travel to Southeast Asia and post-spa experiences. The online survey was conducted between September 2010 and February 2011. The sample profile was again dominated by females (69.4 per cent) and by individuals in their twenties and thirties (78 per cent). About 54 per cent of the respondents had actually made plans to visit spas prior to travel.

Liminality, thresholds and the benefits of spa experiences

Liminality and thresholds are conceptual schemes in tourist behaviour to which spa experiences can be linked. The liminality construct has been frequently adopted to understand the role and behaviour of a tourist (Pearce, 2005; Graburn, 1989; Ryan, 1997). It is understood that liminality, which is entrenched in earlier works on thresholds and transition zones, helps define the nature of tourist encounters which are challenging and novel (Pearce, 2005). According to scholars, the three zones or phases in relation to liminality are: (1) the normal state, which refers to one's regular life and experiences at home; (2) the liminoid state (a threshold phase), which refers to the state of transition and often abnormal; and (3) the post-liminoid state, which signifies the reversion back to normal life.

Clawson and Knetsch's (1966) idea of the different phases of travel behaviour is also linked to this notion of liminality. They suggested that a pre-purchase/planning phase, travel to the destination, onsite experiences, travel back to origin and reflection make up the cycle of tourist behaviour. The constant transition of states between these phases helps define the varieties of the travellers' experiences. In this study, the degree to which tourists benefit from spa experiences were explored and were found to be closely linked to the changing phases of tourist behaviour. Spa-going, like many other destination-based tourist activities, is a voluntary pursuit. It is therefore a valid assumption to say that tourists deemed a spa experience to be beneficial to an extent but the point at which this assessment can be made is important. The data provided an opportunity to link benefits to the tourists' experiences during any particular trip.

A 7-point Likert scale was used to measure the positive impacts of the spa activity to the respondents' trip. The set of 12 statements indicating potential positive contributions of the spa activity were based on Pearce and Lee's (2005) travel career pattern (TCP) model which involves 14 motive factors such as novelty, escape/relax, relationships, autonomy, nature, personal development, self-actualisation, isolation, stimulation, recognition, nostalgia and romance. In addition, the statements were based on the different dimensions of wellness (physical, emotional, intellectual, social, spiritual and occupational). The respondents reported that the three most beneficial factors of spa-going while travelling involved:

- Escape/relaxation
    - a relaxing way to unwind and get away from the usual stress and demands of travelling ($\bar{x}=6.16$); and
- Novelty
    - the chance to be pampered, which they did not often get at home ($\bar{x}=6.11$); and,
    - an opportunity to try a new and different experience while travelling ($\bar{x}=5.94$).

Similarly, the respondents were asked to indicate their agreement about post-spa benefits which involved a set of 12 items which were positive statements of potential benefits of a spa experience. Following the previous approach, the statements were based on the TCP model and the multidimensionality of wellness. Overall, the respondents reported a high degree of relaxed feeling ($\bar{x}=6.16$) and the ability to sleep better ($\bar{x}=5.86$). They also reported a sense of youthfulness and energy ($\bar{x}=5.69$), and of peacefulness and calmness ($\bar{x}=5.63$).

These findings suggest that the benefits that tourists obtain from spa experiences are closely linked to the physical and psychological (emotional, intellectual) dimensions. Although travel can be relaxing for many, it also involves a degree of physical and mental stress for an individual. The liminoid zone, which usually encompasses the travel to and from the destination and the onsite experiences of a tourist, can be truly challenging. The physical dimensions of tourist behaviour and experience can be demanding. Driving, flying, waiting at airports, hyper and hypothermia, jet lag and changing climates are just some examples of the physical challenges to a traveller. Often connected to these physical constraints are mental barriers that a traveller may face such as lack of information, getting lost and other constraints.

It can therefore be argued that the while the changing phases of tourist behaviour can be truly stimulating, exciting, puzzling and perplexing at the same time, spa experiences can be very beneficial to a traveller. The benefits, although short-lived, contribute to the physical and psychological well-being of a traveller. The quick relief from physical and psychological stress is becoming more of a need. This is underpinned by Goldstein and Coyle Hospitality Group (2010) in their report of why consumers visit spas; they found that relaxation/stress management (89 per cent) was the key motivating factor for individuals who visit spas. This finding was supported by the current study.

On a more long term basis, however, there were reports of an improved social dimension for individuals. These reported benefits are characterised by a strengthened relationship between the tourist and their partner/family/friends which lasted up to a month after the spa experience. Although it is difficult to identify the other factors that may have contributed to an improved relationship as reported by the participants, it is maintained that the question was asked in a very specific fashion and was stated as 'if you think your spa experience during the trip contributed to your well-being, approximately how long did the benefits last?' Apart from a temporal scale that ranged from days to a year, the choices included 'no benefit' and 'can't remember' options. A total of 58 respondents (42.3 per cent of the total sample) completed this section of the questionnaire and provided responses within the specific temporal scale (i.e. did not have 'no benefit' and 'can't remember' responses).

The data showed that most of the respondents felt the benefits for each of the dimensions for about one month after the spa experience, with the total accounting for 32.6 per cent for the well-being dimensions. The longest lasting effects of the spa experience were felt by most respondents on the social dimension (6–12 months = 31.7 per cent). The results of Pearson's chi-square showed a significant relationship between the dimensions of well-being and the duration by which the benefits of the spa experience were felt by the spa-going tourists (x^2 (20)=61.90, $p<.05$). This result indicates that spa experiences can indeed contribute to one's overall well-being for a certain period of time. For this data, the Cramer's statistic is .113, which represents a small association between the dimensions and the duration of benefits as perceived by the respondents. This value, however, is significant ($p<.05$) which also indicates that the strength of the association is significant, confirming the chi-square results.

This finding is seen as an embodiment of the reflection phase of the tourist behaviour. In the context of responding to the questionnaire, the participants were compelled to recall their experience with their companions during that trip. Indeed, the memory that they had from the spa experience, whether it was because of the treatment or the company that they had, was arguably a positive experience to them which was worth remembering.

Conclusions and implications

This chapter suggests that spa-going is an experiential journey because spa-goers are enticed by new textures, aromas and sounds that are inherent in many spa treatments and products, particularly while travelling in Asia. Spa-goers also often expect that elements of their spa experience can extend to their everyday lives. In this study of tourist spa-goers' flow experiences and the benefits that they have gained from such experiences, implications can be drawn in terms of the meshing of tourism and positive psychology.

The notion of the *positive-tourism* relationship provides an opportunity to further develop theoretical linkages between the specialisms. The integration of the flow concept, and specifically testing the FSS-2 in a passive tourist activity underpins the notion that tourism businesses, which make up one of the most global and people-oriented industries, are implicitly striving to be profitable by offering positive experiences.

Tourist well-being is core to the tourism-positive psychology relationship. The practical applications that this chapter offers lie in the cultivation of various ways of enhancing tourist well-being. As participants reported a high degree of positive response about their spa experiences while travelling, it can be inferred that a spa experience per se can be a rewarding activity. This perceived benefit of spa experiences suggests that even though moderate to limited flow experiences have been reported in the study, the spa-going activity can be a source of experiences that are beneficial to tourists' wellness. As the findings suggest, spa experiences are beneficial to different well-being dimensions. Overall, the results can be utilised not only to understand how tourists perceive spa experiences, but also to support tourist well-being through spa experiences.

References

Alave, K.L. (2008) 'Taking "hilot" or touch therapy into the 21st century', *Philippine Daily Inquirer*.

Beardsley, M.C. (1982) 'Some persistent issues in aesthetics', in Wreen, M.J. and Callen, D.M. (eds), *The Aesthetic Point of View*. Ithaca, NY: Cornell University Press, pp. 285–287.

Carruthers, C.P. and Hood, C.D. (2004) 'The power of the positive: leisure and well-being', *Therapeutic Recreation Journal*, 38: 225–245.

Chapman, J. (2006) *Ultimate Spa: Asia's Best Spas and Spa Treatments*. Singapore: Periplus Editions.

Clawson, M. and Knetsch, J.L. (1966) *Economics of Outdoor Recreation*. Baltimore: John Hopkins Press.

Cohen, E. (1996) 'A phenomenology of tourist experiences', in Apostolopoulos, Y., Leivadi, S. and Yiannakis, A. (eds), *The Sociology of Tourism*. Oxford: Routledge, pp. 51–74.

Connell, J. (2006) 'Medical tourism: sea, sun, sand and ... surgery', *Tourism Management*, 27: 1093–1100.

Csikszentmihalyi, M. (1975) *Beyond Boredom and Anxiety*. San Francisco: Jossey Bass.

Csikszentmihalyi, M. (1990) *Flow: The Psychology of Optimal Experience*. New York: Harper and Row.

Csikszentmihalyi, M. and Csikszentmihalyi, I. (1988) *Optimal Experience: Pscyhological Studies of Flow in Consciousness*. Cambridge: Cambridge University Press.

Devereux, C. and Carnegie, E. (2006) 'Pilgrimage: journeying beyond self', *Tourism Recreation Research*, 31: 47–56.

Didascalou, E.A., Nastos, P.T. and Matzarakis, A. (2007) 'Spa destination development using a decision support system: the role of climate and bioclimate information', *Developments in Tourism Climatology*, 2007: 158–165.

Douglas, N. (2001) 'Travelling for health: spa and health resorts', in Douglas, N., Douglas, N. and Derrett, R. (eds), *Special Interest Tourism*. Milton, Queensland: John Wiley and Sons, Australia, pp. 260–282.

Dunn, H.L. (1959) 'High-level wellness for man and society', *American Journal of Public Health*, 49: 786–792.

Ellis, G.D., Voelkl, J.E. and Morris, C. (1994) 'Measurement and analysis issues with explanation of variance in daily experience using the flow model', *Journal of Leisure Research*, 26: 336–356.

Fain, N.C. and Lewis, N.M. (2002) 'Wellness: the holistic approach', *Journal of Family and Consumer Sciences*, 94: 6–8.

Filep, S. (2008) 'Applying the dimensions of flow to explore visitor engagement and satisfaction', *Visitor Studies*, 11: 90–108.

Finnicum, P. and Zeiger, J.B. (1996) 'Tourism and wellness: a natural alliance in a natural state', *Parks and Recreation*, 31 (9): 84.

Furrer, W. (2010) 'Top 20 spa trends in 20 years', *Pulse Magazine*. Lexington, KY: International Spa Association.

Gilbert, D. and Abdullah, J. (2002) 'A study of the impact of the expectation of a holiday on an individual's sense of well-being', *Journal of Vacation Marketing*, 8: 352–361.

Gilbert, D. and Abdullah, J. (2003) 'Holidaytaking and the sense of well-being', *Annals of Tourism Research*, 31: 103–121.

Global Spa Summit (GSS) (2008) *The Global Spa Economy 2007*. Stanford Research Institute (SRI) International.

Global Spa Summit (GSS) (2010) *Spas and the Global Wellness Market: Synergies and Opportunities*. Istanbul, Turkey: Stanford Research International.

Goldstein, S.P. and Coyle Hospitality Group (2010) *New Priorities of Today's Spa Consumers*. Coyle Hospitality Group.

Graburn, N.H. (1989) 'Tourism: the sacred journey', in Smith, V. (ed.), *Hosts and Guests: The Anthropology of Tourism* (2nd edition). Philadelphia: University of Pennsylvania Press, pp. 21–36.

Hall, M. (2003) 'Health and Spa Tourism', in Hudson, S. (ed.), *Sport and Adventure Tourism*. New York: Haworth Hospitality Press, pp. 273–292.

Henry, R.D. (2005) 'Spa state of mind', in Henry, R.D. and Taylor, J.D. (eds), *Spa: The Sensuous Experience*. Mulgrave, Victoria: Images Publishing Group, pp. 6–8.

Horowitz, M.D. and Rosensweig, J.A. (2007) 'Medical tourism: health care in the global economy', *The Physician Executive*, http://proquest.umi.com/pqdweb?index=2&did=1453290851&srchmode=2&sid=2&fmt=6&vinst=prod&vtype=pqd&rqt=309&vname=pqd&ts=1219126087&clientid=20960 [Accessed 20 April 2008].

Hunter-Jones, P. and Blackburn, A. (2007) 'Understanding the relationship between holiday taking and self-assessed health: an exploratory study of senior tourism', *International Journal of Consumer Studies*, 31: 509–516.

International Spa Association (ISPA) (2008) *Types of Spas*, www.experienceispa.com/ispa/visit/spa+101/types+of+spas.htm [Accessed 31 July 2008].

Iovine, J.V. (2005) 'The history of spa', in Henry, R.D. and Taylor, J.D. (eds), *Spa: The Sensuous Experience*. Mulgrave, Victoria: Images Publishing Group, pp. 8–12.

Jackson, S.A. (1996) 'Toward a conceptual understanding of the flow experience in elite athletes', *Research Quarterly for Exercise and Sport*, 67 (1): 76–90.

Jackson, S.A. and Eklund, R.C. (2004) *The Flow Scales Manual*. Morgantown: Fitness Information Technology.

Kaspar, C. (1990) 'A new lease on life for spa and health tourism', *Annals of Tourism Research*, 17: 298–299.

Kerala Ayurveda Tourism (2009) *Kerala ayurveda*, www.keralaayurvedatourism.com/ [Accessed 15 January 2010].

Laing, J. and Weiler, B. (2008) 'Mind, body and spirit: health and wellness tourism in Asia', in Cochrane, J. (ed.), *Asian Tourism: Growth and Change*. Oxford: Elsevier Ltd, pp. 379–389.

Lehto, X.Y., Brown, S., Chen, Y. and Morrison, A.M. (2006) 'Yoga tourism as a niche within the wellness tourism market', *Tourism Recreation Research*, 31: 25–35.

Messerli, H. and Oyama, Y. (2004) *Health and Wellness Tourism, Travel and Tourist Analyst*. London: Mintel International Group.

Miller, J.W. (2005) 'Wellness: the history and development of a concept', *Spektrum freizeit*, 2005: 84–102.

Mind, Body and Soul (2009) *Cupping*, www.mindbodysoul.tv/health/cupping.html [Accessed 23 June 2010].

Mueller, H. and Kaufmann, E.L. (2001) 'Wellness tourism: market analysis of a special health tourism segment and implications for the hotel industry', *Journal of Vacation Marketing*, 7: 5–17.

Myers, J., Sweeney, T. and Witmer, J. (2000) 'The wheel of wellness counselling for wellness: a holistic model for treatment planning', *Journal of Counselling and Development*, 78: 251–266.

North Haven Spa (2007) *Spa Services*, http://northhaven.multiply.com/ [Accessed 23 June 2010].

Pearce, P.L. (2005) *Tourist Behaviour: Themes and Conceptual Schemes*. Clevedon: Channel View Publications.

Pearce, P.L. (2007) 'The relationship between positive psychology and tourist behaviour studies', *International Academy for the Study of Tourism Conference*. Mugla, Turkey.

Pearce, P.L. and Lee, U.-I. (2005) 'Developing the travel career approach to tourist motivation', *Journal of Travel Research*, 43: 226–237.

Pernecky, T. and Johnston, C. (2006) 'Voyage through numinous space: applying the specialisation concept to new age tourism', *Tourism Recreation Research*, 31: 37–46.

Pilzer, P.Z. (2007) *The New Wellness Revolution*. Hoboken: John Wiley and Sons.

Puczko, L. and Bachvarov, M. (2006) 'Spa, bath, thermae: what's behind the labels?' *Tourism Recreation Research*, 31: 83–91.

Ryan, C. (1997) *The Tourist Experience: A New Introduction*. New York: Cassell.

Sanctuario Spa (2009) *Sanctuario Spa: Filipino Traditional Healing*, http://sanctuariospa.com/services-and-packages/id/filipino-traditional-healing [Accessed 23 June 2010].

Seligman, M.E.P. and Csikszentmihalyi, M. (2000) 'Positive psychology: an introduction', *American Psychologist*, 55: 5–14.

Smith, M. and Kelly, C. (2006) 'Wellness tourism', *Tourism Recreation Research*, 31: 1–4.

Smith, M. and Puczko, L. (2009) *Health and Wellness Tourism*. Oxford: Butterworth-Heinemann.

Spa Wellness Council (2008) *About APSWC*, www.spawellnesscouncil.com/ [Accessed 30 July 2008].

Spitzer, D. (2009) 'Ayurvedic tourism in Kerala: local identities and global markets', in Winter, T., Teo, P. and Chang, T.C. (eds), *Asia on Tour: Exploring the Rise of Asian Tourism*. London: Routledge, pp. 138–150.

Steiner, C.J. and Reisinger, Y. (2006) 'Ringing the fourfold: a philosophical framework for thinking about wellness tourism', *Tourism Recreation Research*, 31: 5–14.

The Spa Village (2008) *Traditional Spa Experience*, www.spavillage.com/pangkorlaut/spa-packages/traditional.htm [Accessed 23 June 2010].

Travis, J.W. and Ryan, R.S. (2004) *The Wellness Workbook* (3rd edition). Berkeley: Celestial Arts.

Part II
Meaning and self-actualisation

6 Meaning making, life transitional experiences and personal well-being within the contexts of religious and spiritual travel

Glenn Ross

It was the great traveller Herodotus of Halicarnassus who noted the ubiquity of religious expression over two millennia ago (Kapuscinski, 2007; Marozzi, 2008). Among the people who travelled in the ancient world there were many who did so to visit religious shrines such as the temple of Apollo at Delphi; they came there to consult the oracle and frequently to quieten a restless mind about their fate. Wood (2004) makes the point that many who consulted the oracle were hoping for a clear and detailed response; indeed they often believed that their well-being depended upon both the content and the clarity of the pronouncement. Yet clarity was often not evident, rather, equivocation and opacity were frequently delivered to the pilgrims at Apollo's shrine. Not only did they experience disappointment when the oracle's responses were given; so too might there be little happiness if, later, the opaque prognostications of the oracle were to be misinterpreted and then acted upon. The pursuit of well-being has been a characteristic of human endeavour throughout history, and in many contexts including religion and spirituality. Moreover, many travellers have gone to great lengths so as to increase their level of well-being. The reception of oracular pronouncements has not always been at the centre of pilgrim purpose; very often it has rather involved personal meaning and even a measure of self transcendence that may be derived from out of the many experiences of the journey.

Well-being has in recent times come to the fore as an interest within the discipline of psychology. In this century psychology has shifted its almost singular focus from that of negative functioning so as to include positive aspects of human life. There is now a greater emphasis on elucidating those factors that are associated with meaningful and satisfying life experiences, often described as well-being. This shift in emphasis is often dated to the 1990s, and initially to the efforts of the then president of the American Psychological Association, Martin Seligman, who argued vigorously for a reorientation of psychology towards the positive aspects of human functioning such as strengths and virtues. Peterson and Seligman (2004) have subsequently developed a *Character Strengths and Values Handbook* that presents six core virtues of human well-being: wisdom and knowledge, courage, humanity, justice, temperance and transcendence. It is the case that among the character strengths that are said to make up transcendence is spirituality.

There have now been a number of studies that have examined positive strategies said to promote well-being and assist in the control of depression. Seligman *et al.* (2005), in assessing these character strengths and virtues together with their effects upon people's lives, have found that the exercise of gratitude, a reflection on the good aspects of a person's life and the creative exercise of a person's perceived strengths all promoted higher levels of well-being. Sin and Lyubomirsky (2009) have also found that factors such as forgiveness, kindness and mindfulness can be instrumental in enhancing well-being and reducing depression. Collicut (2011) finds that positive psychology can have great synergies with the psychology of religion and spirituality. Both, she avers, are typically purposed toward individual growth and life meaning. Drawing on the work of Peterson (2006), she names character strengths such as forgiveness, integrity, kindness and gratitude, and makes the point that these are among the virtues of major faith traditions. She further notes that these faiths are accorded respect by positive psychology, as well as an acknowledgement that these characteristics and virtues have been long valued and perpetuated by them. Well-being has thus been found to be associated with transcendence and religious expression. This chapter will examine these associations within the context of travel; it will do so by providing an overview of a number of major issues current in the area of religious tourism, will present a basic understanding of the various differences such as those between religion and spirituality, will go on to highlight the various contributions that draw an association between religious expression and well-being, and will then present a model that seeks to encompass these various domains. It will further explore the value of the narrative in providing insights associated with religious and spiritual travel, meaning making and well-being; this chapter will then conclude with some suggestions for future research regarding the examination of enarratives in so far as they illuminate religious and spiritual experiences together with perceptions of meaning, identity and personal well-being.

Religious tourism: issues and perspectives

Religious tourism has for some time now been characterised by the energetic exploration of the pilgrim-tourist dichotomy (Collins-Kreiner, 2010; Olsen and Timothy, 2006; Olsen, 2010). The point is made that the clear differentiation between the role of a pilgrim and of a tourist of previous decades has now faded; the emphasis on commonalities has in its place emerged. Yet religious tourism would seem to have taken place for as long as travel itself (Rinschede, 1992; Vukonic, 1996). Herodotus noted such patterns and motivations in travel (Kapuscinski, 2007; Marozzi, 2008; Smith, 1992). Indeed Rinschede argues that religious tourism identifies itself by its motivation, and would hold that it is a form of travel associated to varying degrees with religious purposes or activities (Rinschede, 1992). Today religious travel, that form of activity which might include both religious activity and also secular experiences, is widely practised by many adherents of the major world religions including Buddhism, Christianity, Hinduism, Islam and Judaism.

There has also been a change, suggests Collins-Kreiner, with regards to the manner in which theories are approached. It is said to have changed from that of an either/or approach to that of a both/and way of comprehending the role of theory. As an example, she cites the work and theoretical contributions of Turner and Turner (1969, 1978) and the somewhat different perspective on pilgrimage advanced by Eade and Sallnow (1991). Now, it is asserted, a researcher does not have to make judgements as to which one is correct. Instead, a researcher is said most likely to choose a method and perspective deemed most appropriate for the topic, whilst freely acknowledging their own background, beliefs and assumptions in terms of social and individual behaviour. The point is made by Collins-Kreiner that truth and error is much less likely to feature; more likely there will be the inclusion of a clarification as to the nature of interpretations relied upon. Pilgrimages, it is concluded, are much more likely to be embedded in and products of the socio-cultural milieu of the individual producing the narrative. Thus the narratives that religious tourists offer are able to reflect both the culture and also the life story of the individual.

A variety of models have now been proposed so as to represent the core concepts and processes associated with religious tourism. They aim at illustrating the structural components as well as providing descriptions of patterns and categories. Among the better known models of religion and tourism are those proposed by Cohen (1992), Rinschede (1992) and Smith (1992). Cohen, addressing a Thai Buddhist context, proposes a useful distinction between temples that may be described as concentric-formal and those termed peripheral-popular. Within this model, travellers might be described as falling into one of two categories, the traveller pilgrim, identified as belonging to the culture and religion of the temple, and the traveller tourist, a person not formally associated with the culture of the religious tradition. Rinschede takes a somewhat different approach, wishing to distinguish between a short-stay traveller and a longer-stay one; for Rinschede the former may be regarded as the pilgrimage, whereas the latter is said to be an expression of the pilgrimage journey. Smith proposes a third and again, somewhat different typology to those above. Religious travel might usefully be regarded as falling somewhere along a continuum that stretches from secular tourists at one extremity to that of devout pilgrims at the other extremity.

Ron (2009) has proposed a more recent typological model of Christian travel. This particular typology seeks to distinguish between activities, destinations and practices that are relevant to both pilgrimage and also non-pilgrimage Christian tourists. He has outlined a number of assumptions associated with this, of which a major one is to do with the relationship between pilgrimage and religious tourism. The two terms for Ron are not synonymous; pilgrimage is regarded as being but one form of religious tourism. Ron provides an example concerning a Jewish traveller who visits religious places of significance such as synagogues and centres of Jewish learning in Europe; this person Ron points out ought not be regarded as a pilgrim, but rather, a Jewish religious tourist. The conceptualisation regarding pilgrimage and religious travel is said to emerge from the two types that generally describe pilgrimage; the first, the more particularised proposed by Ron would highlight the sanctity of a religious destination. The second type of pilgrimage definition is described as being of a broader and more encompassing kind, involving descriptions such as inner travel and New Age travel; it can also involve secular and civil religion, involving football stadia, war graves and the homes of the famous. Ron also makes the point that he does not regard the notions of pilgrimage and tourism as being at opposite ends of a continuum; rather he avers that pilgrimage is embedded within the general idea of tourism. Quoting Olsen and Timothy (2006), Ron understands pilgrims as falling within the classification of tourists of a religious kind whose motivations are associated with religion or spirituality.

Reader (2007) has also drawn attention to the importance of meaning in the life of the individual religious tourist. He has studied the Shikoku pilgrimage in Japan extensively and over a lengthy period of time; he has also had an interest in European pilgrimage sites such as Santiago de Compostela, those in the Mediterranean region and also pilgrimages in the United States. He has noted some of the more traditional motivations for pilgrimage, such as the encouragement of religious authorities as well as the greater ease that now exists in undertaking such journeys. To these he adds another – it is and has traditionally been a way in which a person could seek meaning in life, and do so within a spiritual context. This latter motivation he sees as assuming a much greater importance for some present-day pilgrims in an age of modernity; he points out that technological advances and the centrality of economic purposes in life are perceived to have left many in a dissatisfied, even an anomic state. Alternative styles of living, essentially of meaning making in an individual's life by way of escape or of discontinuity if only for a limited period of time, would seem increasingly attractive to many, he concludes. This is said to be happening in conjunction with another effect of modernity that is a lessening of the ties to traditional religious expressions. These structures he avers were widely regarded as the providers of a philosophical and theological worldview to which people formerly had recourse when faced with the need to find comfort and meaning. Many people are said no longer to accord them such respect or even utility.

It has been argued by Reader that these two major forces for change within many societies (that is, the advent of a rationalised, prosaic and materialistic worldview and also the drift of many people away from organised religion and toward a more individuated search for meaning) are powerful explanatory factors in the popularity of pilgrimages such as the Camino in Spain or Shikoku in Japan. Reader has found from the many interviews completed over a number of years that some pilgrims report a rising sense of insecurity engendered by aspects of modern industrial society; the modern world from which many of these pilgrims have come is reported to have changed and done so drastically in their lifetime, yet this new culture and worldview has, they averred, given them few if any answers to their inner perplexities or fears.

He further suggests that the traditional religious structures, in the case of the Shikoku those within Buddhism, apparently for an increasing number of people had done little to provide meaning or assurance in the face of modern society's superficial conception of individual meaning. Reader argues that there appears to be two pilgrimage traditions here, one involving individuals pursuing the traditional Shikoku, and beside it, another more secular and modern movement. Quoting Frey (1998), he concludes that this movement has had an influence upon many of the people who undertake routes such as the Camino; the themes of greater knowledge of self and personal meaning are in such movements writ large. He also quotes Basu (2004) who notes that many pilgrims are said to have a tendency to take along with them what are described as New Age personal growth and instruction books. These would seem to have served as guides and sources of arcane knowledge and insight.

Traditional places of pilgrimage are not the only ones to be influenced by the growing attractiveness of New Age ideas; so too have some more recent sites of religious tourism. Reader, drawing on the work of Preston (1992), suggests that these ideas have now assisted in the emergence, or re-emergence, of a number of sites such as Glastonbury in the UK and Sedona in the US. Findings of a similar nature among the visitors of the Glastonbury site have been found by Farias *et al.* (2005) and Farias and Lalljee (2006, 2008). Reader makes the point that Sedona had been a pilgrimage site for native Indians, with Glastonbury having a similar provenance in Christianity. Glastonbury now, it is concluded, has emerged as a New Age centre of considerable importance for a number of reasons. It was seen to be bound up with the culture of the Celtic peoples, former rulers of the region; it is also associated with the spiritual traditions of King Arthur, as well as being deemed to be at the centre of ley lines regarded as pathways that connect sources of spiritual energy. Sedona, Reader notes, is acknowledged by some as a place containing great power, a convergence place whereat the vital spiritual entity of the planet is regarded as manifest. Many spiritual energy forces are said to centre on Sedona, and this some hold produces miraculous events. Reader, referring to the work of Ivakhiv (2001), observes that there is a belief that a wide range of New Age phenomena can be experienced in Sedona, including UFOs, extraterrestrials, healing centres, as well as vortex tours of revered sites said to be famed for their spiritual potency.

The motive of personal autonomy would seem to be at the core of Reader's findings in regard to the understanding of pilgrimage as a form of modern religious tourism. Moreover, this quest for personal autonomy is said to be quite separate from conventional religious beliefs for many people; this was much less likely to be the case in previous eras of pilgrimage. Today, pilgrimages to places such as Santiago de Compostela, Shikoku, Glastonbury and Sedona have all now frequently been regarded as affording a person the opportunity of a change so as to experience their very own spiritual transformation, perhaps in a form of their own choosing. And while such motives may not have been new, they are said to be much more common now; they are less likely to be undertaken under the auspices of or even associated with an organised religious tradition. Reader is however careful to note that the more traditional pilgrimages associated with the Buddhist, Christian, Hindu and Islamic traditions do still occur and sometimes in very large numbers; they are moreover still a major part of their spiritual heritage. The point however he does make is that the resurgence of pilgrim numbers ought not to necessarily and in every circumstance be seen as some type of organised religious revival. There are many religious tourists now who see pilgrimage as an opportunity to explore spiritual ideas and practices that could give them personal meaning, could assist them to cope with the world today, and could perhaps above all else, imbue their lives with meaningful purpose and well-being. A wide range of ideas and meaning systems, such as New Age philosophies, and in an age of uncertainty regarding economic and cultural institutions, may be considered as but one response to the need for personal meaning, so concludes Reader.

A similar theme is highlighted by Power (2006) in regard to Celtic spirituality. People attracted to Celtic spirituality and sites such as Iona in Scotland may include those feeling disillusioned or disempowered by religious systems; they thus find themselves attracted to a version of Celtic spirituality that endows their life with greater meaning and purpose. Power points out that the current Celtic spirituality revival has become very popular, despite its beliefs and practices having relatively little in common with that which may be encountered in university courses on this subject. Instead, she finds that the origins of current Celtic spirituality are to be found in popular culture, most notably that shared by white middle class people; this she asserts has not normally been so for such a group. There are said to be quite distinct similarities as those between Pagan and Christian expressions of this type of spirituality; in particular it may be seen that both forms have a focus upon the individual and his or her personal development, with inner personal growth and spiritual enlightenment assuming prime importance.

For some of those people presently belonging to a traditional religious organisation there may be a suspicion or dislike of the power vested in ecclesiastical institutions. Another group attracted to Celtic spirituality, she finds, are women who might have relatively little trust in the traditional religious institutions and who report feeling disempowered within these structures by the denial of any meaningful role therein. Individual spiritual development is typically fostered by way of individual or group retreats, through the dissemination of literature and by Celtic spirituality conferences; this, Power finds has led to a heightened acceptance of Celtic religious practices as an alternative to the traditional church structures and practices. Celtic spirituality is also said to view the Christian church as having a strong tendency to be monolithic and culturally dominant. It is also the case, she finds, that this form of spirituality can exhibit relatively little interest in social action. So too it is said to have a distrust of intellectualism and thus lacks any effective means of critical reflection on the origins of the movement.

Forms of religious expression

A growing body of literature now exists that explores the relationship between religion and various indicators of well-being in the physical, social and psychological domains. Dillon and Wink (2007) report that people who evince some degree of religious belief are likely to hold altruistic views; Koenig *et al.* (2001) suggest that religiously inclined individuals are associated with higher degrees of physical and psychological well-being. It has been argued by Argyle (2000, 2002), and Argyle and Hills (2000) that a range of human values are associated with the holding of some religious beliefs. The notion of religion however may be understood to embrace two somewhat different yet related ideas, that of religiousness and of spirituality. Religiousness generally encompasses church attendance and a formal association with some religious organisation; these in more recent decades have been seen to experience a considerable decline (Hout and Fischer, 2002). Spiritual beliefs on the other hand have not seen the same changes. Indeed, their attractiveness is clearly on the rise. Spirituality typically encompasses spiritual beliefs, practices and interest involving no specific church or ecclesiastical organisation (Fuller, 2001; Roof, 1999).

Religiousness – that which involves the beliefs and behaviours of those who choose to observe the tenets of formal ecclesiastical organisations – has been found to be associated with being pro-social, tender minded, responsible, controlled and caring (Eysenck, 1998; Saroglou, 2002; Saroglou and Fiasse, 2003). Koenig *et al.* (1990) have also found this group of people less likely to be dominant and aggressive, whereas McCullough *et al.* (2003), Saroglou and Fiasse (2003), and Taylor and MacDonald (1999) have, in studies relating to topics such as religious engagement and personality, also found religiousness to be associated with higher levels of agreeableness and conscientiousness. Friendly and self disciplined individuals, it is suggested, may be more likely to seek out social and organisational contexts such as those involving church-based activities. Such a suggestion is supported by McCullough *et al.* (2003) who find that individuals high on agreeableness and conscientiousness in their younger years were, as young adults some years later, more likely to elect for an association with a traditional religious organisation.

Spirituality is a term frequently used to describe a form of seeking that may resemble various types of religious activity; predominantly though, it can have little or nothing to do with a formal religious organisation. Whilst the term has been employed to describe particular practices within some traditional religious organisations, it is more widely understood as referring to practices such as Eastern meditation techniques, as well as the beliefs and practices of movements such as those of the New Age. This spirituality became more widely known in the decade of the 1960s in the Western world (Fuller, 2001; Roof, 1999). One notable personality dimension – that of openness to experience – has been found to be associated with this type of spirituality. Saroglou and Faisse (2003) find that individuals embracing a form of spirituality are more likely to regard themselves as open to the experiences of life, wherever they may be found; Piedmont (1999) has also found that spirituality seekers see an interconnectedness in all of life, whereas Kosek (1999) has revealed the group to be active in the questioning of traditional explanations. Spirituality seekers are also said to be more likely to pursue transcendental experiences in whatever context and form they may be encountered (MacDonald, 2000).

Further characteristics of this growing group have been illuminated by Fuller (2001), Roof (1999) and Wuthnow (1998). Fuller has found that many in this group regard themselves as essentially spiritual in nature, though do not identify themselves as being religious. Both Roof and Wuthnow make the point that people in this group believe they possess the right, and indeed a need, to forge their own distinctive identity, a fundamental part of which is spiritual in nature. They are said to do this very often with beliefs and practices that would be very different to those found in mainstream ecclesiastical traditions. Roof and Wuthnow make the point that this growing interest in spirituality is associated with those cultural upheavals that occurred in Western societies in the 1960s and onwards; a considerable focus on individualism in both private and socio-cultural life was said to be a major feature of this period, and continues to be so for spiritual seekers. In regard to personality, Wink *et al.* (2007) aver that there is a long-term association between the personality dimension of openness to experience and that of spiritual seeking at a later point in a person's lifespan; individuals rating highly on openness to experience when younger are found to have a greater likelihood to have an interest in spiritual seeking in later years. Wink *et al.* have generally concluded that personality factors are associated with the preferences evinced and decisions made regarding religious expression across the lifespan.

Religious expression and well-being

Myers (2000), in a contribution to the *American Psychologist*'s 2000 special edition on positive psychology, has addressed some of the issues associated with religious expression and well-being. He includes in his section on faith and well-being a challenge to Freud's claim that religion is destructive in that it is said to cause an obsessional neurosis involving guilt together with repressed emotions and sexuality. Not so, concludes Myers; religion he asserts is more often associated with expressions of joy. Whilst some forms of religion he acknowledges do appear associated with guilt and prejudice, many people are said to find happiness within their faith. It is said more likely to be the case that people with an active involvement have higher levels of mental health. Findings by Batson *et al.* (1993), and Colasanto and Shriver (1989) he quotes in support of the contention that religiously active people are less likely to take their own lives or to have problems with the abuse of drugs or of alcohol. Myers also cites the findings of Koenig (1997), and Matthews and Larson (1997) that religiously active individuals often enjoy high levels of physical health; this, it is suggested, is because they have a lesser likelihood of smoking or drinking to excess.

Responses to life crises seem to be more effective among groups such as widows who are active in religious organisations, suggests Myers. Their beliefs and practices are thought to be likely to provide them with a higher level of comfort and joy in their lives. From the work of Friedrich *et al.* (1988), Myers concludes that the mothers of children facing developmental challenges and who evince an active religious engagement were less likely to suffer depression and hopelessness. Myers also refers to the work of Inglehart (1990) on happiness and that by Okun and Stock (1987) on life satisfaction among older people; religiously engaged individuals were found more likely to report happiness. For older people life satisfaction was found to be related to good health and being religiously active. In regard to older people, Coleman (2005) has found a range of physical benefits to be associated with spiritual engagement, including higher quality of life, lower levels of stress, higher levels of physical well-being and years more of survival.

Religious or spiritual beliefs would appear to have been found beneficial for many in the face of life's challenges, such as growing frailty and dependence upon other people or upon institutions. Benjamin and Finlayson (2007) suggest that this may not only be so for older people; they report that it is also the case in several other life stages such as middle age, when personal challenges may confront an individual such as that posed by the onset of multiple sclerosis. In this case, Benjamin and Finlayson aver that an active involvement with some form of religious expression was found to be associated with improved health and personal satisfaction. Myers would posit that there is quite a strong relationship between religious expression and various measures of personal well-being. It is proposed by Myers that this effect is to be found among various groups in society, and is moreover not simply one relating to any particular culture; rather it is said to be found in many international settings and religious expressions.

The question may then arise as to what might be the factors that account for this link between religious expression and measures of well-being. Myers considers two possible explanations, one involving social support and the other representing the benefits derived from meaning making; it is also suggested that indeed both may be important. Religious engagement typically occurs within the context of communities of like-minded people; in such an arena social support, particularly in times of adversity, can be quite readily accessible. This conclusion is also reached by Cacioppo *et al.* (2005) who make the point that sociality and spirituality are quite often closely interconnected in most human societies. Humans are essentially a social species and religious expression is most often seen within that context; indeed sociality plays an essential role in the facilitation of spiritual experiences, whether they occur in church services, yoga groups or New Age ceremonies.

Myers also points out that an essential element of life is the making of meaning. This, as McAdams (2001, 2006), McAdams and Olsen (2010), and Bauer and McAdams (2004) have demonstrated, is an outcome that has involved the construction of a life narrative that brings together people and events and aims at blending them into a coherent whole; this is done so that these narratives may then provide explanation, both to the person and also to others, as to the salience and direction of their life. Myers advocates the utility of meaning making in the understanding of religious engagement; a person's religious or spiritual beliefs and practices, it is suggested, will likely provide that person with a sense of meaning and purpose. It is within this context that Seligman's suggestion that the lack of life meaning might well be linked to higher rates of depression among many is noted. Myers would conclude that well-being derived from religiousness might be associated with the acquisition of optimism when confronted with the vicissitudes of life, or even eventual death. He would thus take issue with Freud's diagnosis of religiousness as typically a toxic causal agent of painful emotional trauma. It is suggested here that the notion of meaning making may provide a useful framework within which to examine religious expression, well-being and tourism.

Religious expression and meaning making

Silberman has in recent times made a valuable contribution to the explication of religious expression as a meaning system (Silberman, 2003, 2004, 2005; Silberman *et al.*, 2001, 2005). This has been achieved within the context of a social/personality psychology framework wherein meaning systems are regarded as both descriptive and prescriptive/motivational beliefs. The descriptive beliefs concern the self, others around the individual and also the surrounding environment; prescriptive beliefs in Silberman's model encompass what an individual ought or ought not to do. Across a lifetime each person is said to assemble a unique meaning system and it is this motivational system in which religious beliefs are said to appear. A person's religious meaning system, she suggests, citing McIntosh (1995), will function in the manner of a lens through which the individual will perceive his or her reality; they will furthermore continue to construct this religious meaning system across the lifespan. It is also proposed by Silberman that religious meaning systems have the power to evoke or shape emotions and behaviour; so too may meaning systems influence self-regulatory processes. Essentially, religious meaning systems are said to focus upon that which is deemed to be sacred. This may include conceptualisations of a higher power, a divine entity, God, and also the notion of the transcendent, that class of phenomena typically regarded as holy and separate from the mundane or familiar in a person's life. These, she holds, may be seen as evoking or deserving of veneration or at least respect. For this reason they may be said to represent an elevated type of meaning, purpose or direction in a person's life.

The religious meaning system proposed by Silberman is articulated as a set of psychological processes. The first of these concerns the self along with the person's beliefs about the world around them. She regards the individual self as that which is essential about the person, together with that which the person regards as sacred and set apart from the mundane. The second of Silberman's processes involves contingencies and expectations; religious meaning systems, she avers, can regulate both contingencies and expectations. Contingencies typically involve that which is regarded as good or bad, right or wrong, approved or forbidden; the just and the good are said to deserve reward whereas those involved in injustice, oppression or harm of others are likely deserving of opprobrium or punishment. Outcome expectations in this religious meaning system involve self-efficacy beliefs; individuals are generally assumed to have a degree of personal agency and at sufficient levels so as to make alterations to the direction of their own lives. They are also said to have some agency so as to contribute to change within the society in which they reside.

Goals are another element in Silberman's schema. Here the paramount motivation involves connecting with and remaining constant with what is deemed to be the sacred. Silberman finds that a number of researchers such as Schwartz and Huismars (1995), Tang et al. (2005) and Batson et al. (1993) have previously investigated this area, and notes that goals here have been found to include benevolence, forgiveness and altruism; goals she points out may also at times involve motivations such as dominance and destruction for some individuals. All of these may, on occasions, take on a religious context if they become associated with the sacred or divine. Actions too are part of Silberman's meaning system. Religious systems may prescribe certain behaviours as being important; so too might these systems forbid other behaviours regarded as inimical to their basic tenets. And whilst some of these actions are easily recognised as being a component of a religious meaning system, such as prayer, others can be from daily life and may not be so identified. Citing the work of Oman and Thoreson (2003), she suggests that actions such as compassion and charity to those in need would fall into the latter goal; they too are said to be important elements in the religious meaning system for many people.

Emotional states also play an important role in Silberman's system. Religious expressions of various kinds can be powerful determinants of emotional reactions and they can do this in a number of ways. Individuals, it is suggested, can feel intensely accepted, even, in part, incorporated into some spiritual entity. She also finds that a person's emotions may be enhanced or even diminished if the religious meaning system that they embrace promotes joyful and satisfying responses as well as discouraging other emotions such as hate, anger or even hopelessness. Thus religious meaning systems may well impart principles and aspirations that are likely to have a direct bearing upon the emotional state of adherents. Citing Sethi and Seligman (1993) and Silberman (2003, 2004), she notes that this process related to emotional states can have both positive and negative outcomes. As examples, she suggests that beliefs regarding the inherent goodness of the world, and also the possibility of individual agency in improving the self and the world around them, may augment the well-being of people embracing such beliefs. Religious meaning systems, in so far as they are pointed toward the sacred, are also said to have a facility to address the widespread personal desire for transcendence among many people. Silberman, citing Emmons (1999, 2005), makes the point that this apparent need for transcendence, and so often found in quests involving spirituality, is closely connected to perceptions of well-being.

The components of a religious meaning system, when considered together, are suggested to have a considerable capacity to provide a sense of well-being for many people. Indeed these processes are to be seen reflected in the findings of researchers such as Ron (2009), Reader (2007) and Power (2006). These components of a religious system moreover have, Silberman concludes, a comprehensiveness that can endow an individual with an appreciation of meaning in regard to history, to human life across the lifespan, and at various points in time and space. These elements of the meaning system also, it is held, can afford meaning to life's roles, to rites of passage, to cultural events and artefacts as well as to other people and environmental phenomena. They do further provide the possibility of meaning to those many everyday situations that go to make up a human life. The religious meaning system is said to apply to the most profound dilemmas that can confront an individual. Both answers and hope can be offered when other possible strategies may not prove sufficient. Silberman warns however, quoting Kushner (1989) and Pargament *et al.* (2005), that religious meaning systems may also be constructed in such a manner as to furnish beliefs and behaviours that are profoundly problematic for an individual. These beliefs may become the cause of personal distress, of harm to the self and to others, and even of destruction on a large scale. Acts of violence, of terrorism and of bloodshed directed at many innocent people can, it is argued, in this way become synonymous with the sacred for a person whose religious meaning system is so created (Pargament *et al.*, 2005; Silberman, 2003; Silberman *et al.*, 2005).

Narratives and meaning systems

A variety of commentators in the field of narrative psychology have now made the point that it is within the stories people tell, often to themselves as well as to others, that meaning can be found (Adler *et al.*, 2007; McAdams, 2001; McAdams and Olson, 2010; Bauer and McAdams, 2004; Bauer *et al.*, 2005; McLean *et al.*, 2007; Singer, 2005). Others have used such narrative insights in examining factors that might distinguish among groups of religious travellers (Farias and Lalljee, 2006; Noy, 2004a, 2004b). Essentially meaning is seen to emerge from the narrative and is relevant not only to a researcher but also to the narrator in understanding the life course of the individual; the stories are said to be a part of the self-development process in that they have the action of explaining the experiences to the story teller and thereby add to the person's self concept as well as their ongoing life story (McLean *et al.*, 2007). Narratives would thus hold promise in the understanding of religious travel, and in particular how experiences come to influence the religious tourist's self image and identity by way of experiences such as those that might be described as self transforming. Collins-Kreiner (2010) and Olsen (2010) have described how changes have taken place in the ways in which pilgrimage is regarded; there has been, finds Collins-Kreiner, a major shift in regard to how this type of travel is now understood. More traditional conceptualisations would see pilgrimage as affording particular specified experiences that are basically related to the object of the exercise, the pilgrimage. However the focus now is said more likely to be upon the tourists' own experiences, and in particular how they may see and interpret those experiences to the self. This change of focus Collins-Kreiner describes as moving from object to subject, and from objectivity to subjectivity. These changes would seem to be in accord with the notions of McAdams and others who seek to understand the experiences within the narratives that individuals produce; it is out of these narratives that meaning can emerge.

It is argued by McAdams *et al.* that the accounts an individual both constructs and communicates to others about themselves and the happenings in their life have the capacity to provide considerable insight into the narrator's identity and major life concerns. It is also held that these narratives seek to explore, to integrate and to comprehend important events and experiences in their life course; it is so, they conclude, so that the person can gain a sense of both purpose and unity. McAdams *et al.* make the point that there are some quite basic elements to the narrative. It is the recounting of a story, quite often in a sequential form; it can at one level be understood as a vital expression of the person as a social being. Here the narrator is said to convey a story within the context of other people. The narrative may be associated with various motivations: it may be aimed as conveying information, or it may be primarily to teach or to urge others to achieve higher standards in their lives. The narrator's motives may also involve a desire to be critical, to be condemnatory or even to deliver threats of retribution if there is not an elevation of standards. And within these various types of narratives, the narrator's purpose fails if those reading, listening or even watching cannot understand the message of the narrator. Coherence thus is of critical importance within a narrative; it must convey effectively the narrator's basic message. If the target audience fails to comprehend the message, then this social process is said to have failed (Labov, 1972; McAdams, 1985, 2001).

Transformative narratives

Narratives, as McAdams *et al.* have concluded, are typically concerned with major and easily identifiable themes. One such theme is that concerned with life transformative experiences. Transformative narratives concern personal change and the critical growth challenges of life (Bakan, 1966; Bauer and McAdams, 2004; Bauer *et al.*, 2008; McAdams, 1985). The transitions of life, those experiences and growth points, are often unexpected and sometimes unwelcome events of change; every individual will not likely avoid such events in his or her life. They come moreover in all of the activities of life. Cantor and Kihlstrom (1987) have understood these life transitions as representing times of elevated self-reflection and as periods wherein a person may discern meaning in their life. In similar vein, Bauer and Bonanno (2001) regard these as periods of opportunity and of self-development. Some have also suggested that it not so much what happens during these periods of life transition that is critical; rather it is how the person interprets the experiences that will more likely define the outcome of the transition process. It would seem that those individuals who choose to see these life transitions as opportunities for reflection and growth, perhaps even for profound change, are the ones more likely to attain positive outcomes in the sense of meaning making and personal well being. In essence it is suggested that happiness and life satisfaction as outcomes of many life transitions, even some of those that on first encounter may appear negative and bleak, would likely be influenced in large measure by the templates of reflection and growth that the person applies to the life transition experiences.

Personal growth oriented perspectives on life transitions are regarded as those to do with purposive self-development of a person's wisdom and maturity in the life course (Brandtstadter, 1999; Lerner and Walls, 1999). In order to understand these life transitions, Bauer and McAdams (2004) have suggested two growth themes, integrative and intrinsic, corresponding to two dimensions of personality development: social-cognitive maturity and social-emotional well-being. They argue that the integrative theme is concerned with high levels of mature thinking, complexity of meaning making, assimilation, differentiation and accommodation of new information. Essentially they hold that this theme is to do with levels of complexity that an individual might employ in reflecting on self and on others. This theme is contrasted with the intrinsic theme, with ideas concerning highly developed capacities for adjustment, psychological health, happiness and well-being. This they would sum up as how a person feels about him or herself within the context of other people. It is this latter theme that has been explored in this chapter.

In regard to social-emotional well-being themes, Bauer and McAdams (2004) draw attention to motivating values, particularly those that are intrinsic versus those that are extrinsic. Intrinsic motivational values are those that foster feelings of life satisfaction and well-being; they are also said to focus upon personal growth, a genuineness in relationships with others and altruism toward those in their society. By way of contrast, Bauer and McAdams (2004) point out that extrinsic values are to do with status, wealth and physical appearances. Intrinsically motivated goals and activities are said to be more likely to produce desirable psychological outcomes for the individual in areas such as personal goal attainment and age-related adjustment. Bauer and McAdams (2004) have also noted the well-being that is associated with intrinsically-motivated memories, particularly those narratives that reveal the perceived importance of intrinsic rather than extrinsic values as their source of meaning making; they further make the point that it is not an event or even an activity that they would focus on to classify as intrinsic or extrinsic, but rather the personal meaning that the individual attributed to it in the narrative. Thus for Bauer and McAdams (2004), interest ought to be amongst the reasons for why a person would regard a particular memory as important in their life. In summary, it would seem that those life transition themes concerned with higher levels of intrinsic motivation within narratives were the ones found to be related to higher levels of satisfaction, happiness and well-being; those narratives that evidenced greater adjustment to life transitions were much more likely to emphasise personal growth and interpersonal relationships as well as an awareness of the needs of others around them. The works of Reader (2007) and of Power (2006) would seem to reveal the power of narratives, particularly those of the transformative type, in the reporting of an attainment of well-being within a spiritual context.

There is now a growing body of evidence that allows an understanding of various groups of travellers who do seek out places and experiences that are likely to produce life transitions. Groups included here are those of backpackers and younger travellers; since the 1970s a number of studies have shed light upon the various motivations, patterns of behaviour, emotions and cognitions associated with groups such as these. Noy (2004a, 2004b) has investigated narratives of self-change among backpackers, and suggests two major self-change genres: romanticists and semi-religious or religious. He has revealed that the recounted self-change narratives are founded on unique experiences to do with authenticity and adventure, and suggests that the external travel as described in the narratives may be understood as running parallel with the self-change process as a form of internal travel.

Noy also finds that these travellers, when they return home, recount stories concerning places visited as well as recounting the life transition experiences had during the trip. Noy points out that whilst backpackers and younger travellers are not the only groups who desire to encounter authenticity, their desire to engage with the unfamiliar, the exciting, even the somewhat dangerous, does seem to identify them as distinct in an experiential sense. In regard to the romanticist traveller, Noy holds that the authentic quest would involve the experiences of authentic places and of genuine people; it is thus suggested that such contact and engagement would lead to transformational experiences. The semi-religious or religious traveller, Noy finds, is more likely to regard authenticity in terms of a sacred centre, an experience of the divine, the spiritual or the authentic Other. Here Noy also finds a parallel between the actual or outer voyage and the inner voyage that is connected with a form of transformational change.

Finally, it is suggested that meaning making, life transitional experiences and personal well-being within spiritual or religious narratives in an online context might offer a promising research direction. There are now a number of etravel sources websites publishing the experiences and perceptions of travellers which include spiritual and religious enarratives; relatively few of these enarratives, though, would seem to involve conventional religious travel experiences. Rather these narratives appear more likely to reflect spiritual experiences and accompanying transformative personal events; sometimes a conventional religious establishment may serve as a backdrop for an experience that is reported as life transforming, whereas other narratives describe happenings that are more in the nature of a New Age encounter or event that can occur in a variety of circumstances. The enarratives contained in these sources clearly represent a variety of contexts, spiritual traditions, awe-inspiring occasions and transformative experiences that, for the narrator, are believed to have resulted in greater perceptions of well-being. Moreover they aim to describe socio-emotional themes that reflect intrinsic strivings, often for transformational personal change and new levels of life meaning, as well as how such strivings are believed to have endowed the narrator's life with higher degrees of well-being. The roles of transcendence and of meaning making in the enhancement of well-being have long been central in the understanding of spiritual and religious travel. Etravel narratives now offer new perspectives in this domain of travel. Whilst it may be argued that the motives for spiritual and religious travel have changed relatively little since the time of Herodotus of Helicarnassus, there would now appear to exist comparatively new opportunities to explore modalities such as context, process and outcome.

References

Adler, J.M., Wagner, J.W. and McAdams, D.P. (2007) 'Personality and the coherence of psychotherapy narratives', *Journal of Research in Personality*, 41: 1179–1198.

Argyle, M. (2000) *Psychology of Religion: An Introduction*. London: Routledge.

Argyle, M. (2002) 'Religion', *The Psychologist*, 15: 22–24.

Argyle, M. and Hills, P. (2000) 'Religious experiences and their relations with happiness and personality', *International Journal for the Psychology of Religion*, 10: 157–172.

Bakan, D. (1966) *The Duality of Human Existence: Isolation and Communion in Western Man*. Boston, MA: Beacon Press.

Basu, P. (2004) 'Route metaphors of "roots-tourism" in the Scottish Highland diaspora', in Coleman, S. and Eade, J. (eds), *Reframing Pilgrimage: Cultures in Motion*. London: Routledge, pp. 150–175.

Batson, C.D., Schoenrade, P.A. and Ventis, W.L. (1993) *Religion and the Individual: A Social Psychological Perspective*. New York: Oxford University Press.

Bauer, J.J. and Bonanno, G.A. (2001) 'Continuity and discontinuity: bridging one's past and present in stories of conjugal bereavement', *Narrative Inquiry*, 11: 123–158.

Bauer, J.J. and McAdams, D.P. (2004) 'Growth goals, maturity, and well-being', *Developmental Psychology*, 40: 114–127.

Bauer, J.J., McAdams, D.P. and Pals, J.L. (2008) 'Narrative identity and eudaimonic well-being', *Journal of Happiness Studies*, 9: 81–94.

Bauer, J.J., McAdams, D.P. and Sakaeda, A.R. (2005) 'Interpreting the good life: growth memories in the lives of mature, happy people', *Journal of Personality and Social Psychology*, 88: 203–217.

Benjamin, M.R. and Finlayson, M. (2007) 'Using religious services to improve health: findings form a sample of middle-aged and older adults with multiple sclerosis', *Journal of Aging and Health*, 19: 537–553.

Brandtstadter, J. (1999) 'The self in action and development: cultural, biological and ontological bases of intentional self-development', in Brandtstadter, J. and Lerner, R.M. (eds), *Action and Self Development: Theory and Research through the Lifespan*. Thousand Oaks, CA: Sage, pp. 3–26.

Cacioppo, J.T., Hawkley, L.C., Rickett, E. and Masi, C.M. (2005) 'Sociality, spirituality and meaning making: Chicago health, aging and social relations study', *Review of General Psychology*, 9: 143–155.

Cantor, N. and Kihlstrom, J.F. (1987) *Personality and Social Intelligence*. Englewood Cliffs, NJ: Prentice-Hall.

Cohen, E. (1992) 'Pilgrimage centres: concentric and excentric', *Annals of Tourism Research*, 19: 33–50.

Colasanto, D. and Shriver, J. (1989) 'Mirror of America', *Gallup Report*, 284: 34–38.

Coleman, P.G. (2005) 'Spirituality and ageing: the health implications of religious belief and practice', *Age and Ageing*, 34: 318–319.

Collicutt, J. (2011) 'Psychology, religion and spirituality', *The Psychologist*, 24: 250–251.

Collins-Kreiner, N. (2010) 'Researching pilgrimage: continuity and transformation', *Annals of Tourism Research*, 37: 440–456.

Dillon, M. and Wink, P. (2007) *In the Course of a Lifetime: Tracing Religious Belief, Practice and Change*. Berkeley, CA: University of California Press.

Eade, J. and Sallnow, M.J. (eds) (1991) *Contesting the Sacred: The Anthropology of Christian Pilgrimage*. London: Routledge.

Emmons, R.A. (1999) *The Psychology of Ultimate Concerns: Motivation and Spirituality in Personality*. New York: Guilford Press.

Emmons, R.A. (2005) 'Striving for the sacred: personal goals, life meaning, and religion', *Journal of Social Issues*, 61: 731–745.

Eysenck, M.W. (1998) 'Personality and the psychology of religion', *Mental Health, Religion and Culture*, 1: 11–19.

Farias, M. and Lalljee, M. (2006) 'Empowerment in the New Age: a motivational study of autobiographical life stories', *Journal of Contemporary Religion*, 21: 241–257.

Farias, M. and Lalljee, M. (2008) 'Holistic individualism in the Age of Aquarius: measuring individualism and collectivism in New Age, Catholic and Atheistic/agnostic groups', *Journal of the Scientific Study of Religion*, 47: 277–289.

Farias, M., Claridge, G. and Lalljee, M. (2005) 'Personality and cognitive predictors of New Age practices and beliefs', *Personality and Individual Differences*, 39: 979–989.

Frey, N. (1998) *Pilgrim Stories On and Off the Road to Santiago: Journeys along an Ancient Way in Modern Spain*. Berkeley, CA: University of California Press.

Friedrich, W.N., Cohen, D.S. and Wilturner, L.T. (1988) 'Specific beliefs as moderator variables in maternal coping with mental retardation', *Children's Health Care*, 17: 40–44.

Fuller, R.C. (2001) *Spiritual, but not Religious*. New York: Oxford University Press.

Hout, M. and Fischer, C. (2002) 'Explaining the rise of Americans with no religious preference: polarities and generations', *American Sociological Review*, 67: 165–190.

Inglehart, R. (1990) *Culture Shifts in Advanced Industrial Society*. Princeton, NJ: Princeton University Press.

Ivakhiv, A.J. (2001) 'Claiming sacred ground: pilgrimage and institutional religion', *Folklore*, 117: 33–53.

Kapuscinski, R. (2007) *Travels with Herodotus*. London: Penguin.

Koenig, H.G. (1997) *Is Religion Good for your Health? The Effects of Religion on Physical and Mental Health*. Birmingham, NY: Hawarth Press.

Koenig, H.G., Siegler, I.C., Meader, K.G. and George, L.K. (1990) 'Religious coping and personality in later life', *International Journal of Geriatric Psychiatry*, 5: 123–131.

Koenig, H.G., McCullough, M. and Larson, D. (2001) *Handbook of Religion and Health*. New York: Oxford University Press.

Kosek, R.B. (1999) 'Adaption of the Big Five as a hermeneutic instrument for religious constructs', *Personality and Individual Differences*, 27: 229–237.

Kushner, H.S. (1989) *When Bad Things Happen to Good People*. New York: Avon Books.

Labov, W. (1972) *Sociolinguistic Patterns*. Philadelphia: University of Pennsylvania Press.

Lerner, R.M. and Walls, T. (1999) 'Revisiting individuals as producers of their own development: from dynamic interactionism to developmental systems', in Brandtstadter, J. and Lerner, R.M. (eds), *Action and Self Development: Theory and Research through the Lifespan*. Thousand Oaks, CA: Sage, pp. 3–26.

McAdams, D.P. (1985) *Power, Intimacy and the Life Story*. New York: Guilford Press.

McAdams, D.P. (2001) 'The psychology of life stories', *Review of General Psychology*, 5: 100–122.

McAdams, D.P. (2006) *The Redemptive Self: Stories Americans Live By*. New York: Oxford University Press.

McAdams, D.P. and Olson, B.D. (2010) 'Personality development: continuity and change over the life course', *Annual Review of Psychology*, 61: 517–542.

McCullough, M.E., Tsang, J. and Brion, S. (2003) 'Personality traits in adolescence as predictors of religiousness in early adulthood: findings from the Terman longitudinal study', *Personality and Social Psychology Bulletin*, 29: 980–991.

MacDonald, D.A. (2000) 'Spirituality: description, measurement, and relation to the five-factor model of personality', *Journal of Personality*, 68: 153–197.

McIntosh, D.N. (1995) 'Religion as a schema, with implications for the relation between religion and coping', *International Journal for the Psychology of Religion*, 5: 1–16.

McLean, K.C., Pasupathi, M. and Pals, J.L. (2007) 'Selves creating stories creating selves: a process model of self-development', *Personality and Social Psychology Review*, 11: 262–278.

Marozzi, J. (2008) *The Way of Herodotus: Travels with the Man who Invented History*. Philadelphia, PA: DaCapo/Murray.

Matthews, D.A. and Larson, D.B. (1997) *The Faith Factor: An Annotated Bibliography of Clinical Research on Spiritual Subjects* (vols I–IV). Rockville, MD: National Institute for Health Care Research and Georgetown University Press.

Myers, D.G. (2000) 'The funds, friends, and faith of happy people', *American Psychologist*, 55: 56–67.

Noy, C. (2004a) 'This trip really changed me: backpackers' narratives of self change', *Annals of Tourism Research*, 31: 78–122.

Noy, C. (2004b) 'Performing identity: touristic narratives of self change', *Text and Performance Quarterly*, 24: 115–138.

Okun, M.A. and Stock, W.A. (1987) 'Correlates and components of subjective well-being among the elderly', *Journal of Applied Gerontology*, 6: 95–112.

Olsen, D.H. (2010) 'Pilgrims, tourists and Max Weber's "Ideal Types"', *Annals of Tourism Research*, 37: 848–851.

Olsen, D.H. and Timothy, D.J. (2006) 'Tourism and religious journeys', in Timothy, D.J. and Olsen, D.H. (eds), *Tourism, Religion and Spiritual Journeys*. London and New York: Routledge, pp. 1–21.

Oman, D. and Thoreson, C.E. (2003) 'Spiritual modeling: a key to spiritual and religious growth?' *International Journal for the Psychology of Religion*, 13: 149–165.

Pargament, K.I., Maygar-Russell, G. and Murray-Swank, N.A. (2005) 'The sacred and the search for significance: religion as a unique process', *Journal of Social Issues*, 61: 665–687.

Peterson, C. (2006) 'The values in action classification of character strengths', in Csikszentmihalyi, M. and Csikszentmihalyi, S. (eds), *A Life Worth Living: Contributions to Positive Psychology*. New York: Oxford University Press, pp. 29–48.

Peterson, C. and Seligman, M.E.P. (2004) *Character Strengths and Virtues: A Handbook and Classification*. Oxford: Oxford University Press.

Piedmont, R.L. (1999) 'Does spirituality represent the sixth factor of personality? Spiritual transcendence and the five-factor model', *Journal of Personality*, 67: 985–1013.

Power, R. (2006) 'A place of community: "Celtic" Iona and institutional religion', *Folklore*, 117: 33–53.

Preston, J.J. (1992) 'Spiritual magnetism: organizing principles for the study of pilgrimage', in Morinas, A. (ed.), *Sacred Journeys: An Anthropology of Pilgrimage*. Westport, CT: Greenwood, pp. 31–46.

Reader, I. (2007) 'Pilgrimage growth in the modern world: meanings and implications', *Religion*, 37: 210–229.

Rinschede, G. (1992) 'Forms of religious tourism', *Annals of Tourism Research*, 19: 51–67.

Ron, A. (2009) 'Towards a typological model of contemporary Christian travel', *Journal of Heritage Tourism*, 4: 287–297.

Roof, W.C. (1999) *Spiritual Marketplace: Baby Boomers and the Remaking of American Religion*. Princeton, NJ: Princeton University Press.

Saroglou, V. (2002) 'Religion and the five factors of personality: a meta-analytic review', *Personality and Individual Differences*, 32: 15–25.

Saroglou, V. and Fiasse, L. (2003) 'Birth order, personality, and religion: a study among young adults from a three-sibling family', *Personality and Individual Differences*, 35: 19–29.

Schwartz, S.H. and Huismars, S. (1995) 'Value priorities and religiosity in four Western religions', *Social Psychology Quarterly*, 58: 88–107.

Seligman, M.E.P., Steen, T.A., Park, N. and Peterson, C. (2005) 'Positive psychology progress: empirical validation of interventions', *American Psychologist*, 60 (5): 410–421.

Sethi, S. and Seligman, M.E.P. (1993) 'Optimism and fundamentalism', *Psychological Sciences*, 4: 256–259.

Silberman, I. (2003) 'Spiritual role modeling: the teaching of meaning systems', *International Journal for the Psychology of Religion*, 13: 175–195.

Silberman, I. (2004) 'Religion as a meaning system: implications for pastoral care and guidance', in Herl, D. and Berman, M.L. (eds), *Building Bridges over Troubled Waters: Enhanced Pastoral Care and Guidance*. Lima, OH: Wyndham Hall Press, pp. 51–67.

Silberman, I. (2005) 'Religion as a meaning system: implications for the new Millennium', *Journal of Social Issues*, 4: 641–663.

Silberman, I., Higgins, E.T. and Dwerk, C.S. (2001) 'Religion and well-being: world beliefs as mediators', Paper presented as the 109th Annual Convention of the American Psychological Association, San Francisco, CA.

Silberman, I., Higgins, E.T. and Dwerk, C.S. (2005) 'Religion and world change: violence and terrorism versus peace', *Journal of Social Issues*, 61: 761–784.

Sin, N.L. and Lyubomirsky, S. (2009) 'Enhancing well-being and alleviating depressive symptoms with positive psychology: a practice-friendly meta-analysis', *Journal of Clinical Psychology*, 65: 467–487.

Singer, J.A. (2005) *Personality and Psychotherapy: Treating the Whole Person*. New York: Guilford Press.

Smith, V.L. (1992) 'Introduction: the quest in guest', *Annals of Tourism Research*, 19: 1–17.

Tang, J., McCullough, M.E. and Hout, W.T. (2005) 'Psychometric and rationalization accounts of the religion-forgiveness discrepancy', *Journal of Social Issues*, 61: 785–805.

Taylor, A. and MacDonald, D.A. (1999) 'Religion and the five factor model of personality: an exploratory investigation using a Canadian university sample', *Personality and Individual Differences*, 27: 1243–1259.

Turner, V. and Turner, E. (1969) *The Ritual Process*. London: Routledge.

Turner, V. and Turner, E. (1978) *Image and Pilgrimage in Christian Culture*. New York: Colombia University Press.

Vukonic, B. (1996) *Tourism and Religion*. London: Elsevier.

Wink, P., Ciciolla, L., Dillon, M. and Tracey, A. (2007) 'Religiousness, spiritual seeking and personality: findings from a longitudinal study', *Journal of Personality*, 75: 1051–1070.

Wood, M. (2004) *The Road to Delphi: The Life and Afterlife of Oracles*. London: Chatto and Windus.

Wuthnow, R. (1998) *After Heaven: Spirituality in America since the 1950's*. Berkeley, CA: University of California Press.

7 Experiencing flamenco
An examination of a spiritual journey

Xavier Matteucci

Introduction

This chapter is concerned with how foreign tourists experience intangible heritage taking the example of flamenco as an art form. Every year thousands of people travel to Spain, and particularly to the southern region of Andalusia, to attend flamenco festivals, flamenco concerts and participate in flamenco music and dance courses. Aoyama (2009) and Steingress (2004) can be counted among the commentators who argue that with the rise of globalisation, flamenco has become a transnational phenomenon which is evidenced by the growing number of people who do flamenco beyond the Spanish or Andalusian borders. While there are no statistics that attest to the number of non-Spanish flamenco enthusiasts in the world, the ever-increasing presence of foreign visitors at flamenco festivals within Andalusia is a sign of this internationalisation. Not only do tourists congregate to Andalusia to experience flamenco, but also many flamenco artists from Andalusia teach and perform at flamenco festivals outside Spain. To illustrate the fervour that flamenco engenders beyond the Andalusian boundaries, Shikaze (2004) tells us that in Japan alone about 80,000 people study flamenco at about 600 academies throughout the country.

Recently, due to the growth in popularity of flamenco, more attention has been paid to flamenco as a tourist attraction on the part of the regional authorities. For example, every two years the regional government of Andalusia collects data on flamenco tourism on the occasion of the bi-annual flamenco festival *Bienal de Flamenco de Sevilla*. Flamenco tourists use both tourist and non-tourist places so that their economic contribution goes far beyond the traditional tourism money circuit. For instance, the flamenco tourism income more directly spreads to local flamenco artists and other heritage-related stakeholders such as flamenco specialised shops, clothes and accessories designers, musical instrument makers, regional record companies, and flamenco venues, among others. The new consumptive practices of the growing mass of creative individuals (Florida, 2002; Richards, 2011) in search of unique, authentic and place-specific cultural experiences may explain the consolidation of flamenco both as an art form originating from Andalusia and as a tourism product. However, despite the contemporary trends towards intangibility, subjectivity and co-creation of cultural tourist experiences, both the production and consumption of flamenco have received little attention (Aoyama, 2007; Cantero, 2009; Perujo, 2008). Therefore, it is not surprising that, to date, little information is available on those tourists who have a special interest in flamenco music and dance. Additionally, despite the recent institutionalisation of the study of flamenco throughout Andalusia, in particular at the universities of Seville and Córdoba, few, if any, attempts have been made to understand the experiences of flamenco tourists.

The material presented in this chapter aims to fill those knowledge gaps and, therefore, documents the tourist experience of flamenco in Seville, Spain. Following a grounded theory research strategy, qualitative data were collected through in-depth interviews, photo-elicitation and participant observations. The fieldwork was carried out between September 2009 and May 2010; the study participants included eleven French native speakers from France, Luxembourg, Switzerland and Canada and nine English speakers from Australia, Wales and England, Canada and the United States who participated in flamenco music (guitar) and dance courses in Seville. The 20 respondents included 16 females and 4 males with an average of 31 years of age. All respondents were tourists with some staying only a few weeks and others up to one year, and all experienced flamenco in its different forms (e.g. classes, concerts, self-performances, flamenco shows, etc.). Interviews were not only complemented with observational notes taken before and after most interviews but also with reflections on various shared and personal experiences of flamenco. In the subsequent section, I use selected quotes from the tourists' accounts to describe their experience of flamenco in the Andalusian capital.

The tourist experience as a spiritual journey

Some commentators have described tourism as a form of pilgrimage (Cohen, 1979; Graburn, 1989) with some tourists searching for authenticity in the exotic Other (MacCannell, 1976). This study provides some evidence of this and, therefore, argues that the flamenco tourist is indeed a modern pilgrim attracted to a sacred centre. While religious pilgrims congregate at Mecca, St Peter's square or in the Golden Temple in the Indian city of Amritsar, flamenco pilgrims find their spiritual centre in Seville or in other such places within Andalusia. Thus, it does not seem far-fetched to state that God, in the monotheist tradition, is replaced by 'flamenco gods', or is juxtaposed with a multitude of flamenco artists who enact (and are perceived as) authentic spiritual leaders. Like religious pilgrimages, secular tourism or leisure activities (e.g. flamenco courses) are described as rituals by their temporality and liminality (Turner, 1979). Psychologists who have been grappling with the spirituality construct have evaluated it in three main ways: spirituality has been either seen as a general trait, as a process reflecting personal goals or as an outcome (Emmons, 2006). For example, Pargament (1999, p. 12) defines spirituality as 'a search for the sacred' thus highlighting the process orientation of the concept. Unlike Pargament, Kelly (1995 cited in Emmons, 2006), underscores the experiential dimension of spirituality and defines it as 'a deep sense of belonging, of wholeness, of connectedness, and of openness to the infinite' (pp. 4–5). Emmons (2006) attempts to grasp the multi-dimensionality of the construct and describes spirituality as 'something spontaneous, informal, creative, universal, ... authentic inner experience and freedom of personal expression, of seeking, even of religious experimenting' (p. 64). The experience dimensions expounded in this chapter echo Emmons' definition as these reflect the tourists' personal goals to learning flamenco, which in turn have led to a variety of emotional states. The research participants experienced spirituality in diverse situations and places as shown in Table 7.1.

The data analysis has uncovered a number of dimensions which indicate that the tourist experience of flamenco (as experienced by most of the study participants) closely resembles the spiritual experience. These dimensions have been tentatively labelled as: environment, challenge, arousal, ineffable and self. The *environment* has to do with the experience of place and the relationship with peers, instructors and the local community. *Challenge* refers to the experience of risk, sacrifice and hardship. *Arousal* has to do with visceral experiences, such as body awareness and intense emotional states. The *ineffable* is concerned with those extraordinary experiences that translate into states of transcendence and feelings of unity. Last, *self* relates to notions of enrichment, meaningfulness, transformation and eudaimonic well-being. The first two dimensions (environment and challenge) are seen as triggers in that they are the complementary

Table 7.1 Respondents' spiritual experiences

Respondents	Activity	Context
Celina	Dancing	Flamenco dance studio (Seville)
	Being in Seville	Seville
Jil	Listening to the trumpet	Street parade during *Semana Santa*
	Meeting artists	Flamenco dance studio (Jerez and Seville)
Maya	Dancing/music	Flamenco dance studio (Seville)
	Interacting with instructors	Flamenco dance studio (Seville)
Irena	Being in class with instructor	Flamenco dance studio (Seville)
Alice	Being in Seville	Seville streets
	Being at a peña	Performance at a local Peña
	Dancing	Flamenco dance studio (Seville)
Ana	Performing with peers/music	Stage performance/rehearsal (Seville)
Aglaé	Dancing	Improvised street party (Seville)
	Dancing	Flamenco dance studio (Seville)
	Doing flamenco	Being in Seville
Sandra	Dancing	Flamenco dance studio (Seville)
Aaron	Participating in street party (hand clapping)	Jerez festival (Feria de Jerez)
	Doing flamenco	Stage performance/rehearsal (Seville)
Aron	Experiencing music	Performance at a local bar
	Doing flamenco	Being in Seville

conditions for attaining spiritual experiences. The following two dimensions (arousal and the ineffable) correspond to the direct emotional reactions and feelings that people have in relation to those triggers. The last dimension (self) refers to the surfacing outcomes which result from the experience. The following text briefly describes each of these dimensions, emphasising the positive aspects of the tourists' subjective experiences.

Environment

In their variety, physical spaces influenced the study participants in different ways. Seville was spoken about in terms of the holy place of flamenco where one must come to in order to experience authentic flamenco. Additionally, the atmosphere experienced in the intimacy of other spaces such as the flamenco clubs (peñas) and the flamenco studios was also described as authentic. These extraordinary spaces are real but also imagined and fantasised. For the participants, what these different spaces have in common is that they offer a very special space where individuals derive meanings, act in accordance to those meanings and embody their identities. Foucault (1984) calls such places 'other spaces' or *heterotopias*. To illustrate what he means by heterotopia, Foucault provides the example of a boat that he describes as 'a place without a place'; although materially bounded, the boat is a floating space on the immensity of the sea which is used to pursue a variety of dreams (p. 49). Seville itself and these other places where flamenco can be genuinely experienced are Foucault's boat, or heterotopic zones where one seeks meaning, invents him/herself and aspires to an ideal. Foucault notes that heterotopic spaces serve two functions: they are either sites where one may live up to his or her illusions, or sites where one may create his or her own real and perfect world. Such sites serve as compensation for the dreary spaces of workaday life. Such places imply particular performances in the form of rites; those rites find legitimacy within the physical limits of those spaces. For example, for Jil the stage clearly represents a liminal space that empowers her to adopt behaviour different from her everyday conduct. The theatre stage offers Jil a safe environment in which her fantasies and emotions can be freely expressed. Like Jil on stage, within the boundaries of the class Catherine feels empowered to unleash her emotions and it is clear that the physical environment alone does not suffice to generate such heightened states; rather, the presence of other dancers as well as the leadership of an inspiring instructor largely accounts for this. The flamenco artists and instructors were frequently given a privileged status such as being elevated to idols, mentors or even flamenco gods. In a similar vein, the respondents' interactions with their peers often resulted in positive feelings of togetherness which created a close social bond between them. Victor Turner (1969) refers to this feeling as *communitas*. Turner says that it is a blend of 'lowliness and sacredness, of homogeneity and comradeship' that emerges from the liminal experience (p. 96). While participants evoked feelings of belonging to a group of like-minded people, it is precisely the sharing of experiences and the elision of social and ethnic status, which operates within the class environment that constitutes communitas. Indeed, what people do in the outside world does not matter anymore, and it is only because it does not matter that communion is possible. This flattening of origin and status is clearly visible in the words of Celina:

> I think it's cool being around a bunch of other people from all over the world who are trying to do the same thing.
>
> (Celina)

Other respondents referred to the wide but at the same time small 'flamenco family' in which they felt a part of. Some talked about their new friendships.

The data reveal that it is not only the sharing of experience that produces such heightened feelings of communion. Music was also found to be a powerful coalescing factor. Indeed, respondents have undergone meaningful feelings of social relationship through the shared experience of music. This special bond mediated by the experience of music could be described as an intense feeling of togetherness:

> For me dancing next to someone who's singing is a very emotional thing. Often on stage, talking about a dancer, we say 'le entra'.[1] When someone tells me 'le entra' [laugh], it's that I'm really sensitive to the song. For example, if there is a very good singer behind me, it can emotionally affect me that it can change the way I dance.... A singer with a powerful voice who's like two meters behind me and he sings to you stretching his arms like that towards you [laugh], it's very touching ... I don't know how to explain this. It makes it easier for you to live the soleá, the seguiryia or l'alegría; live like to truly experience what you're listening to.
>
> (Ana)

In the above quotation, Ana has experienced music in the presence of other people who have equally contributed to the performance in some way. Put differently, all the participants co-created their experience of the music. These social interactions inspired by music resulted in intense, unique and meaningful experiences. For example, Ana uses the Spanish expression '*le entra*' (being instilled/understanding) to explain the infusing effect of the co-created music performance on her. The phrase '*le entra*' unmistakably describes a transcendental experience, i.e. an experience beyond the physical self. Ana feels filled by something special which emanates from someone else, someone who is not under her control. We can relate this phenomenon to the *mutual tuning-in relationship* (Schütz, 1964). In investigating musical performances, social phenomenologist Alfred Schütz (1899–1959) found that participants had gone through meaningful experiences as a result of an acute, simultaneous experience of the other. He writes, 'this relationship is established by the reciprocal sharing of the Other's flux of experiences in inner time, by living through a vivid present together, by experiencing this togetherness as a "We"' (p. 177). Therefore, as with communitas, what seems crucial in the *tuning-in relationship* is the simple nexus of doing and sharing. Like for a number of my research participants, Schütz asserts that it is the harmonious accord with and the consciousness of the other participants that makes the experience exceptionally meaningful. The relevance of the tuning-in relationship is that it captures 'what it is that is experienced in religious rituals' (Neitz and Spickard, 1990, p. 31).

Challenge

The challenge dimension was found in most of the respondents' accounts and was articulated in terms of risk, doubt, sacrifice and hardship. This is perhaps explained by the fact that the study participants are driven by clear existential goals and to reach these goals, participants venture into the unknown. For instance Alice left her family and Australia behind with no idea of when she will return home, and Celina and Jil both quit their well-paid jobs to live their passion and expose themselves to an uncertain future. Whether it was through learning and mastering new physical skills (flamenco dance or music instruments), or expanding their emotional boundaries (being on their own for the first time or coping with moments of doubt), the flamenco enthusiasts reported hard times which they expressed with words and phrases such as *sacrifice, hard work, discipline, pressure, pain* and living on a *tight budget*. Some of the participants had been confronted with doubts and different types of pressure mostly before but also during their stay in Seville. For example, Aglaé expressed her lack of sense of purpose in life before deciding to do flamenco in Spain. She has also experienced doubt and anxiety about her decision to focus on flamenco rather than on a more conventional career. In a similar vein, Sandra, Rémi, Celina, Jil and Maya reported unfulfilling working lives before coming to Seville. Likewise, both Aron and Ebony felt the urge to come to Seville, and Natalia alluded to her life crisis. The following excerpt attests to those moments of doubt and disquietude:

> I mean for my work back there, she had to hire a contractor who probably cost more than I do to cover me for those six months that I took off. You work for 5 years and you can take six months off and not get fired [laugh]. 'Cause you're either burnt out and quit or you take a sabbatical, so I've chosen a sabbatical.... With me I think I was ... I was always trying to be that person that everybody expects me to be, and it was just easier to do things like to focus on other people instead of myself. And this is really the only time I had where, I really have to depend on myself, I have to book my train tickets, I have to figure where I'm going, I have to find a place on a map, and I think that's where a lot of experiences are coming from. It's taking this time for myself that I just haven't really done. You know. I've been in a relationship for 15 years solid, so [chuckles], so it's just never been about me ... I think that's the whole Catholic upbringing too [laugh] ... I've never really realised how strong it was until I was travelling. Just the

whole idea of self sacrifice and you know, pride being a negative thing, vanity being a negative thing, like all those you need to be a strong person.... Well, I've learnt a ridiculous amount about myself, things I didn't know were there and so I know when I go home there's gonna be some significant changes that not everybody is gonna be happy about.

(Natalia)

Natalia's example is illustrative in that it clearly shows the profound transformation that she has gone through. Her detailed account reveals a number of significant disruptions, such as the disintegration of her sentimental relationship, her stressful and consuming job, as well as the challenges to her basic values and beliefs. Despite moments of doubts and stressful life events, Natalia exhibited determination and faith in pursuing her aspirations which demonstrates her motivation to change. What Natalia's example indicates is that negative feelings as in life crises may not only 'force the self to evolve in numerous directions', but these also present opportunities for personal change and for the promotion of character strengths (Harter, 2002, p. 390).

Arousal and the ineffable

I've been in a kind of daze this whole time where everything is a great experience.

(Alice)

Arousal refers to the stimulation of the sensuous body in a way that the individual becomes aware of her or his own body and affective states (Bond and Stinson, 2000). It is difficult to separate the dimension of *arousal* from the dimension of *ineffable* because of their kinship and strong interdependence. The next passage not only provides a perfect illustration of this interrelationship, but it also serves to further illustrate the liminality of the flamenco space and practice:

Well, I guess that personality wise I am pretty introvert, and it's not that when I am dancing I go crazy or anything like that, but I feel things more acutely. I don't know how it comes out and how other people view it? But when I am enjoying like Andrés Peña's class, with the bulería, I love it! And, like I feel like I am – you know – I'm grooving [intonation of excitement] – you know – and it's awesome. And so I got that enjoyment thingy, I don't know, it's not something that I feel often normally in my daily life, but when I am dancing and when they're singing, it's like ... I don't know, it's hard to explain.... How do I feel? I don't know why but like, it does not matter, I mean if I am dancing a soleá[2] and stuff, it's a really sad song, right? But afterwards it's like; it's like runner's high, afterwards. What do they call it? Endorphins? I don't know.

(Celina)

Flamenco, tourism and spirituality 117

Celina's words convey feelings of enjoyment and well-being. *Body resonance* is the term used by Bond and Stinson (2000) to describe this heightened bodily feeling which, they argue, entails 'emotional and cognitive awareness or transformation' (p. 56). Her heightened sensuousness is encapsulated in the phrase: 'I feel things more acutely'. Expressions like 'grooving', 'the runner's high', and the repetitive use of the verb 'feel' not only imply the full activation of her sense organs, but also suggest that the intensity of the sensory stimulations approximates a trance-like experience which the body cannot contain. These expressions also indicate that Celina's experience is extremely enjoyable. Csikszentmihalyi (1990) uses the term *autotelic* to describe such desirable and rewarding experiences (Filep, 2008). Moreover, the phrases 'it's like … I don't know' and 'it's hard to explain' indicate that Celina's emotional experience is hard to describe.

In her study of tourism dance performances, Daniel (1996) defines this extraordinary state of being as *experiential authenticity*, a moment in which 'time and tensions are suspended' (p. 789). When Daniel goes on to say that 'for many tourists, the dance becomes their entire world at that particular moment' (p. 789), she alludes to a sense of personal synthesis where body, mind and environment become one. Like for the *tourist moment* described by Hom Cary (2004, p. 64), in which the subject becomes 'entirely subsumed by the dance', Celina ceases to be a tourist, Asian or Canadian, in that particular moment, which suggests a loss of separate identity. By putting the body at the centre, Celina experiences a religious-like feeling, a feeling that transcends her. Here, it is suggested that it is precisely by unleashing her body expressions that Celina is able to attain such feelings of transcendence. It seems that Celina's emotional experience is to some degree triggered by the sound of music. Evidence for this is found in the phrases: 'when they're singing, it's like' and 'when he sang, I could feel it'. Another reason for Celina's strong reaction to music may be explained by the process of musical empathy. Scherer and his colleague Zentner (2001) explain empathy (Einfühlung) as a kind of contagion which is felt when listening or moving to a certain rhythm. They suggest that 'musical empathy will be more likely in the case of listening to an admired performer … who is performing in a highly emotional manner' (p. 371). The way Rafael Campallo, who is a famous flamenco dancer, sang *Soleá* in class may have augmented Celina's emotional arousal. This state of communion through music, which Celina experiences here, parallels other informants' experiences which are akin to Schütz's *tuning-in relationship*. Additionally, because she is far away from her family and boyfriend, Celina says that she relates even more to the loneliness conveyed in the song and by the sound of Campallo's voice. This may suggest that some relationship exists between actual emotional states and the pre-existence of similar and unconscious feelings. In other words, Celina's strong emotional experience may have been reinforced by an underlying emotional effect.

Besides, in her account when she reports the positive emotions felt while deeply feeling the sad character of the *Soleá*, Celina touches the mysterious and paradoxical affective quality of music. While Celina feels sad and lonely, her feeling of loneliness is not just exacerbated through dancing but also made bearable and is even converted into an ecstatic state of being. This ecstatic feeling is encapsulated by the phrases: 'it's like runner's high' and 'endorphins'. In order to elucidate the magical powers of music on human beings, Saldanha (2002) draws upon the philosophy of Deleuze and Guattari (1980). She writes that 'music is the cultural form best suited to extract the energies already oscillating in and in-between human bodies and their surroundings, to *carry them elsewhere*, to enhance their powers' (p. 58). Following the same argument, Bond and Stinson (2000) refer to the seminal work of John Dewey, *Art of Experience*, published in 1934. They argue that, in his description of *imaginative unification*, Dewey provides the most influential 'conceptualization of the arts as integral to learning and life experience' (p. 73). In music and activities like dancing, Dewey concisely notes that 'we are carried out beyond ourselves to find ourselves' which results in a feeling of wholeness that is analogous to the religious experience (Bond and Stinson, 2000, p. 73). Indeed, flamenco takes Celina away from her ordinary life through states of intense emotional and sensory arousals to then throw her back into a more meaningful life. This process is akin to a spiritual transformation.

Another example comes from Alice who explains how she feels while dancing in her class:

> I don't know. It's just like a moment where you're doing, so you're so self-absorbed in something you don't think about, like eating or drinking or breathing or ... you just really.... At the same time, it is important that you ..., you have to be aware of everything in your body. So, what your finger is doing, you know, what your face is doing. You have to be really aware. So yeah, when you're dancing, it's kind of like you've got this energy, like a current that's running through your whole body. And that's how you just, you have to stay aware of everything. But not be too aware, and still lose yourself a little bit. That makes it really hard to achieve. Yeah, I mean, even if the class is the hardest, still I have to say they're really fun.
>
> (Alice)

Alice alludes to her sense of control when she says that she feels aware of everything that she does while dancing. She is totally focused on what she is doing, meaning that her mind is not wandering somewhere else. As one dimension of the concept of *flow*, Csikszentmihalyi (1975) construes this state as the merger of action and awareness. The phrase 'you're so self-absorbed in something you don't think about, like eating or drinking or breathing' suggests Alice's deep involvement and the spontaneity of her action. She says that the class, overall, is pleasurable which indicates that dancing for Alice is an intrinsically rewarding activity. Alice's dancing experience is a good example of Csikszentmihalyi's experience of flow. Similar to flow, the concept of mindfulness is also relevant to describe Celina and Alice's learning experiences. Being mindful means being alert and receptive to new situations while being situated in the present (Langer, 2002). Following Langer (2002), by learning mindfully, Celina and Alice are making the most of their dance lessons and, at the same time, their flamenco performance is improved. As such, mindfulness enables Celina and Alice to enjoy themselves more and therefore be happier.

Self

This study reveals that at the core of the flamenco journey is the impact on the self. By fully engaging in intrinsically motivated activities, the respondents strongly felt flow-like experiences and evoked a variety of personal rewards, such as self-enrichment and greater sense of self. These positive feelings resemble the notion of eudaimonic well-being.

Pearce *et al.* (2011) explain that the notion of eudaimonia has to do with virtues such as those concerned with the conduct of a sensible life. Waterman *et al.* (2008) more precisely define eudaimonia as 'the feelings present when one is moving toward self-realization in terms of the developing one's unique individual potentials and furthering one's purposes in living' (p. 42). The construct of eudaimonic well-being has clearly emerged from the data. Evidence for this can be found in the following quote:

> These moments are priceless. It's just unique. For me, life is worth to be lived for these particular moments. And if I can multiply these moments to the maximum, live those moments throughout my entire life, making money, making a living of it [flamenco], like of those moments, it would be pure happiness. It would simply be happiness. This experience is existentially wonderful.... Two years ago, I became a believer. And from that time on, I really wanted to be authentic; I looked for authenticity in my life. And it was while searching that I've come across flamenco. I didn't expect it, but apparently it [flamenco] was something that truly fitted my way of being. So now, I want to do this as within an act of faith. And of course, now, letting myself transported by the music, flamenco music, it's a spiritual thing.
>
> (Maya)

The words used by Maya reveal that her experience was felt as meaningful and extremely fulfilling when she says, 'these moments are priceless' and 'life is worth to be lived for these particular moments'. Maya also mentions the search for her authentic self, for being the person who she thinks she truly is. Living in accord with her true self is not only a goal to which she aspires, but the core benefit of behaving authentically is that she merely feels happier. Psychologist Susan Harter (2002), in her work with adolescents, found that true-self behaviour was linked to a number of personal benefits such as higher self-esteem, optimism and cheerfulness. Finding her true self equates with the expressive realisation of one's highest potential; it requires sustained efforts and the process itself is unmistakably a lifelong existential and spiritual pursuit. This lifelong pursuit is mostly undertaken in connection to the self, whereas sometimes, as for Maya, a religious feeling can be the driving force. Although the way to happiness is not without pitfalls, every little achievement is an encouragement which keeps people on track and proves that life is worth living.

Csikszentmihalyi (1975) suggests that people are happiest while undergoing flow states and while engaging in activities which match their level of skills. This is found in Maya's account when she says that the moments during which she dances flamenco are moments of 'pure happiness'. As the following account suggests, eudaimonic well-being is also clearly related to having a purpose in life and, perhaps, more specifically to engaging in intrinsically motivated activities:

> you decide to study and keep going because you run in so many walls, so many walls, and you say 'there's just no way I can play this picado[3] faster'; 'There's no fucking way'; 'I cannot do this technique; I just won't be able to do it'. That passion to keep going is what keeps you going instead of just saying – you know – 'maybe Flamenco isn't for me'. You know? And – you know – a lot of people hit their wall and their drive to learn it isn't strong enough. You know – and when you just keep going, you keep hitting wall after wall but every time you hit those walls, you know that is a little further than the last time you hit the wall. It keeps you going – you know.
>
> (Aaron)

The word 'passion' certainly comes close to describing the complex set of feelings which make up the positive, subjective state of eudaimonic well-being. The search for increased well-being is also apparent in the words of Aron and Aglaé who speak of their experience in Seville in terms of a therapy:

> I mean, I see myself quite a spiritual person. And it's about me. I'm not being self-centered but this trip is about me. You can't get along that well with people in the world if you can't get along with yourself, so my ... that's why I am here for; [it] is to learn to like myself and to better myself, learn to forget the bad things in the past and start a new chapter. You know. Yeah, it's a self bettering experience, as I said; I use the guitar as a form of meditation. 'Cause at that time I'm in my purist bliss. Is that the word? When I'm playing guitar there is no demons nagging my head, you know ... I'm trying to get rid of my scars, you know, try to patch up my scars.
>
> (Aron)

> Actually, for me, flamenco is like a sort of therapy ... because I didn't have a clear goal in life. I was studying something I didn't like, so it was like a way to let out all the things that I had inside, all the emotions.
>
> (Aglaé)

The above two accounts indicate that the flamenco experience in Seville is not a superficial, instant search for pleasure; instead, it corresponds to a deeper search for long lasting changes in life. The two quotes suggest that the respondents' experience is a reaction to or an escape from the alienated structures of the home environment ('no demons nagging my head', 'I didn't have a clear goal in life'). The healing nature of the experience is underscored by the phrases: 'it's a self bettering experience', 'I'm trying to get rid of my scars', 'try to patch up my scars' and 'flamenco is like a sort of therapy'.

Conclusion

The data revealed a number of themes which represent the tourist experience as a spiritual journey. An essential aspect of the spiritual experience is the active involvement of individuals in intrinsically motivated activities. It has been illustrated that both the physical environment and the meaningful interactions between the participants can trigger such experiences. The contribution of positive social interactions to spiritual experiences is consistent with research that underscores the relationship between spirituality and psychological adjustment through factors such as perceived social support (Salsman et al., 2005). This study also suggests that the multi-sensory and kinaesthetic experience of music leads to ecstatic feelings and spiritual fulfilment. In addition to arousing the corporeal and emotional self, the flamenco experience invokes states of transcendence which words alone cannot describe. It was also shown that the experience of challenge, in its various forms, contributes to elevate the respondents' experiences to a spiritual level. Moreover, the flamenco experience proved to be spiritually enriching and transformational. The relevance of the experience of challenge to scrutinise human subjective well-being is that through stressful events people often feel forced to rely on their inner strengths in order to overcome difficult situations (Ryff and Singer, 2003). In this respect, Park (2003) notes that the term *stress-related growth* is commonly used to describe the positive changes resulting from stressful life experiences. Given that the flamenco enthusiasts purposively engaged in flamenco courses to acquire some skills, it is reasonable to suggest that they did not necessarily expect to experience any personal transformation. These unintended transformations found expression through positive subjective states, such as feelings of well-being, meaningfulness and a more congruous sense of self. Figure 7.1 summarises the five dimensions comprising the spiritual experience of flamenco in Seville.

The themes uncovered in this study are consistent with the findings of previous empirical investigations, which addressed the spiritual dimension of tourism or leisure experiences. For example, in a study on various leisure experiences, Schmidt and Little (2007) found that natural environments and the notion of challenge engendered spiritual experiences. Similarly, Li et al. (2006) found that the interactions of young Christian tourists with each other and their contact with nature led to spiritual experiences. Moreover, in an exploratory investigation on Western tourists' experience of the Sri Aurobindo Ashram in India, Sharpley and Sundaram (2005) found that while for some people the Ashram and Auroville were experienced as spiritual places, others felt spiritually fulfilled through activities such as yoga and meditation. The common experiences reported in the three aforementioned studies were an increased sense of self,

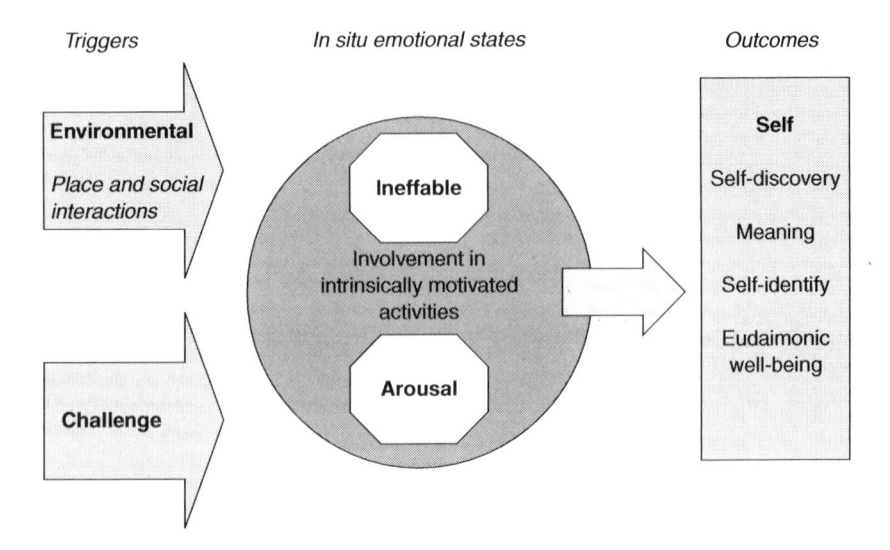

Figure 7.1 Dimensions of the spiritual experience of flamenco.

feelings of self-fulfilment and a sense of connection with God or something beyond the self. Contrary to Bruner's (1991) mass tourists to developing countries who are not radically challenged by the sites and performances they gaze upon, the creative flamenco tourists who are searching for learning opportunities eventually feel as having profoundly expanded their selves in some ways. With regard to the emotional realm, it has been shown that the respondents' deep involvement in the experiential dimensions of the flamenco activities closely resembles the experience of flow as well as the notions of 'experiential authenticity' (Daniel, 1996) and 'the tourist moment' (Hom Cary, 2004). A similar description found in tourism literature is the concept of 'existential authenticity' (Wang 1999) which relates to the authentic inner experience that people feel while engaging in certain activities.

The present research findings are also concordant with the findings of previous studies within the overlapping fields of positive psychology and the psychology of religion. From a psychology of religion standpoint, spiritual experiences are commonly construed as meaningful and/or transformational experiences through the sacred: the sacred encompassing both the strictly religious and the secular domains (Zinnbauer and Pargament, 2005). In line with this description, the study's respondents have proven to be following sacred routes either in connection to religious convictions or mostly in search of emotional well-being, meaning and personal growth through the consumption of flamenco; flamenco being perceived as a sacred cultural object. Pargament and Mahoney (2002) note that those who sanctify objects tend to make considerable efforts in order to preserve and experience those objects. These two psychologists also observe that, in their pursuit of the sacred, 'people are likely to derive more meaning, strength, and satisfaction from sacred dimensions of their lives' (p. 650). Thus, the journey becomes a pathway to positive changes in the tourists' lives. Similarly, Van Dierendonck and Mohan (2006) have described the close connection that exists between spirituality and eudaimonic well-being. In this study, the notion of eudaimonic well-being is particularly useful in describing the respondents' desires for self-exploration, self-betterment and their aspirations to conduct more meaningful lives.

Research within the field of positive psychology has also shown that individuals who pursue important goals are more likely to experience feelings of well-being (Diener *et al.*, 2002). Key proponents of positive psychology, Seligman and Csikszentmihalyi (2000) included spirituality as one individual trait pertinent to positive subjective experiences. In addition, Seligman and Peterson (2003) later developed a list of virtues and strengths in which spirituality was identified as one core element that contributes to shape human behaviour and provides comfort. It is obvious that not all respondents had experienced dramatic changes, yet even the smaller positive changes are illustrative of a positive transformation. The small but still significant changes that were reported by the respondents include, for example, an increased sense of self, maturity, a greater appreciation for the simple things in life, an increased self-confidence, a renewed optimism and greater courage to cope with new situations. New horizons opened up to them and in some cases new paths and new careers might arise as a result of those transformations. For Pargament and Mahoney (2002), a spiritual transformation means that people 'incorporate a sense of the sacred into themselves' (p. 654). No matter how profound these changes may be, they contribute to add meaning to one's life, to provide some degree of comfort and reassurance as well as drive people to pursue their dreams in which flamenco plays a central role.

Finally, the importance of flamenco as a tourist product through which people can feel good and develop character strengths was also highlighted. The latter point suggests the great potential that well-crafted place-specific cultural activities may have for both tourists and destinations alike.

Notes

1 '*le entra*' is said when a performer is experiencing a feeling of authenticity, or any heightened state of emotion such as a trance-like feeling usually referred to as *duende* within the flamenco community.
2 *Soleá* is a dramatic song or *palo* (flamenco music style) within the flamenco repertoire and consists of 12 beats.
3 *Picados* refer to flamenco scales on the guitar.

References

Aoyama, Y. (2007) 'The role of consumption and globalization in a cultural industry: the case of flamenco', *Geoforum*, 38: 103–113.
Aoyama, Y. (2009) 'Artists, tourists, and the state: cultural tourism and the Flamenco industry in Andalusia, Spain', *International Journal of Urban and Regional Research*, 33 (1): 80–104.

Bond, K.E. and Stinson, S.W. (2000) '"I feel like I'm going to take off!": young people's experiences of the superordinary in dance', *Dance Research Journal*, 32 (2) (Winter 2000/01).

Bruner, E.M. (1991) 'Transformation of self in tourism', *Annals of Tourism Research*, 18: 238–250.

Cantero, J. (2009) 'Economía y Flamenco', *La Nueva Alboreá, Revista de la Agencia Andaluza para el Desarrollo del Flamenco*, N. 11.

Cohen, E. (1979) 'A phenomenology of tourist experiences', *Journal of the British Sociological Association*, 13 (2): 179–201.

Csikszentmihalyi, M. (1975) *Beyond Boredom and Anxiety*. San Francisco: Jossey Bass.

Csikszentmihalyi, M. (1990) *Flow: The Psychology of Optimal Experience*. New-York: Harper and Row.

Daniel, Y.P. (1996) 'Tourism dance performances: authenticity and creativity', *Annals of Tourism Research*, 23 (4): 780–797.

Deleuze, G. and Guattari, F. (1980) *Mille Plateaux: Capitalisme et Schizophrénie, tome 2*. Editions de Minuit, Paris.

Diener, E., Lucas, R.E. and Oishi, S. (2002) 'Subjective well-being: the science of happiness and life satisfaction', in Snyder, C.R. and Lopez, S.J. (eds), *The Handbook of Positive Psychology*. Oxford: Oxford University Press, pp. 63–74.

Emmons, R. (2006) 'Spirituality: recent progress', in Csiksentmihalyi, M. and Csiksentmihalyi, I.S. (eds), *A Life Worth Living: Contributions to Positive Psychology*. New York: Oxford University Press, pp. 62–85.

Filep, S. (2008) 'Applying the dimensions of flow to explore visitor engagement and satisfaction', *Visitor Studies*, 11 (1): 90–108.

Florida, R. (2002) *The Rise of the Creative Class: And how it's Transforming Work, Leisure, Community, and Everyday Life*. New York: Basic Books.

Foucault, M. (1984) 'Des espaces autres', *Architecture, Mouvement, Continuité*, no. 5, Octobre 1984, pp. 46–49. http://foucault.info/documents/heteroTopia/foucault.heteroTopia.fr.html. [Accessed on 24 November 2010].

Graburn, N.H.H. (1989) 'Tourism: the sacred journey', in Smith, V.L. (ed.), *Hosts and Guests*. Philadelphia: University of Pennsylvania Press, pp. 21–36.

Harter, S. (2002) 'Authenticity', in Snyder, C.R. and Lopez, S.J. (eds), *The Handbook of Positive Psychology*. Oxford: Oxford University Press, pp. 382–394.

Hom Cary, S. (2004) 'The tourist moment', *Annals of Tourism Research*, 31 (1): 61–77.

Kelly, E.W. Jr. (1995) *Spirituality and Religion in Counseling and Psychotherapy*. Alexandria, VA: American Counseling Association.

Langer, E. (2002) 'Well-being: mindfulness versus positive evaluation', in Snyder, C.R. and Lopez, S.J. (eds), *The Handbook of Positive Psychology*. Oxford: Oxford University Press, pp. 214–230.

Li, B., Niininen, O. and Jacobs, K. (2006) 'Spiritual well-being through vacations: exploring the travel motives of the young Christian travelers', *Tourism*, 54 (3): 211–224.

MacCannell, D. (1976) *The Tourist: A New Theory of the Leisure Class*. New York: Schocken.

Neitz, M.J. and Spickard, J.V. (1990) 'Steps toward a sociology of religious experience: the theories of Mihaly Csikszentmihalyi and Alfred Schutz', *Sociological Analysis*, 51 (1): 15–33.

Pargament, K.I. (1999) 'The psychology of religion and spirituality? Yes and no', *International Journal for the Psychology of Religion*, 9: 3–16.

Pargament, K.I. and Mahoney, A. (2002) 'Spirituality: discovering and conserving the sacred', in Snyder, C.R. and Lopez, S.J. (eds), *The Handbook of Positive Psychology*. Oxford: Oxford University Press, pp. 646–662.

Park, C.L. (2003) 'The psychology of religion and positive psychology', *Psychology of Religion Newsletter*. American Psychological Association, Division 36, 28 (4).

Pearce, P.L., Filep, S. and Ross, G. (2011) *Tourists, Tourism and the Good Life*. New York: Routledge.

Perujo Serrano, F. (2008) 'El Flamenco: la visión del arte jondo de la Agencia Andaluza para el Desarrollo del Flamenco', *La Nueva Alboreá, Revista de la Agencia Andaluza para el Desarrollo del Flamenco*, no. 8.

Richards, G. (2011) 'Creativity and tourism: the state of the art', *Annals of Tourism Research*, 38 (4): 1225–1253.

Ryff, C.D. and Singer, B. (2003) 'Ironies of the human condition: well-being and health on the way to mortality', in Aspinwall, L.G. and Staudinger, U.M. (eds), *A Psychology of Human Strengths*. Washington, DC: American Psychological Association, pp. 271–287.

Saldanha, A. (2002) 'Music tourism and factions of bodies in Goa', *Tourist Studies*, 2 (1): 43–62.

Salsman, J.M., Brown, T.L., Brechting, E.H. and Carlson, C.R. (2005) 'The link between religion and spirituality and psychological adjustment: the mediating role of optimism and social support', *Personality and Social Psychology Bulletin*, 31 (4): 522–535.

Scherer, K.R. and Zentner, M.R. (2001) 'Emotional effects of music: production rules', in Juslin, P.N. and Sloboda, J.A. (eds), *Music and Emotion: Theory and Research*. Oxford; New York: Oxford University Press, pp. 361–392.

Schmidt, C. and Little, D.E. (2007) 'Qualitative insights into leisure as a spiritual experience', *Journal of Leisure Research*, 39 (2): 222–247.

Schütz, A. (1964) 'Making music together: a study in social relationship', in Brodersen, A. (ed.), *Collected Papers II: Studies in Social Theory*. The Hague: Martinus Nijhoff, pp. 159–178.

Seligman, M.E.P. and Csikszentmihalyi, M. (2000) 'Positive psychology: an introduction', *American Psychologist*, 55 (1): 5–14.

Seligman, M.E.P. and Peterson, C. (2003) 'Positive clinical psychology', in Aspinwall, L.G. and Staudinger, U.M. (eds), *A Psychology of Human Strengths*. Washington, DC: American Psychological Association, pp. 305–318.

Sharpley, R. and Sundaram, P. (2005) 'Tourism: a sacred journey? The case of Ashram tourism, India', *International Journal of Tourism Research*, 7: 161–171.

Shikaze, K. (2004) 'Fifteen thousand kilometres around the corner', Flamenco-world. com. www.flamenco-world.com/magazine/about/japon/japon15062004–1.htm. [Accessed on 4 December 2011].

Steingress, G. (2004) 'La hibridación transcultural como clave de la formación del Nuevo Flamenco (aspectos histórico-sociológicos, analíticos y comparativos)', *Revista Transcultural de Música/Transcultural Music Review*, no. 8.

Turner, V. (1969) *The Ritual Process: Structure and Anti-Structure*. New York: Aldine De Gruyter.

Turner, V. (1979) 'Frame, flow and reflection: ritual and drama as public liminality', *Japanese Journal of Religious Studies*, 6/4 December issue.

Van Dierendonck, D. and Mohan, K. (2006) 'Some thoughts on spirituality and eudaimonic well-being', *Mental Health, Religion & Culture* 9 (3): 227–238.

Wang, N. (1999) 'Rethinking authenticity in tourism experience', *Annals of Tourism Research*, 26 (2): 349–370.

Waterman, A.S., Schwartz, S.J. and Conti, R. (2008) 'The implications of two conceptions of happiness (hedonic enjoyment and eudaimonia) for the understanding of intrinsic motivation', *Journal of Happiness Studies* 9: 41–79.

Zinnbauer, B.J. and Pargament, K.I. (2005) 'Religiousness and spirituality', in Paloutzian, R.F. and Park, C.L. (eds), *Handbook of the Psychology of Religion and Spirituality*. New York: Guilford Press, pp. 21–42.

8 Personal transformation through long-distance walking

Robert Saunders, Jennifer Laing and Betty Weiler

Introduction

Walking is a popular leisure activity throughout much of the world, and is widely endorsed for its benefits to health. Contemporary bushwalking in Australia and New Zealand, while sharing the romantic origins of British, European and American leisure walking cultures (Edensor, 2000; Solnit, 2000), has evolved within the distinctive settings, history and symbolism of the region (Harper, 2007). In recent decades the development of hut-based and designated trails, the availability of lightweight camping equipment, and the growth of support services have encouraged participation in multi-day walking by novices and active older adults. Given the frequent association of long-distance walking with contemplation, self-development and achievement (Edensor, 2000; Pearce, 2011), a closer examination of the walking experience and its outcomes has the potential to offer insights into the under-researched transformative potential of travel, and associated benefits to well-being through positive personal change.

This chapter presents and discusses findings of a study exploring ways in which adults come to make positive changes in their lives following long-distance walks. Guided and self-guided walking experiences are included in the study, in settings recognised for their natural or cultural significance. The research presented here is part of a broader qualitative exploration of transformative experiences associated with long-distance walks within Australia and nearby regions. Participants, recruited through walking clubs, websites of popular tracks and snowball sampling, were self-selected after having 'personally significant' experiences on a walk of at least three days duration.

In-depth, semi-structured interviews (Wengraf, 2001) were carried out with 25 adults, including follow-up interviews with participants who reported significant change. Additional insights were obtained from personal journals and other written material provided by participants. A phenomenological approach is taken in the analysis, with themes and interpretations emerging from participants' articulation of their walking experiences, reflections and subsequent actions. The nature of any self-reported change is explored, along with insights participants provided about their change processes.

128 R. Saunders et al.

The chapter begins with an overview of key literature relevant to transformative travel and long-distance walking. It then presents five major outcomes or 'themes' emerging from interviews with walkers, regarding personal changes they associate with their long-distance walking experiences. Outcomes and transformative processes are then discussed in the context of positive psychology, and a model is proposed linking transformative processes with the five PERMA elements of well-being postulated by Seligman (2011). The relevance of character strengths (Peterson and Seligman, 2004) not included in the PERMA formulation is also noted, although a detailed analysis of this aspect is beyond the scope of the present chapter.

A synopsis of key literature on personal transformation and long-distance walking

The contemporary world generates many situations that can catalyse personal transformation. Changes in relationships, careers, health, finances, family situations and technological developments have an impact on the life course of many people. While not all role changes and turning points in life's journey are negative, the associated feelings of disorientation often are. Effectively negotiating change involves what Bridges (2004, p. 186) describes as *transition*: 'the psychological process of disengagement from the old, going through the nowhere between old and new, and then embracing and identifying with the new'.

The pace, complexity and uncertainty of present-day life can generate anxiety, depression and personal crisis. Kottler (1997) advises that appropriate styles of travel can be effective mediations in many situations routinely seen in counselling, by facilitating new perspectives and building resilience and other coping skills. Seligman (1993) also suggests that anxiety and mild depression may be more amenable to treatment by methods that address attitudes, ways of thinking and behaviours than by treatment with drugs, which often merely reduces the symptoms of these conditions.

A complementary, proactive perspective on personal transformation is that of growth through self-directed change. Widespread belief in the possibility of managing personal change over the life course is a relatively recent phenomenon, and 'represents one of the most fundamental and important revolutions in modern thought' (Seligman, 1993, p. 17). Self-development has become a major industry, targeting or exploiting almost every aspect of contemporary life, including tourism. Pine and Gilmore (1999), in advocating the integration of experiential elements into service industries as a way of adding economic value, suggest that transformation is the ultimate form of experience. Travel is an ideal vehicle for experiential services, and the last two decades have seen substantial growth in both product and participation, as well as some research in the emerging field of transformative tourism (Lean, 2009).

Of course, not all travel is expected to be transformative. Many people are content with themselves as they are, or 'aren't up to the task of confronting any major challenges such as those that might be a part of making significant life changes' (Kottler, 1997, p. 14). But personal change can also be subtle and unintentional. It can arise from a variety of processes including learning new skills; having novel experiences that trigger emotional drivers; temporarily altering one's social identity or entering a new social world; experiencing mindfulness and deep processing through immersion in a setting; or realising the reflective value of learning about others in one's own life (Pearce, 2011).

Nash (1996, p. 50) points to three characteristics which are likely to constrain the life-changing potential of travel, contending that 'too many tours are too short, too superficial and have qualities too much like home to result in enduring personal transformations'. In this study, long-distance walking has been selected as a vehicle for exploring transformative travel because it is an extended, often absorbing activity offering a range of levels of comfort through supported and self-reliant styles. Long-distance walking is also widely accessible, attracting many adult participants, and is currently undergoing growth in popularity and product creation (Curtis and Zanon, 2010).

There is a growing body of research on the impact of travel experiences on participants' knowledge, attitudes and values within specific tourist segments. Contemporary forms of tourism associated with growth, personal development and rites of passage, especially during the transition from youth to adulthood, include overseas study programmes (Nash, 1996); backpacking (Noy, 2004) the 'gap year' (Hall, 2007). Long-term travel as a ritual of life stage, personal growth and the discovery of new meaning in life has also b in the context of early mid-life (Ateljevic and Doorne, 2000) a (Rosh White and White, 2004), with such journeys offering no tunity to escape from everyday life but also a liminal space for rel. and O'Cass, 2001).

While many kinds of journey may be associated with a search for me. .ng, long-distance walking particularly calls to mind the traditions of pilgrimage. Digance (2006) argues that modern, secular pilgrimages embody historical archetypes including 'the quest', hardship, and the journey to a special, 'sacred' place. Although the notion of what is sacred has blurred in modern society (Digance, 2006, p. 37), aspects of long-distance walking can be seen as contemporary expressions of persistent cultural tropes, many of which imply the potential for personal transformation.

Lean's (2009) study of transformative travel finds that 'those who experienced the most significant transformation visited settings far removed from their home', and 'the factor most commonly identified by participants as affecting transformation was social contact' (p. 199–200). While Lean (2009) finds no particular correlation between transformation and motivation or trip length, his findings support the idea that 'reflection is a key to transformation' (p. 201). Lean (2009) concludes that an immense range of travel generated transformations are possible and that 'future research ... needs to be conducted on a smaller scale with a fixed scope, so as to reduce complexity' (p. 203).

A range of studies investigated long-distance walking and related adventure activities undertaken for the purposes of outdoor education. Many Australians are introduced to long-distance walking through school camps, scouting or commercial adventure activities. Programme objectives range from learning bushwalking skills; through experiential environmental education and adventure activity designed to promote personal responsibility and team work; to 'bush adventure therapy' for those considered socially or psychologically at risk (Pryor et al., 2005). The majority of Australian outdoor education programmes focus predominantly on youth and young adults. This parallels the wilderness experience programme industry in the United States (Friese et al., 1998), which 'despite serving a full spectrum of people, is primarily focused on youth, youth at risk or college/university students' (p. 42).

The authors regard developmental changes which occur during the teenage years and early twenties as formative rather than transformative, and for this reason have selected research subjects who are aged 30 years and over. Longitudinal studies in social psychology suggest that personality in most people is fully established by the age of 30, although it does not stop developing at that point but 'appears to grow increasingly consistent with age and reach a plateau later in life than previously thought (e.g. age 50)' (Caspi and Roberts, 2001, p. 51).

In one of the few published studies which consider the impacts of long-distance walking on adult participants, Mueser (1998) surveyed people completing the more than 3,500 kilometre-long Appalachian Trail in the United States. He found, amongst other things, that,

> before the hike, only one hiker out of 136 had been working in a job involving the environment; but after months of following the Appalachian Trail, some 18 individuals said they had changed or were going to change jobs to work in ecology and the environment.
>
> (Mueser, 1998, p. 15)

Major changes in core life domains such as career suggest that profound impacts on values and attitudes are possible.

The experiences of long-distance walkers seem rarely to have been investigated, with Mills and Butler's (2005) analysis of flow experiences among Appalachian Trail hikers, and den Breejen's (2007) study of walkers on the West Highland Way in Scotland important exceptions. Mills and Butler (2005, p. 366) report that more than 60 per cent of hikers sampled experienced flow, 'and for the majority of them it was a daily occurrence'. Den Breejen's (2007) use of an innovative in-situ diary captured the lived experience of 15 long-distance walkers who enjoyed meeting other hikers, appreciated the scenery and a sense of being close to nature, felt varying degrees of solitude and freedom, and found time to think and reflect during their 152 km trek. The end of their walk was experienced as a climax of enjoyment, suggesting scope for further research into the role of achievement and its contribution to positive affect (den Breejen, 2007).

A recent exploratory study of long-distance walking in the United Kingdom (Crust et al., 2011) utilised in-depth interviews with six long-distance walkers.

While their study did not specifically explore transformative experiences, the age range, walk length and track characteristics chosen by Crust *et al.* (2011) are consistent with criteria used in the current research. Crust *et al.* (2011, p. 258) report that 'the three main outcomes were bittersweet feelings [at the end of the walk], sense of well-being, and personal growth'. Conclusions from the Crust *et al.* (2011) study relate directly to the framework of positive psychology, and suggest that 'long-distance walking can elicit positive emotions, undo the effects of stress, promote an increased sense of well-being, and personal growth' (p. 261).

The current study seeks to extend the exploration of outcomes and benefits of long-distance walking by identifying positive changes people make in their lives following a long-distance walk, and elucidating associated processes of change. Findings are discussed within the context of positive psychology. In particular, this chapter explores the relevance of Seligman's (2011) five elements of well-being to the outcomes of long-distance walking: positive emotion, engagement, relationships, meaning and achievement (PERMA). The qualitative nature of the current study means that these elements were elicited from the content analysis of interviews and written journals.

Study context and major transformative themes emerging from interviews

A range of settings and styles of long-distance walking are included in this study. Walking tracks mentioned by more than one participant include Tasmania's Overland Track, the Larapinta Trail of Central Australia, Western Australia's Bibbulmun Track, the Kokoda Trail of Papua New Guinea and New Zealand's Milford Track. While most are nature-based treks, the Kokoda Trail is also an iconic Second World War battlefield site. Walks undertaken by interviewees range from three days to three months, and include guided and self-guided styles. Interview participants include males and females, novice long-distance walkers and those with hiking experience dating back to their youth.

The selective and qualitative nature of this study means that it is difficult to assess the frequency of personally significant experiences and transformative outcomes amongst long distance walkers. While several guides (who were also interviewed as part of the larger study on which this chapter is based) suggest that the majority of people walking the Kokoda Trail are significantly affected by their experiences, one Overland Track guide suggested that only about 30 of the 600 participants he has led have had transformative experiences:

> For some of them you know it's just ticking off something on a list of things they want to do. It doesn't mean any more than that. For others there is a deeper meaning and connection they make – you can see it in them.

Most interviewees had completed their long-distance walk within the three months prior to the interview. In cases where significant change was reported, a longitudinal perspective was obtained by follow-up interviews between six months and two years after the initial interview to test the enduring nature of the change. Analysis of interviews from the 25 long-distance walkers suggests that thematic saturation has been reached (Boeiji, 2002). While the wide range of raw themes and detailed stories is beyond the scope of this chapter, five major themes have emerged from the analysis that are positive expressions of personal transformation and are directly relevant to enhanced well-being:

1 Therapy and problem solving
2 Challenge and achievement
3 Relationships and belonging
4 Health and fitness
5 Meaning and connection

The remainder of this chapter draws on interview findings to illustrate these themes and consider antecedent and in-situ elements and processes that may contribute to personal transformation and enhanced well-being. All names used in reporting the findings are pseudonyms.

Therapy and problem solving

Transformative changes are perhaps most evident when they relate to the resolution of a chronic problem. Five of the 25 interviewees fit this category. Susan and Valerie had suffered clinical depression for some years before their long-distance walks. Keith had left his job and had become depressed, overweight and unmotivated at a stage in life when he had taken on the responsibility of a mortgage and become a father. Ollie had a fear of heights which was impacting on his enjoyment of hiking and other activities. Trish was suffering the effects of a traumatic separation from her partner, which also left her with sole responsibility for their school-age children. In all cases, long-distance walking provided relief and helped facilitate a resolution to these problems.

Susan explained the background to her eight week walk with her husband:

> I had been on anti-depressives for about seven years. I have had various jobs ... taking on difficult programs ... and feeling just unappreciated.... So yeah, I think I was pretty stressed, pretty run down, pretty depressed.

During the early stages of the walk, there was a process of disengagement from Susan's normal life, which provided respite from the stresses of her work:

> It took several days before I even wanted to write in the diary and then three weeks before I really felt like I was relaxed and into the way of life.

Susan gradually became engaged in all aspects of the walk: the physical challenges; social interactions with her husband and other people they met; and observation of the natural environment through which they walked. After a month she had a revelation:

> I can remember, yeah, not really thinking too much about the work situation but after four weeks just saying 'Yeah it's clear. I'm not going back'. So I didn't actually need to sort of wrestle with that at all, it just seemed to come to me in not thinking about it for several weeks. It just came to me that that was how it should be.

Susan loved her work, but it was affecting her health. Medication helped her through each day, but wasn't curing her depression. Walking gave her space and time to reflect, to put her problems into a new perspective and to see a solution: she could do similar work somewhere else. Putting her resolution into practice took effort and courage, but the achievement of completing the walk and conquering her fears about river crossings along the way was empowering. Reflection and resolution continued after the walk, when Susan worked as a volunteer before finding a new position. Two years later she is still not taking any medication.

For Trish the unexpected separation from her partner 'was awful' and generated a lasting sense of grief. Long-distance walking brought her closer to family members who supported her emotionally, and allowed her to develop in new ways. Her first long-distance walk at Wilsons Promontory was a pivotal moment:

> In a sense that was a turning point, that I did realise was something if we had stayed together I'd never have done.... You do grow in ways that you'd never have dreamed. And so while I'd still prefer to be married, to the same person actually, it was just, it was wonderfully liberating to be able to do these things.

Later, long-distance walking became a frequent source of stress-relief for Trish, and provided new perspectives from which to review her life and her work:

> It was just strange that I realised what I needed to change ... and how I could just generally improve everything for everyone, on a track on the way to Everest. Why can't I do that at home?

Challenge and achievement

The most common transformative theme emerging from interviews relates to the sense of achievement derived from completing a long-distance walk. This theme was reported by males and females; experienced and novice walkers; on guided and self-guided treks; and from those who walked for only three or four days and others who walked for up to three months. Interviewees also reported gaining confidence in relation to other aspects of their lives and setting new goals.

Follow-up interviews confirmed the behavioural expression of change. New goals set following walks varied from undertaking more frequent or longer walks, to specific targets like completing a marathon on each continent. In some cases interviewees reflected on their priorities in life and this led to other goals such as seeking to change jobs, spending more time with family or incorporating exercise into daily activities. A clear aspect of this theme is empowerment: interviewees felt that the walk gave them the courage, strength and determination to follow through on their goals.

Keith described how the personal significance of successfully climbing a remote mountain was immediately apparent, and experienced emotionally:

> It poured all night and half the next day and we just lay in our tents glowing warm from having got there ... I couldn't believe that after at least a dozen years of walking in Tasmania I had achieved what I thought was the ultimate: getting to the top of Federation Peak. So I was ecstatic ... even the initial adrenaline that comes from being exposed to danger wasn't the only reason I was ecstatic ... I had started to face down the fears that I had, and that if I was able to do that in terms of a physical intimidation like a hard mountain climb, then that was transferable to the rest of life, to the difficulties I faced in terms of employment and self-esteem.

For Keith the achievement of climbing Federation Peak prompted a progression of self-directed life changes including obtaining employment in his chosen field. This suggests self-efficacy and growth may be facilitated by increased self-confidence.

Self-efficacy and growth were also demonstrated by Roy, together with an element of disengagement from the past. After completing a three month walk 'to put some distance between our lives in the workforce and our future lives; a time to walk, a time to reflect and a time to rejuvenate', Roy observed that 'some of the cynicism built up during 30 years of work has been shed and we certainly have no fears for what life now holds'. Challenge, achievement and goal setting have become central to Roy's new life:

> The Great South Coast Walk taught us that, to feel fulfilled, you need to constantly provide yourself with a challenge, of which an adventure such as this is only one form. The dreaming, the planning, the doing, the remembering while the next dream evolves all contribute to an increasing sense of achievement and purpose.

For Barbara the empowerment derived from walking has led to new goals and achievements, and tackling things she previously had not envisaged:

> It just enabled me to see that I am capable of doing things. Since 2007 I've run five marathons.... And I bought a house too ... that is a big thing! Because it was about, particularly as a single woman buying a property ...

my mindset was I'd have to have somebody else to help me do it but in reality I did it all by myself.

The sense of achievement among interviewees also generates positive affect: people feel happy and satisfied, proud to have achieved something they value.

Relationships and belonging

The social benefits of walking can be transformative. In meeting other like-minded people, some participants find and enter a new social world, commonly undertaking further walks with the same group. Social benefits of this nature were more often mentioned by novice long-distance walkers. For Elaine, walking the Milford Track in New Zealand and staying in huts overnight was initially challenging:

> For me it was really quite life-changing because first of all ... in the first hut you sleep with 20 people. So that was very different for me, I'd never done anything like it, the roughing it. I've never roughed it like that.

Elaine found it hard to sleep the first night of her trek, but began to form a relationship with some younger American women who subsequently looked out for her, and helped to make her more comfortable at the next hut:

> One of the girls had got there before me and she'd kept a space for us ... which was nice because we'd got friends with all these youngsters and ... they wanted us with them.

There are clear suggestions of communitas (Turner, 1974) in Elaine's narrative, emphasised by the age and social differences between participants. Elaine found the experience enjoyable and rewarding, and has kept in touch with people she met on the walk:

> All those youngsters kept on saying we hope we're like you when we're your age ... so it was great, we made friends with all these kids. I occasionally get emails from people, and I like it ... [On return to Australia] I picked them up and we went and had dinner. And I'm sure that if they ever come here again they'll contact us, or if I will go to San Francisco, I'll contact them.

Another example of this theme is Dianne, who met her new life-partner during a long-distance walk. Within a year she had left her job, moved interstate to live, travelled extensively overseas and given up another long-term leisure activity which had previously been a central life interest. The development of such a close relationship could be seen as incidental to the walk, however several interviewees noted that sharing the difficulties and the emotional journey of an extended walk is a bonding experience, and some suggested that walking is a good way to see the real person behind the facade some may present to the world.

In Andrew's case, the relationship formed with an indigenous porter on the Kokoda Trail was an important element of his trip, and a reason to continue his involvement with the people living along the Trail:

> I met his wife and his kids. When we went through his village he took me to the school and showed me around his village and he had such pride in it ... you don't hear about the beautiful side of these people and that's what we saw with the villagers ... I think we've formed a relationship and ... I'm going to help him in whatever way I can.

Health and fitness

While the effort of pack-carrying, tired muscles and blisters were mentioned by many interviewees, there was a common view that these are small costs compared to the benefits in overall health and fitness that accrue from long-distance walking. Claire noticed an improvement in her strength after she returned from long-distance walking in New Zealand:

> I go to the gym on a regular basis, and I got back to the gym and I was doing weights that I would normally do, and they were easy. And I didn't, until then, realise how strong I'd become in New Zealand on that trip. So, yeah, for fitness, it was fantastic.

For Susan, weight loss and fitness gains also contributed to her resilience and self-esteem:

> I lost 10 kilograms during the hike ... I can wear the clothes that my daughters wear which is lovely ... I think it's probably made me feel stronger in character overall because I can do these physical things and I can follow things through ... and so you get the recognition of other people, that you're hard-core walkers, you can do these things.

Some interviewees mentioned the benefits of going to sleep many hours earlier than they would at home, and waking with the dawn. Sleeping soundly and reconnecting with natural cycles are seen by many as part of the slowing down and simplification of life that comes with long-distance walking. Susan spoke of:

> Really satisfying physical tiredness ... I could sleep for 12 hours, 11 or 12 hours, no worries at all ... because it was dark; it was the middle of winter. ... It was just lovely to feel like I could, I needed that sleep because I was physically tired.

For Ursula, physical and other aspects of health and well-being are intimately connected:

> The body becomes more resilient, strong, lean, grows in its capacity to cope with extremes of temperature and terrible rain and that kind of thing ... I think that there isn't a clear division between our physical body and our – the other dimensions of our being.... For myself I found that the physical resilience opened up or brought about a mental resilience as well ... like a focus and a clarity of thought.

Meaning and connection

A transformative theme associated with walking some tracks more than others is finding or creating meaning and connection with something bigger. There also seems to be a sense of growth associated with the discovery of new meaning, or the intensification of existing attitudes, values and beliefs. On nature-based treks, deep engagement with the setting can generate a sense of spiritual awareness, of connection with the infinite. Keith expresses this as follows:

> I feel just the tiniest speck of life in a vast universe and yet somehow the fact that I'm able to have feelings of transcendence and sublime feelings somehow enlarge you, make you feel that you expand into the vastness of that universe too. I believe in paradox – I like holding those kinds of tensions. Yes I'm insignificant and yet somehow I count, I matter, and not just to myself.

Interviewees who walked the Kokoda Trail reported deeply emotional experiences and an embodied sense of connection with the soldiers of the Second World War. They frequently found personal meaning in these experiences. Jeff's journal entry about Brigade Hill, the site of a major battle, illustrates how he came to empathise with the soldiers and their predicament:

> The battle site is certainly very significant and the stories amazing ... the Japanese killed many Australians here and it was sacred soil in my book. I thought about what it must have been like during the night here, dug into a foxhole not knowing if the Japanese were ten metres in front of you ... not knowing if you would be dead in a while.

Jeff was ill throughout his trek and at the end he collapsed on the side of the track physically and mentally drained. However, in hindsight he was deeply satisfied with how he had performed:

> I reflected that I actually showed quite strong leadership skills and ... I was a character amongst the group. There were a lot of people who were insular and they didn't want to help with anything whereas even while I was sick I

was still trying to be involved.... And then I guess one of the other reflections is I thought, maybe I could actually do this, I wouldn't mind being one of the guides.

Jeff's perspective suggests *eudaimonic* well-being, or doing those things that are conducive to growth, as opposed to *hedonic* well-being which consists of seeking pleasure for its own sake (Ryan and Deci, 2001). It seems that the eudaimonic well-being Jeff gained from his Kokoda trek was important to him and sparked a sense of purpose.

A reflexive insight into the relationship between meaning and emotional reaction was offered by Ursula:

I realised really clearly on this walk ... that my experience of hardship versus suffering was entirely dependent on the thoughts that were going through my head. Hardship ... like walking with a blister ... becomes suffering when there's a layer of interpretation ... such as 'you're doing something wrong' ... or 'we're not going to get there now' ... those kinds of meaning-makings absolutely change my experience of the hardship and make it horrible to be with.

Discussion in relation to transformation and positive psychology

To make sense of these themes by linking them to changes people make in their lives, it is useful to consider interviewees' descriptions covering the phases before, during and after their walks. Connections with enhanced well-being are then interpreted by considering outcomes in relation to the five elements of well-being postulated by Seligman (2011), as a basis for proposing a process model.

Before the walk: motivation, preparation and antecedent conditions

Stated motivations for undertaking a long-distance walk included both escapism and attraction to a particular trail. Challenge, a desire to get back in touch with nature, and mental relaxation were frequently mentioned, similar to the findings of den Breejen (2007) for the West Highland Way. Training and preparation was sometimes evident, particularly for the more arduous treks. Interestingly, personal change was rarely described in intentional terms. Some interviewees sought relief and respite from personal crisis through long-distance walking, but there was little evidence of any expectation that they would experience profound change.

In some cases, people are conscious of life-stage transitions, but as Kottler (1997, p.ix) emphasises, antecedent conditions may be unconscious aspects of travel motivations. In the words of one of the guides interviewed for this study:

Sometimes people are searching for something, you know they are. Other times people don't even know they are looking for something, but they are open to things when they happen. They've got to be ready for it. You can transform someone who isn't ready for it.

Interviews suggest that there are many reasons why people may be open to personal change. It could be curiosity and open-mindedness, or a vague sense of something missing or out of balance in their life. The absence of a close relationship seems to have been a factor in the case of Dianne, who met her future partner on a long-distance walk. A more general social and nurturing need may have been important for Ivan, who became a scout leader after enjoying long-distance walking in national parks. Needs relating to growth and development are suggested by some of Jeff's comments quoted earlier, regarding leadership.

For others, there may be deeper, hidden or unrecognised needs and drives. Susan's depression did not appear to be a conscious reason for undertaking her walk, nor did she expect that walking would resolve her issues. However, prior to the walk she discussed with her doctor the possibility of reducing her medication during the walk. She also prepared a page for diary notes each day, as if she tacitly understood the value of reflection. Despite these actions, Susan's pre-walk perspective towards her depression can only be described as hopeful, and she was genuinely surprised at her realisation during the walk that changing jobs could restore her mental health.

Specific long-distance walks seem to have been chosen based on previous knowledge and expectations. As Mueser (1998) observed in relation to Appalachian Trail hikers, many had thought about doing an extended walk for some time. Especially in the case of the longer trails, timing was often opportunistic, based around access to a period of extended leave from work or the organisation of a group activity by a friend or colleague.

During the walk: processes of engagement and reflection

People who feel that they have had a personally significant experience on a long-distance walk have engaged deeply with the *task* of walking, with other *people* or with the *setting* of the walk, and often with all three. Disengagement from the participant's normal life (Bridges, 2004) also seems to be important and may be facilitated by engagement with something new and different. It seems to be through distancing oneself from normal life that the opportunity to reflect from a different perspective is accessed, allowing issues to be reviewed and major decisions made.

Task engagement is usually experienced by trek participants as the challenge of the walk. Long-distance walking often requires persistence through inclement weather, route finding, demanding track conditions and fatigue. At times, risks such as walking alone in remote and unknown countries, obstacles such as river crossings and exposed rock-climbs tested the courage of interviewees. Successfully completing the walk or achieving a key goal of the trip usually generated a strong sense of achievement.

There are glimpses here of an underlying process involving the development or expression of personal traits such as courage and persistence, which are part of the strengths and virtues framework of positive psychology (Peterson and Seligman, 2004). Specific traits appear to contribute to a number of themes. For example, the development of courage and persistence seems to facilitate therapy and problem solving (theme 1), challenge and achievement (theme 2), and health and fitness (theme 4).

Engagement with other people including guides, and in the case of the Kokoda Trail, with indigenous porters, developed relationships through social interactions, shared experiences and emotions. Sometimes a sense of communitas (Turner, 1974) emerged. Relationships that develop on a walk can lead to a participant entering a new social world of shared interests and values, extending those relationships and developing a sense of belonging.

Flow-like states (Csikszentmihalyi, 1975; Mills and Butler, 2005) seem mostly to be experienced when people are alone in challenging, scenic or meaningful settings within a walk. However, some group situations suggested co-active social flow and in-depth conversations may have generated interactive social flow (Walker, 2010). In all of these states people lose their self-consciousness and this may contribute to the liminality of the experience.

Engagement with the setting of a walk can lead to the emergence of meaning. In the case of the Kokoda Trail, cognitive, affective and behavioural aspects of meaning became evident as the physical challenge of the walk led to a sense of re-enactment amongst trekkers (Saunders, 2013). Deep engagement with the battlefield setting of the Kokoda Trail sometimes led to numinous experiences: a deeply felt connection 'to the people and spirit of an earlier time' (Cameron and Gatewood, 2003: 55).

The richness of the walking experience seems to depend on the level of engagement with the task, people and setting of the walk. Interestingly, many of the strong emotions felt during the walk were not what one would associate with pleasure: they include fears about safety and the walker's capacity to meet challenges; negative reactions to other trail users such as dirt-bike riders and hunters; and deep sadness associated with stories of horrific battles on the Kokoda Track.

Although interviewees generally enjoyed their walking experiences, strong positive emotion was most often associated with the end of the walk, as observed by den Breejen (2007). Trish found this energising, and a source of renewed enthusiasm for her work: 'I often come back to work bouncing, grateful for the [clients] that are coming in, because that's where a lot of life happens for me'. The strong sense of elation on completing a long-distance walk was sometimes tinged with loss, reminiscent of the 'bittersweet feelings' identified by Crust *et al.* (2011). The strength of the positive emotion also faded over a week or two. Ursula wrote on her return after seven weeks of solo walking:

> When the track was fresh in me ... I could feel light in my eyes. I don't know how else to describe it. All of the elements of such a journey, the outdoors-ness of it, the walking, the watching and breathing of it ... they work a magic ... I feel that that radiance is quietly lessening, going underground?

Disappearing? Being veiled? I think that's what I find a bit sad, and not super-sad ... just wistful, maybe. Because I want to keep that. And I can't.

After the walk: behavioural expression of enduring change

Returning to the five themes of personal transformation presented earlier in this chapter, the most widespread outcome evident among interviewees was the feeling of confidence that results from achievement (theme 2). This was typically expressed after the walk by setting new goals and working towards achieving them. An example of this is Barbara who, after walking the Kokoda Trail, decided to run a marathon on every continent. She has completed marathons on five continents to date.

Interviewees tended to refer to this outcome in terms of a feeling of confidence, which supports the findings of Crust *et al.* (2011); however its consistent expression through subsequent actions suggest it could also be interpreted in terms of empowerment and self-efficacy. Ryan and Deci (2001, p. 156) note that self-efficacy 'is associated with enhanced well-being'. Outcomes for some people may also include increased optimism as they find the personal resources to deal with life's ups and downs: 'optimism, the conviction that you *can* change, is a necessary first step in the process of all change' (Seligman, 1993, p. 253).

Enhanced health and fitness (theme 4) is usually related to the walk itself, although some interviewees have subsequently integrated regular walking into their normal lives in order to maintain their improved fitness. Regular doses of long-distance walking were seen by several interviewees as important in helping them cope with life's stresses, and even the knowledge that one can always go for a walk when times are tough was seen by some as valuable for stress management. The combination of confidence and persistence that comes from long-distance walking also seems to enhance resilience.

In all cases where interviewees described behavioural expressions of change following their walk, strong emotional engagement with some aspect of the walking experience was mentioned, along with reflection during or after the walk. In the case of the Kokoda Trail experience, the strongest emotions were expressed in relation to meaning and connection (theme 5). Most Kokoda trekkers reported reading books about the wartime history of the trail on their return. After his walk Andrew also sought out veterans of the Kokoda campaign living in nursing homes, and now visits them regularly. He also joined one of the Kokoda Battalion Associations and attends their dinners and Anzac Day services.

Emotional impact seems to be important in generating the motivation necessary to integrate change into the lives of interviewees after a walk. Challenge and achievement (theme 2) had the most widespread emotional impact on interviewees. In some cases, relationships and a sense of belonging (theme 3) through meeting people with shared interests also generated strong emotions. Together with the sense of meaning and connection (theme 5), these outcomes often seem to generate a new sense of purpose. Powerful positive emotions are associated

142 R. Saunders et al.

with the end of a walk and appear to be a generalised outcome of the holistic experience rather than being tied to any one aspect.

Figure 8.1 draws on concepts from positive psychology and the findings from interviews to suggest how a long-distance walking experience may enhance well-being through personal transformation. A combination of antecedent conditions and motivations prior to a long-distance walk facilitates engagement in three key aspects of the experience: the walking task; social interactions with people during the walk and the walk setting. *Engagement*, one of Seligman's five elements of well-being, thus becomes a central process in transformation. Three other elements of well-being: *achievement, relationships* and *meaning* are outcomes that arise from the engagement with task, people and settings. Seligman's fifth element of well-being, *positive emotion*, is a product of all these aspects. All five of Seligman's (2011) elements of well-being are potentially enriched by the transformative experience.

Implicit in the model are also the three components of Bridges' (2004) change process: disengagement from normal life occurs in the early stages of the walk, followed by an extended period of liminality in which participants are open to new perspectives. Integration of changed perspectives and behaviours into normal life occurs after the walk, with goal setting, growth and self-efficacy being important aspects. For this reason, therapy and problem solving (theme 1)

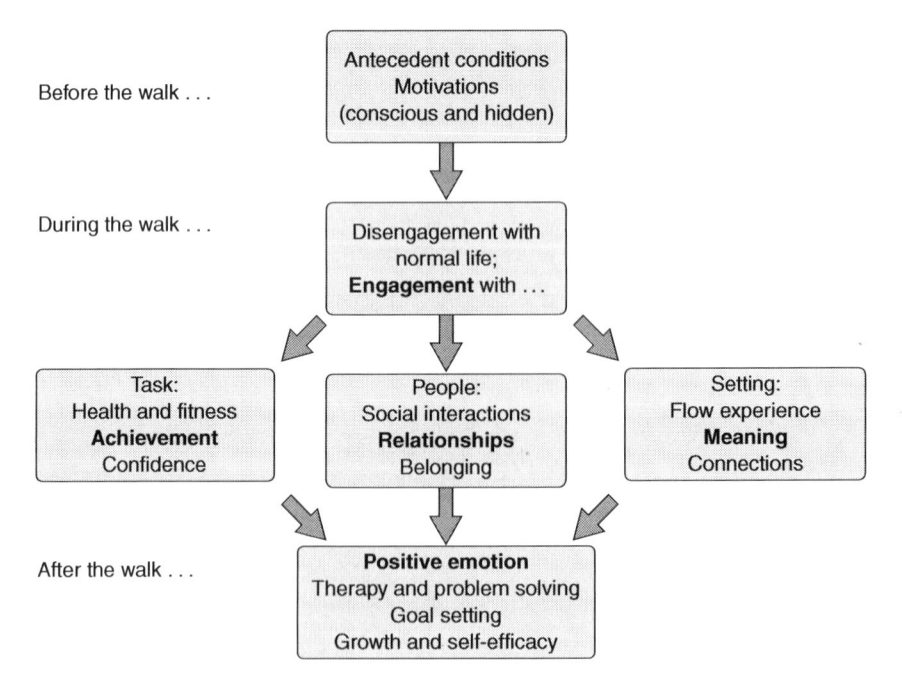

Figure 8.1 Transformative effects of long-distance walking.

Note
Bold text highlights Seligman's (2011) five elements of well-being.

is shown in the model as a holistic outcome at the end of the walk. Although critical insights may occur during reflective moments of the walk, in each case from interviews, important additional actions occurred after the walk.

In linking achievement, relationships and meaning directly with the walking task, other people, and the walk setting, the model simplifies complex interactions. Walking in itself can generate longer-term meaning, especially through guiding and sharing experiences with other people. Since completing their walks, Jeff has become a tour guide and has led several treks along the Kokoda Trail, Ivan has become a Scout leader and Roy has found a new central life interest by developing a website to share information about his long-distance walks.

Conclusion

This chapter has explored the outcomes and benefits of long-distance walking; outlined positive changes interviewees made in their lives following such an experience and elucidated associated processes of change. Interviews suggest that long-distance walking can facilitate processes of relief and disengagement from common stresses and problems in life and can help people find ways to resolve their issues. Moreover, long-distance walking can foster enduring positive self-directed change in participants' lives by building confidence and a sense of purpose. Process elements highlighted in interviews include opportunities for reflection and reappraisal, which may be important in adjusting to life crises and major life transitions.

The framework of positive psychology helps further elucidate the process of transformation and its positive effects on well-being. In particular, all five elements of well-being in Seligman's (2011) PERMA scheme are evident in the transformation process, as presented in Figure 8.1. Engagement with the task and challenge of long-distance walking generate a sense of achievement, which frequently leads to increased confidence and goal setting. Relationships formed and developed through long-distance walking can be strong and enduring, with shared experiences and associated emotions deepening bonds. Meaning emerges particularly from engagement with setting, changed perspectives and time spent in reflection while walking; but can also be facilitated through interaction with other people such as guides. Positive emotion is a product of all these aspects. Perhaps most powerfully, the achievement of completing a challenging and meaningful walk can boost self-efficacy and generate growth.

This study supports the findings of Crust *et al.* (2011) that long-distance walking in itself can contribute to well-being. Findings also support Kottler's (1997) contention that appropriate travel can act as a substitute or supplement to counselling and other interventions, and suggests that long-distance walking may have potential to help older adults in ways which build on established programmes directed at youth and young adults. The potential contribution of long-distance walking to the development of character strengths (Peterson and Seligman, 2004) not included in the PERMA formulation is an area in need of further research, as is research examining how certain character traits may contribute to a range of outcomes and benefits to participants.

A limitation of the current study is its exploratory nature. Elements of well-being have been elicited from the content analysis of interviews and written journals rather than being identified through validated, quantitative measures. The extent to which well-being is enhanced, whether this is an enduring effect, and the frequency of personally significant experiences and transformative outcomes have not been measured. Quantitative research may be able to elucidate these aspects and the importance of transformation in ongoing personal well-being. The field of guiding and guide training may benefit from further research into the role of emotion and flow-like states including social flow (Walker 2010), and ways in which these experiences can be facilitated. The transformative benefits of long-distance walking suggest that research may also be worthwhile into the relationship between achievement, confidence and the broader constructs of self-efficacy and learned optimism.

Transformative travel is under-researched, despite recent growth in the types of experiences available around the world and the numbers taking up these activities. This chapter contributes to knowledge about transformative travel by exploring long-distance walking in an Australian context and examining change processes which benefit adult well-being. A model is developed which draws on themes elicited from a qualitative study of long-distance walkers, together with the elements of well-being identified by Seligman (2011). This chapter illustrates how these experiences can become life-changing for participants, by setting new goals and directions which become central to some aspect of their lives. Walking, far from being a passive leisure experience, appears to have had profound effects on the participants in this study. Future research will explore these experiences in greater detail, including the antecedents and longevity of transformative outcomes.

References

Ateljevic, I. and Doorne, S. (2000) 'Tourism as an escape: long term travelers in New Zealand', *Tourism Analysis*, 5: 131–136.

Boeiji, H. (2002) 'A purposeful approach to the Constant Comparative Method in the analysis of qualitative interviews', *Quality and Quantity*, 36 (4): 391–409.

Bridges, W. (2004) *Transitions: Making Sense of Life's Changes* (2nd edition). Cambridge, MA: Da Capo Press.

Cameron, C.M. and Gatewood, J.B. (2003) 'Seeking numinous experiences in the unremembered past', *Ethnology*, 42 (1): 55–71.

Caspi, A. and Roberts, B.W. (2001) 'Personality development across the life course: the argument for change and continuity', *Psychological Inquiry*, 12 (2): 49–66.

Crust, L., Keegan, R., Piggott, D. and Swann, C. (2011) 'Walking the walk: a phenomenological study of long distance walking', *Journal of Applied Sport Psychology*, 23 (3): 243–262.

Csikszentmihalyi, M. (1975) *Beyond Boredom and Anxiety: The Experience of Play in Work and Games*. San Francisco: Jossey-Bass.

Curtis, J. and Zanon, D. (2010) 'The influence of population and recreation trends on the future use of parks managed by Parks Victoria', Melbourne: Parks Victoria.

den Breejen, L. (2007) 'The experiences of long distance walking: a case study of the West Highland Way in Scotland', *Tourism Management*, 28: 1417–1427.

Digance, J. (2006) 'Religious and secular pilgrimage: journeys redolent with meaning', in Dallen, J.T. and Olsen, D.H. (eds), *Tourism, Religion and Spiritual Journeys*. New York: Routledge, pp. 36–48.

Edensor, T. (2000) 'Walking in the British countryside: reflexivity, embodied practices and ways to escape', *Body and Society*, 6 (3–4): 81–106.

Friese, G., Hendee, J.C. and Kinziger, M. (1998) 'The wilderness experience program industry in the United States: characteristics and dynamics', *The Journal of Experiential Education*, 21 (1): 40–45.

Hall, C.M. (2007) *Introduction to Tourism in Australia: Development, Issues and Change* (5th edition). Frenchs Forest, NSW: Pearson.

Harper, M. (2007) *The Ways of the Bushwalker: On Foot in Australia*. Sydney: University of NSW.

Kottler, J. (1997) *Travel that can Change your Life: How to Create a Transformative Experience*. San Fransisco: Jossey-Bass.

Lean, G.L. (2009) 'Transformative travel: inspiring sustainability', in Bushell, R. and Sheldon, P.J. (eds), *Wellness Tourism: Mind, Body, Spirit, Place*. New York: Cognizant Publisher, pp. 191–205.

Mills, A.S. and Butler, T.S. (2005) 'Flow experience among Appalachian Trail thru-hikers', Proceedings of the 2005 Northeastern Recreation Research Symposium GTR-NE-341.

Mueser, R. (1998) *Long-Distance Hiking: Lessons from the Appalachian Trail*. Camden, Maine: Ragged Mountain Press.

Muller, T. and O'Cass, A. (2001) 'Targeting the young at heart, seeing senior vacationers the way they see themselves', *Journal of Vacation Marketing*, 7: 285–301.

Nash, D. (1996) *Anthropology of Tourism*. Oxford: Pergamon.

Noy, C. (2004) 'This trip really changed me: backpackers narratives of self-change', *Annals of Tourism Research*, 31 (1): 78–102.

Pearce, P.L. (2011) *Tourist Behaviour and the Contemporary World*. Bristol: Channel View Publications.

Peterson, C. and Seligman, M.E.P. (2004) *Character Strengths and Virtues: A Handbook and Classification*. Oxford: Oxford University Press.

Pine, J.B. and Gilmore, J.H. (1999) *The Experience Economy: Work is Theatre and Every Business a Stage*. Boston: Harvard Business School Press.

Pryor, A., Carpenter, C. and Townsend, M. (2005) 'Outdoor education and bush adventure therapy: a socio-ecological approach to health and wellbeing', *Australian Journal of Outdoor Education*, 9 (1) 3–13.

Rosh White, N. and White, P.B. (2004) 'Travel as transition: identity and place', *Annals of Tourism Research*, 31 (1): 200–218.

Ryan, R.M. and Deci, E.L. (2001) 'On happiness and human potentials: a review of research on hedonic and eudaimonic well-being', *Annual Review of Psychology*, 52: 141–166.

Saunders, R.E. (2013) 'Identity, meaning and tourism on the Kokoda Trail', in Norman, A. (ed.), *Journey and Destinations: Studies in Travel, Identity and Meaning*. Newcastle-Upon-Tyne: Cambridge Scholars Press (in press).

Seligman, M.E.P. (1993) *What You Can Change ... and What You Can't: The Complete Guide to Successful Self-Improvement*. Columbine, New York: Fawcett.

Seligman, M.E.P. (2011) *Flourish: A Visionary New Understanding of Happiness and Well-Being*. New York: Free Press.

Solnit, R. (2000) *Wanderlust: A History of Walking*. USA: Viking Penguin.

Turner, V. (1974) *Dramas, Fields and Metaphors: Symbolic Action in Human Society*. Ithica, New York: Cornell University Press.

Walker, C.J. (2010) 'Experiencing flow: is doing it together better than doing it alone?' *The Journal of Positive Psychology*, 5 (1): 3–11.

Wengraf, T. (2001) *Qualitative Research Interviewing: Biographic Narrative and Semi-Structured Methods*. London: Sage Publications.

9 The development of self through volunteer tourism

Zoë Alexander and Ali Bakir

Introduction

The aim of this chapter is to consider an experience which is highly likely to change its participants, and in beneficial ways. In so doing, this study identifies the psychological impacts of volunteer tourism on tourists, for example volunteer tourists are highly likely to return from their trip to busier, more active and adventurous lives. This chapter describes the volunteer tourism experience and any resulting changes in people's everyday lives.

Volunteer tourism, also known as 'Voluntourism', is the 'engagement in volunteer work as a tourist' (Alexander and Bakir, 2011). In Alexander and Bakir's (2011) grounded theory study of volunteer tourism, 'engagement' emerged as the core category which subsumed the other two categories of 'volunteer work' and 'tourist' and, combined, differentiated volunteer tourism from other forms of tourism and its allied notions, such as, cultural tourism. Alexander and Bakir's notion of 'engagement' describes volunteers being meaningfully engaged in activities through interaction with others and doing worthwhile tasks. They use the components of 'Relate–Dedicate–Donate' to summarise the experience. Volunteer tourists 'relate' and collaborate by interacting and integrating with other volunteers and the communities themselves. They 'dedicate' themselves by participating in purposeful work and applying their knowledge and skills to existing worthwhile projects. Last, volunteer tourists 'donate' to an outside customer, the community where the project is located; thus making the project authentic (Alexander and Bakir, 2011, p. 16). Although 'engagement' conceptualises the volunteer tourism experience, through the underlying concepts of Relate–Dedicate–Donate (Alexander and Bakir, 2011) and through the conceptualisation, or commonalities, of the 'experiences' of volunteers, such as 'interaction', 'involvement' and 'participation' (see Alexander, 2012), it is nevertheless not peculiar to volunteer tourism. The concept of 'engagement' has emerged informally in many disciplines, such as in technology-based teaching and learning environments to optimise student learning (Kearsley and Shneiderman, 1998); in wildlife tourism, to encourage visitors to adopt long-term environmentally sustainable practices (Ballantyne *et al.*, 2011); and in psychology, to enhance well-being (see Csikszentmihalyi, 1997).

Alexander's (2012) study attempts to broaden our understanding of engagement in volunteer tourism whilst investigating the resulting impacts on participants. The participants in this study were engaged in community and wildlife projects offered by the Aviva organisation in South Africa; an accredited volunteer tourism provider based in Cape Town. She investigated the likelihood of change in volunteers' personality traits thus building on the existing knowledge of impacts, such as, increased awareness of other people and environments; personal development; and skills to deal with challenging situations (Bailey and Russell, 2010; Broad, 2003; Harlow and Pomfret, 2007; Laythorpe, 2009; Lepp, 2008; McGehee and Santos, 2005; Sin, 2009; Wearing, 2001; Wickens, 2011). This new knowledge attempts to address the call for developing more evidence to establish the effectiveness of volunteer programmes, particularly government programmes because there is a lack of rigorous, publicly available and easily accessible research, especially on youth projects outside of North America and Europe (Mattero, 2008). In South Africa, Benson and Seibert (2009), and Stoddart and Rogerson (2004) note that the literature associated with volunteer tourism's outcomes is limited; most provide rich subjective data of impacts with very few studies providing statistical evidence.

A noticeable weakness of these earlier volunteer tourism impact studies is that they do not elaborate on the experiential factors that facilitate change in the volunteer. Generally, these studies limit their explanations to authentic interaction with hosts and other volunteers, working towards common goals, doing meaningful work and establishing networks and friendships (Bailey and Russell, 2010; Harlow and Pomfret, 2007; Laythorpe, 2009; Lepp, 2008; McGehee and Santos, 2005; McIntosh and Zahra, 2007; Sin, 2009; Wearing, 2001; Wickens, 2011). So there was an opportunity for Alexander (2012) to investigate these experiential factors as well as the beneficial impacts for participants. What follows is a description of the study methods used and the results of that study. Also, some other important concepts will be discussed in this chapter, including: flow (Csikszentmihalyi, 1990); self-confidence (Maslow, 1993; Carver and Scheier, 2005); social integration (Chambre, 1987; Stevens-Ratchford, 2005; Wilson and Musick, 2000); interactional temperament model (Ryckman, 2008); and others. These concepts will be used to explain significant changes in the traits of this sample of volunteer tourists.

Study methods

Research design

Alexander's (2012) study adopts a multiple paradigm, mixed methods approach. Burrell and Morgan (1979) argue that inter-paradigmatic shifts are difficult and rare; in contrast, Lincoln and Guba (2000, p. 164) state that 'various paradigms are beginning to "interbreed"', where 'previously thought ... irreconcilable conflict may now appear ... to be informing' each other. Feyerabend (1975, p. 175) also argues for a multi-paradigmatic approach as 'no one methodology can provide all the answers'. Faulkner and Russell (1997) see that the adoption of paradigms according to their usefulness in specific situations as a pragmatic and potentially productive approach.

In support of mixed methods, Creswell *et al.* (2003) argue that it is possible to move from one paradigm to another if the stages are clear and transparent in the research process, but this movement does present challenges in terms of how to use and link the various aspects of different paradigms in one research investigation (Zahra and Ryan, 2005). Similarly, Denzin and Lincoln (1994) urge the researcher to be a bricoleur – to enter into a dialogue with multi-approaches, theories, practices and methods (see also Jamal and Hollinshead, 2001). This bricoleur approach can be advantageous because of its ability to deal with dynamic situations and provide a broader understanding of the substantive area being studied (see, for example, Briedenhann and Wickens, 2002; Dantas *et al.*, 2010). Nevertheless, Potter and Wetherall (1987) point out that each paradigm captures different kinds of information making it difficult, on the basis of their combination, to reach a coherent result, and this criticism is exacerbated in interdisciplinary research (see Olsen, 2004; Silverman, 1993), especially where different epistemologies are brought together (Meetoo and Temple, 2003; Patton, 1990).

In Alexander's (2012) study, mixed methods were used to address different aspects of the research question; each method adds to the next. This study's approach follows Kelle's (2001) suggestion of using each method for a specific purpose, drawing from each one's strengths, with attention paid individually to validity and reliability. This allows the results to stand alone, or link sequentially to provide a more complete picture of reality. The mixed methods approach included a personality inventory (a quantitative method) to identify the impacts of volunteer tourism on the tourists, and structured web-based personal interviews analysed using the interpretive phenomenological analysis (IPA) method for gaining insight into these impacts.

The sample

Two samples were used for both methods: the volunteer tourists and the control group; each of these is discussed in turn below.

The study used a volunteer sample (Albery *et al.*, 2004), consisting of 60 participants, who put themselves forward. The sample was made up of 10 men (17 per cent) and 50 women (83 per cent). It appears that volunteer tourism is biased towards women. This notion is supported by the characteristics of the population of Aviva volunteers who are predominantly female (86 per cent) (Alexander, 2012), as well as other volunteer tourism research (refer to Bailey and Russell, 2010; Harlow and Pomfret, 2007; Lepp, 2008; McIntosh and Zahra, 2007; Wearing, 2001). One explanation of this bias is the biological and sociological differences between men and women reflected in the women's higher pre-trip scores for the altruism and dutifulness traits.

The volunteer sample consisted of 44 (73 per cent) 16–29 year olds and 16 (27 per cent) 30+ years. The participants were from many countries, including

Britain, United States, Europe, Australia, New Zealand and Canada. They had booked their trip through the Aviva organisation. South Africa was chosen, as a destination to research, because it rates as one of the top ten countries where travellers want to volunteer (Gecko, Bradt Travel Guides and Lasso Communications, 2009; Lasso Communications, 2009). South Africa also rates 'mid-way' in terms of its impacts on tourists (Alexander *et al.*, 2010). Email interviews with these volunteers revealed that they spent an average of £4,163 (US$6,737) on their trip including air fares, stayed an average of ten weeks in South Africa and participated in volunteering 59 per cent of their holiday time. The weekends were generally spent relaxing and doing tourism activities such as shark-diving, clubbing, sightseeing and shopping.

A matched control group was used to eliminate alternative explanations of the results, and at the same time improve the validity of the study method (Clegg, 1990; Johnson and Besselsen, 2002). The control group did not undertake volunteer tourism. The use of a non-volunteer comparison group is novel in volunteer tourism research. Thirty-five people (25 aged 16–29 and ten aged 30+; seven men and 28 women) were selected as a control group through opportunity sampling, where people were willing to take part in the research when asked rather than volunteering to participate (Albery *et al.*, 2004). The selection of the control group involved some snowballing which could have potentially introduced bias in the sample, particularly, if people were friends, having certain things in common. The control group was made up of a mixture of European and South African residents. They were matched to the volunteer tourists on age, gender and socio-economic variables, such as, occupation and education. Questions about the adequacy of the control group were addressed by statistical tests carried out at the start to determine how well the control group matched the volunteers on the 15 traits. The Mann–Whitney U-tests revealed no significant differences in 14 of the 15 traits measured; however, there was a significant difference in 'vulnerability'; this outcome is discussed later in the chapter.

Following Clegg's (1990) emphasis on the importance of sample size, an a priori power analysis was carried out to determine the minimum and maximum number of subjects required to make the study worthwhile. A sample of between 35 and 57 people was found to be required for conducting Wilcoxon matched-pairs signed ranks tests on the pre- and post-test scores of each group (effect size = 0.5, error probability = 0.05, power = 0.80–0.95). Although there are no formal standards for power, most researchers assess the power of their tests using 0.80 as a minimum standard for adequacy (Cunningham and McCrum-Gardner, 2007).

Quantitative analysis method: personality inventory

The web-based personality inventories were completed by volunteer tourists and control group members over a three year period, between August 2008 and August 2011. The data analysis involved using the Wilcoxon matched-pairs signed ranks test and Mann–Whitney U-test, depending on whether the samples were matched or not (Clegg, 1990; Sekaran, 2003). Fifteen traits were measured using a standardised questionnaire (the IPIP-NEO personality inventory): anxiety, depression, vulnerability, assertiveness, action, artistic interests, emotionality, adventurousness, intellect, liberalism, trust, altruism, self-efficacy, dutifulness and cautiousness; defined on the IPIP-NEO website www.personalitytest.net/ipip/ipipneo120.htm. The standardised personality inventory also addressed the problem, noted by Lough *et al.* (2009a), that some volunteers have difficulty articulating the specific impacts of the experience when interviewed as the participants need only choose a statement that best applies to them.

Qualitative analysis method: web-based structured interviews

In the web-based structured interview that followed the trip, participants were asked to describe the experiences which they thought may have led to the change/s and what, if anything, they are doing differently now as a result. Analysis of interview data used the IPA method and followed Smith and Osborn's (2004) recommendations. The following section summarises the results of these analyses.

Results/findings

Table 9.1 summarises the likelihood of change amongst volunteers.

Table 9.1 Summary: the percentage of time we would expect to obtain these results

Trait	All volunteers	Control
Sample size	60	35
Anxiety (%)	99.99	11.77
Trust (%)	99.03	34.33
Self-efficacy (%)	90.49	80.13
Artistic interests (%)	96.93	77.41
Depression (%)	99.84	17.07
Assertiveness (%)	99.25	97.45
Emotionality (%)	96.17	94.23
Altruism (%)	92.73	47.97
Dutifulness (%)	78.83	51.00
Activity level (%)	99.80	39.29
Adventurousness (%)	99.31	55.10
Intellect (%)	72.53	69.14
Vulnerability (%)	99.79	23.61
Liberalism (%)	20.86	70.23
Cautiousness (%)	5.55	57.98

Note
The areas highlighted are the areas where there is a significant probability of change.

The areas highlighted in the first column demonstrate significant differences in pre-trip versus post-trip scores in nine of the fifteen traits measured. The findings were significantly different from the control group who were measured over a similar period of time (second column).

Although post-trip volunteers showed significant changes in nine personality traits out of fifteen, the use of a control group, measured over a similar period of time, eliminated the assertiveness trait from the results because of the possible influence of day-to-day events on this trait. The vulnerability trait was also eliminated from the results because of the differences between the volunteers and control group at the start. The remaining seven traits were highly likely to be impacted by the volunteer tourism experience alone; these were: anxiety, trust, artistic interests, depression, emotionality, activity levels and adventurousness.

Subsequently the causes and consequences of the significant trait changes were analysed using the IPA technique. The experience categories (reported 'causes') that emerged from the 36 interviews with volunteers were: 'action', 'involvement', 'responsibility', 'participation', 'immersion', 'interaction' and 'expectations/satisfaction levels'. Here are examples of some of these categories, derived from the volunteers' responses and shown in [bracket]: 'I would fill the babies' bottles in the morning and chop the vegetables for the day' [action]; 'being thrown into a situation where you live and work with people you've never met before' [involvement]; 'travelling on your own to a new country' [responsibility]; 'seeing the good people can do if they take time out for others' [participation]; 'not feeling like tourists' [immersion]; and 'people were astonishingly kind' [expectations/satisfaction].

The impacts categories (reported 'consequences') that arose from the responses were changes in participants': 'behaviour', 'personal circumstances', 'emotions', 'confidence', 'values', 'knowledge or skills' and 'attitudes'. Some examples from interviewees' responses show these categories, again in [bracket], 'I have a lot more get up and go and don't get bored at all. I fill my time a lot better. Rather than watching TV all night, I watch a programme I find interesting and then read a book' [behaviour]; 'The work at Baphumelele made me a lot more resilient and stronger physically' [personal circumstance]; 'Volunteering opened my eyes about other people's way of life' [emotion]; 'I am not quite as nervous now in new situations' [confidence]; 'I realised that no matter how bad things are, you have to make the most of life and live life to the full' [value]; 'I learned a lot especially respect of other cultures and understanding other's feelings and their individuality' [knowledge and skills]; and 'It made me realise "others" are as capable as me' [attitude].

A synthesis of the statistical results described earlier and the interviews with the volunteers is presented in Figure 9.1 (summary). The figure shows how experiential engagement in volunteer tourism results in specific changes in participants' everyday lives; this is further elaborated in the following section.

```
       ┌─────────────┐
       │ Experiental │
       │ engagement  │
       └─────────────┘
              │
              ▼
       ┌─────────────┐
       │Trait changes│
       └─────────────┘
              │
              ▼
       ┌─────────────┐
       │ Changes in  │
       │participants'│
       │ day-to-day  │
       │    lives    │
       └─────────────┘
```

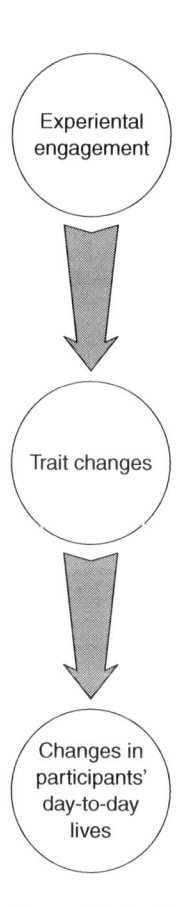

Figure 9.1 A diagrammatic representation of Engagement Theory in volunteer tourism.

Discussion

This section discusses the likelihood of change in the participating volunteer tourists, highlights the study's similarities to other studies and offers explanations for findings which differ from these studies. It also attempts to embed the findings within the notion of experiential engagement, incorporating the concepts of 'flow', and others, in an attempt to explain transformation in the volunteers, and points to the study's limitations.

Alexander (2012) identified beneficial changes in some traits that were not previously identified in the volunteer tourism literature: changes in 'anxiety', 'depression' and 'activity'. Volunteers generally return from their trip calmer and less anxious; less likely to feel sad, dejected and discouraged, and more likely to initiate activities; and more likely to lead busier lives. All three traits contribute to improved well-being as noted in positive psychology research (Baumeister and Vohs, 2005; Williamson, 2005).

Other changes concur with previous studies (e.g. Bailey and Russell, 2010; Laythorpe, 2009): increases in emotionality, trust, artistic interest and adventurousness. Volunteers return from their trip with better access to their own feelings; they assume people are fair, honest and have good intentions; they have more interest in art and nature; and are eager to try new activities, to travel and experience different things.

Some of the study's findings also differ from the findings of previous studies. Unlike Wearing (2001) and Lough *et al.* (2009b, p. 10), this study showed no significant increases in altruism (the concern for other people generally and their feelings, and taking time for others). Also, data from this study's 36 interviews showed that just two volunteers increasing their participation in volunteering or becoming more active citizens in their community after they returned home. One volunteer stated: 'I am grateful for what I have and now have a sense of duty to help whilst I can'; another noted: 'I volunteer regularly at a local school listening to and helping 8 year olds read'. The broader study further found that the probability of changes in altruism increases to 95.56 per cent for volunteers in the younger age group of between 16 and 29, and to 97.27 per cent for those volunteers staying in South Africa for between 5 and 12 weeks. In the above mentioned studies, the volunteers were all below the age of 29 which might have accounted for these different findings.

Alexander (2012) also showed that although self-efficacy (confidence in one's ability to accomplish things, and the belief in one's intelligence, drive and self) levels increased afterwards, it was not statistically significant (probability of 90.49 per cent). This finding differs from both McGehee and Santos (2005), and McIntosh and Zahra (2007) as they have reported increases in self-efficacy in their studies. Although the short-stays of volunteers of around two weeks in McIntosh and Zahra's (2007) research might account for this contrasting finding, this does not explain increased self-efficacy amongst McGehee and Santos's (2005) volunteers as only six of their sixteen volunteers stayed less than a month. McGehee (2012) questioned the use of self-efficacy as a measure of the likelihood to participate in a volunteer tourism experience. In this study, the volunteer group and control group showed no significant differences in this trait on their pre-scores, suggesting that self-efficacy is not a suitable measure.

Moreover, the participants of Alexander's study were unlikely to return from their trip with more liberal attitudes. These findings differ from the findings of some qualitative studies which reported more liberal behaviours and attitudes, for example, Wearing's (2001, p. 129) study highlighted participants gaining new perspectives and 'being more thoughtful and more open' in his conservation and community projects, and Broad's (2003) and Harlow and Pomfret's (2007) studies noted changes in the way the volunteers viewed their lives and the world, and the ability to get on with other people in their wildlife projects.

Last, with regard to the dutifulness trait (the strength of a person's sense of duty and obligation), Zahra and McIntosh (2007) reported an increased 'sense of justice, rights and duties, and the responsibilities one has towards society' (p. 118); whereas, in Alexander's study, this trait was one of the least likely to be impacted by the volunteer tourism experience.

The significant changes in Alexander's volunteer tourists' traits that have occurred as a result of their volunteer tourism experience will now be explained using the literature cited in the introduction and her empirical findings.

Anxiety: the concept of flow

The decreased level of anxiety resulting from the volunteer tourism experience, as this study shows, suggests that the volunteer's anxiety threshold level has increased. This experience offers an opportunity to develop one's skills through action programmes (challenges) which create 'flow' rather than 'anxiety' (Csikszentmihalyi, 1990; Nakamura and Csikszentmihalyi, 2005). Flow is experienced when perceived challenges and skills are above the participant's average levels (Csikszentmihalyi, 1997). However, as challenges increasingly exceed capacities/skills, anxiety is experienced (Nakamura and Csikszentmihalyi, 2005). According to Nakamura and Csikszentmihalyi, in flow, one is engaged in just-manageable challenges/actions; one is completely absorbed in what one is doing. So, an explanation for decreased anxiety amongst this study's volunteer tourists is that the experience provides an opportunity to develop one's skills so that action opportunities (challenges) create 'flow' rather than 'anxiety'. This is demonstrated by volunteer 10:

> I did find the shifts really tough going. It was a physical job. We would fill the babies' bottles in the morning and chop the veg for the day but the hard work was compensated by being with the children and getting to know them. We were always on the go throughout our shift.

In support of this explanation, Broad (2003) and Harlow and Pomfret (2007) found many of their volunteers developed skills to deal with challenging situations; and one of Sin's (2009) volunteers expressed the need to be challenged as an important part of her experience, where 'feeling scared, exhausted and thoroughly tested is sometimes part of the deal' (p. 493). These kinds of challenges have also been found to enhance well-being (Morrow-Howell *et al.*, 2003). The decreased anxiety post-trip found from this study also suggests that these skills might have been transferred to the volunteers' everyday lives at home. One volunteer (no. 13) articulates this impact well: 'I learned a lot especially respect of other cultures and understanding others' feelings and their individuality'.

Trust: increased self-confidence and giving up of control

The trust trait showed a significant increase amongst this study's volunteers. According to Maslow (1993), trust in oneself and in the world involves self-confidence, courage and lack of fear of the world. Increased confidence post-trip and its impact on their day-to-day lives were evident in many participating volunteers. They attributed their increased confidence to 'action', 'interaction', 'involvement' and taking 'responsibility': 'I am not quite as nervous now in new situations' (volunteer 21); 'I feel a sense of achievement and will do more travelling as a woman solo traveller' (volunteer 3); and 'I was constantly with people I didn't know and therefore had to trust them and go with the flow, I got used to trusting people and hoping for the best' (volunteer 31). Maslow (1993) further adds: 'trust involves the temporary giving up of straining and striving, of volition and control, of conscious coping and effort' (p. 65). This consciously 'giving up of control' and trusting others, is experienced by some of this study's volunteers: 'I was thrown into a situation where I lived and worked with people I've never met before' (volunteer 17). Not only is trust a beneficial impact of volunteer tourism, but also optimism. People who are more trusting of others tend to be more optimistic, expecting good things to happen to them (Carver and Scheier, 2005). In this respect, a volunteer tourism experience may help people to become more optimistic. Recent research on 'optimism' (see Carver and Scheier, 2005) suggests that pessimism can be changed despite it being deeply embedded in a person's life either through inheritance or early childhood experience. However, there remain questions about how large a change can be reasonably expected and how permanent the change will be. There also remain questions about whether an induced optimistic view on life will act in the same way – have the same beneficial effects – as does naturally occurring optimistic view. So, volunteer tourism may provide the context for studying this phenomenon further and perhaps address these questions.

Alexander (2012) highlighted the importance of one particular element of 'engagement', the notion of 'taking responsibility' for oneself and for others, as in volunteering. This element can be found in the work of Frankl (2004); Csikszentmihalyi (1997); Maslow (1993) and others as it facilitates personal growth. Mustonen (2006) and Brown (2005) use Maslow's (1970) classic hierarchy of needs to explain people's search for self-actualisation and personal growth through volunteer tourism. Maslow (1993) writes about the impulse we all have towards growth, or towards the actualisation of human potentialities, and how 'the fear of responsibility thwarts this process' (p. 38). He elaborates using the Jonah complex theory, 'So often we run away from the responsibilities dictated (or rather suggested) by nature, by fate, even sometimes by accident, just as Jonah tried – in vain – to run away from *his* fate' (p. 34). Maslow notes that to self-actualise (the need to become more and more what one is, to become everything that one is capable of becoming) is 'to take responsibility', for 'each time one takes responsibility, this is an actualising of the self' (p. 45). Similarly, Csikszentmihalyi (1997) acknowledges the importance of taking responsibility: 'An active responsibility for the rest of humankind, and for the world of which we are a part, is a necessary ingredient of a good life' (p. 132). He suggests that a simple way of improving the quality of life is to take ownership of one's actions. Frankl (2004) endorsed a very similar perspective. In this respect, it is an important factor contributing to personal growth. Wearing's (2001) volunteers recognised 'the importance of their responsibilities in their own personal development and learning' (p. 127). Similarly, Ballantyne *et al.* (2011) acknowledge the importance of responsibility in changing visitor behaviour towards the environment; they said that more attention needs to be given to individual actions (responsibilities). In this respect, Maddux (2005) suggests it (personal responsibility) also offers a replacement for the illness ideology by helping people become more self-directed and self-organised. With regard to this component, and noting the impact that volunteer tourism has on youngsters below the age of 30, volunteer tourism may be thought of as a way of potentially reducing rates of re-offending and other self outcomes (see Moore and Allen, 1996; Paine *et al.*, 2007). Further research is required in this area, particularly with regard to government policy initiatives relating to youth programmes (Mattero, 2008).

Artistic interests: engagement

The artistic interest trait showed a significant increase amongst this study's volunteers. They were more likely to become involved and absorbed in artistic and natural events following a volunteer tourism experience. For example, volunteer 16 commented on how she appreciates art more 'after her eyes were opened in South Africa'. There appears to be very little written about this trait, specifically, although it is a facet of 'openness to experience'; open people tend to be appreciative of art and sensitive to beauty (refer to IPIP-NEO website at www.personalitytest.net/ipip/ipipneo120.htm; Costa and McCrae, 1985, 1992; McCrae and Costa, 2003). Openness is often presented as healthier or mature by psychologists; however, open and closed styles of thinking are useful in different environments, for example, closed thinking is related to superior job performance in police work. Openness has also been identified in positive psychology studies as an antecedent to well-being (Bailey and Russell, 2010). Although the literature does not appear to offer a theoretical explanation for why this trait changed (Bailey and Russell, 2010), interviews with the volunteers in this study suggest the change was due to 'engagement' in volunteer tourism through 'action', 'immersion', 'interaction' and 'participation'. Volunteer 2 describes her 'action': 'I visited art museums to learn about the history of South Africa'; and volunteer 28 described her 'immersion' and 'interaction': 'we didn't feel like tourists and that was a great feeling', 'we got to know people from all over the world and we had so much fun'.

Depression: social integration

The depression trait showed a significant decrease amongst this study's volunteers. It must be noted that depression in this study is more to do with mood, as measured by the IPIP-NEO personality inventory, rather than malfunction. This personality inventory measures the tendency to feel sad, dejected and discouraged. High scorers lack energy and have difficulty initiating activities. A recurring explanation for why depression decreased amongst this study's volunteers and others, is to do with social integration; the extent to which an individual is connected to other people (Chambre, 1987; Csikszentmihalyi, 1997; Stevens-Ratchford, 2005; Wearing, 2001; Wilson and Musick, 2000). These studies concur that activities such as volunteering provide a broad and diverse network of interactions; whereas people report much lower moods when alone, they feel less happy, less cheerful, less strong, more bored and more passive (Albery *et al.*, 2004; Csikszentmihalyi, 1997). Interactions, such as those found in volunteering, are challenging as they require interpersonal skills; also people concentrate their attention on external demands, rather than worries (Csikszentmihalyi, 1997). Having good relationships with others is universally endorsed as being central to optimal living (Ryff and Singer, 2005). In this respect, volunteer tourism may offer an approach to promote well-being. Also, having a good life requires a certain level of activity (Albery *et al.*, 2004; Boniwell, 2006); many of the volunteers in this study reported increases in their activity trait. So, this may also explain why depression decreased amongst this study's volunteers. An increase in activity correlates with a decrease in depression as a result of the social interaction and physical exertion of activity (Albery *et al.*, 2004).

Emotionality: interactional temperament model

High emotionality means that one has good access to and an awareness of one's feelings. This trait showed a significant increase amongst this study's volunteers. When we understand more about ourselves, know our own triggers and develop our emotional intelligence, we are more able to manage situations (Cottrell, 2003). The 'interactional temperament model' offers some insight into why this trait could have changed. Ryckman (2008) explains: the environment and temperament traits (emotionality being one of these) mutually influence each other. This is demonstrated by volunteer 13: 'living in a different country, with different people and different language.... I learned a lot especially respect of other cultures and understanding others' feelings and their individuality'; demonstrating how the environment influenced this volunteer. The interactional temperament model is akin to Wearing's (2001) concept of interactionism, in so far as the 'self' (the temperament traits in the case of the interactional temperament model) is impacted by the space and people that form the destination site.

Activity level: fitness and other self-benefits

The activity level trait showed a significant increase amongst this study's volunteers. Volunteers were more likely to return from their trip energetic and more likely to lead busier lives. Many volunteers improved their fitness as a result of the physical nature of their volunteering and tourism activities. Volunteer 10 'found the shifts really tough going. It was a physical job ... we were always on the go throughout the shift'; volunteer 30 spoke of the contribution the work made to her losing three stone (19 kilograms) in weight; and volunteer 15 spoke of how much there was to do and see and how she 'didn't want to miss out'. Schulman (2005) points out that in order to act one must inquire about his or her motive. Volunteer 34 explains how her action of: 'trying to keep physically active at home' was motivated by her desire to improve her physical health. This trait is important to well-being because having a good life requires a certain level of activity (Boniwell, 2006).

Adventurousness: opportunity to try new things and increased self-confidence

The adventurousness trait showed a significant increase amongst this study's volunteers. Adventurousness is about trying *new* activities, travel and experiencing new things (Costa and McCrae, 1992). Volunteer 'involvement' and 'participation' in activities such as shark-diving, sky-diving, mountain climbing, hiking, caving, handling snakes, eating traditional foods and white-water rafting, seemed to have inspired some of the participating volunteers 'not to hold back if there is something you want to do' (volunteer 32); 'to try new experiences' (volunteer 21); and 'to do more travelling' (volunteer 3). Some of this increased adventurousness seemed to be attributed to increased confidence as a result of trying new experiences (see Bailey and Russell, 2010; Broad, 2003; Harlow and Pomfret, 2007; Lepp, 2008; Wearing, 2001; Wickens, 2011): 'I am not quite as nervous now to try new experiences' (volunteer 21) and 'I feel a sense of achievement and will do more travelling as a woman solo traveller' (volunteer 3).

The impacts, as noted above, that have occurred as a result of participants' volunteer tourism experiences, expand on Alexander and Bakir's (2011) notion of Engagement Theory – 'Relate–Dedicate–Donate' – to explain the volunteer tourism experience. Alexander (2012) takes Engagement Theory one step further to explain transformation in volunteers' daily lives. The engagement in volunteer tourism, as a tourist, emerges as a process that starts with experiential engagement through volunteers' 'action', 'involvement', 'responsibility', 'participation', 'immersion', 'interaction' and 'expectations/satisfaction levels' and ends with specific changes in participants' day-to-day lives, categorised as changes in people's 'personal circumstances', 'behaviour', 'emotions', 'confidence', 'values', 'knowledge or skills' and 'attitudes'. This knowledge provides a greater understanding of engagement as it identifies the elements that will most likely transform volunteers in the mentioned ways.

In practice, an understanding of these experiential elements could assist programme developers in creating projects that not only address community needs but also improve the chances of volunteer satisfaction and other desired outcomes. Birdwell (2011) suggests that the best and most effective programmes focus on ensuring both of these aspects.

Also the use of a control group, in this study, enhanced the validity of the personality inventory results because none of the control group members showed any significant changes in these traits. This study thus adds to the statistical evidence of the impact of volunteer tourism on the participants, as other studies (e.g. Bailey and Russell, 2010, measuring similar traits under the umbrella of 'openness to experience') did not use a control group; and as such might have allowed variables other than the volunteer tourism experience to influence changes in their volunteers.

Limitations

This study, like many of its kind, cannot claim generalisability of the results because non-random sampling techniques were used. Nevertheless, the study's usability is enhanced by the similarities between the sample and the participants of other volunteer tourism studies demonstrated in the broader study. Also personality inventories only capture specific types of data, in this case personality traits, ignoring other areas subject to change, such as a person's skills, abilities, capabilities, interests, values, needs and others. Whilst every effort was made to address this limitation by additionally using structured personal interviews to identify other changes in the volunteers, the study may have missed opportunities to receive unexpected but potentially useful information from a less structured inquiry.

Although this study identified seven categories of experience responsible for transforming volunteers, it does not examine these to any great depth; it only provides examples of these experiences from the interviews with the volunteers. Similarly, for the seven categories of impacts identified in this study, a more in-depth understanding of these may be useful to stakeholders; such as knowing the *types* of skills and knowledge gained from volunteer tourism and the *types* of behaviour outcomes expected including re-assimilation into their home communities (see Machin, 2008).

Conclusion

Notwithstanding the limitations of this study, its findings as identified above, nevertheless, make some significant contributions to knowledge and add to the volunteer tourism literature. The study identifies the traits that are most likely to change as a result of a volunteering trip and points to changes in some traits that were not previously identified by the literature. Additionally, whilst identifying some similarities to other studies, the findings of this study also point to some significant contrasts.

Also, the mixed methods design approach of this study proved useful as it allowed us to gain a broader understanding of the impact of volunteer tourism on the volunteer, and build on Alexander and Bakir's (2011) notion of Engagement Theory in volunteer tourism.

With regard to positive psychology, the evidence presented in this study shows that volunteer tourism represents a proactive catalyst for altering our perspectives and subsequently our actions. Furthermore, this study answers the call from positive psychologists to use a diversity of methods. It used both qualitative and quantitative methods to develop a broader understanding of the volunteer tourism experience and its positive effects. In respect of these positive effects, such as decreased anxiety and depression, and increased trust, emotionality and activity, volunteer tourism offers a context in which to study these traits further. Csikszentmihalyi (1997) argued that 'the best moments usually occur when a person's body or mind is stretched to its limits in a voluntary effort to accomplish something difficult and worthwhile' (p. 3). Volunteer tourism potentially offers such moments. Such experiences contribute to a person's well-being and positive affect, as can be seen from the results of this study.

References

Albery, I., Chandler, C., Field, A., Jones, D., Messer, D., Moore, S. and Sterling, C. (2004) *Complete Psychology*. Dubai: Hodder Arnold.
Alexander, Z. (2012) 'International volunteer tourism experience in South Africa: an investigation into the impact on the tourist', *Journal of Hospitality Marketing & Management*, In Press.
Alexander, Z. and Bakir, A. (2011) 'Understanding voluntourism: a Glaserian grounded theory study', in Benson, A. (ed.), *Volunteer Tourism: Theoretical Frameworks to Practical Applications*. Oxford: Routledge, pp. 9–29.
Alexander, Z., Bakir, A. and Wickens, E. (2010) 'An investigation into the impact of vacation travel on the tourist', *International Journal of Tourism Research*, 12 (5): 574–590.
Bailey, A. and Russell, K. (2010) 'Predictors of interpersonal growth in volunteer tourism: a latent curve approach', *Leisure Sciences*, 32 (4): 352–368.
Ballantyne, R., Packer, J. and Sutherland, L. (2011) 'Visitor's memories of wildlife tourism: implications for the design of powerful interpretive experiences', *Tourism Management*, 32 (4): 770–779.
Baumeister, R. and Vohs, K. (2005) 'The pursuit of meaningfulness in life', in Snyder, C. and Lopez, J. (eds), *Handbook of Positive Psychology*. New York: Oxford University Press, pp. 608–618.
Benson, A. and Seibert, N. (2009) 'Volunteer tourism: motivations of German participants in South Africa', special issue on volunteer tourism, *Annals of Leisure Research*, 12 (3 and 4): 295–314.
Birdwell, J. (2011) *This is the Big Society without Borders*. Service International, Demos, United Kingdom.
Boniwell, I. (2006) *Positive Psychology in a Nutshell*. Hertford: Stephen Austin.
Briedenhann, J. and Wickens, E. (2002) 'Combining qualitative and quantitative research methods in evaluation related rural tourism development research', paper presented at the *Conference on Combining Qualitative and Quantitative Methods in Development Research*, 1–2 July 2002, Swansea, UK: Swansea University.
Broad, S. (2003) 'Living the Thai life: a case study of volunteer tourism at the Gibbon Rehabilitation Project, Thailand', *Tourism Recreational Research*, 28 (3): 63–72.
Brown, S. (2005) 'Travelling with a purpose: understanding the motives and benefits of volunteer vacationers', *Current Issues in Tourism*, 8 (6): 479–496.
Burrell, G. and Morgan, G. (1979) *Sociological Paradigms and Organisational Analysis*. London: Heinemann.

Carver, C. and Scheier, M. (2005) 'Optimism', in Snyder, C. and Lopez, S. (eds), *Handbook of Positive Psychology*. New York: Oxford University Press, pp. 231–243.

Chambre, S. (1987) *Good Deeds in Old Age: Volunteering by the New Leisure Class*. Lexington: Lexington Books.

Clegg, F. (1990) *Simple Statistics*. Cambridge: Cambridge University Press.

Costa, P. and McCrae, R. (1985) *The NEO Personality Inventory. Manual form S and form R, Professional Manual*. Odessa, Florida: Psychological Assessment Resources.

Costa, P. and McCrae, R. (1992) *Revised NEO Personality Inventory (NEO-PI-R) and NEO Five-Factor Inventory (NEO-FFI): Professional Manual*. Odessa, Florida: Psychological Assessment Resources.

Cottrell, S. (2003) *Skills For Success: The Personal Development Planning Handbook*. Basingstoke: Palgrave Macmillan.

Creswell, J., Plano Clark, V., Gutmann, M. and Hanson, W. (2003) 'Advanced mixed methods research designs', in Tashakkori, A. and Teddlie, C. (eds), *Handbook of Mixed Methods in Social and Behavioural Research*. California: Sage Publications.

Csikszentmihalyi, M. (1990) *Flow: The Psychology of Optimal Experience*. New York: Harper Collins.

Csikszentmihalyi, M. (1997) *Finding Flow: The Psychology of Engagement with Everyday Life*. New York: Perseus Book Group.

Cunningham, J. and McCrum-Gardner, E. (2007) 'Power, effect and sample size using GPower: practical issues for researchers and members of research ethics committees', *Evidence Based Midwifery*, 5 (4): 132–136.

Dantas, A., Ferreira, L., Oliveira, M. and Aires, J. (2010) *International Tourism and Human Development: The Perspective of the Local Population in the City of Natal, Brazil*. International Conference on Sustainable Tourism: Issues, Debates and Challenges, Crete.

Denzin, N. and Lincoln, Y. (1994) *Handbook of Qualitative Research*. Thousand Oaks, CA: Sage.

Faulkner, B. and Russell, R. (1997) 'Chaos and complexity in tourism: in search of a new perspective', *Pacific Tourism Review*, 1: 93–102.

Feyerabend, P. (1975) *Against Method*. London: New Left Review.

Frankl, V. (2004) *Man's Search for Meaning*. New York: Pocket Books.

Gecko, Bradt Travel Guides and Lasso Communications (2009) *Volunteer Travel Insights Report: 2009*, USA.

Harlow, S. and Pomfret, G. (2007) 'Evolving environmental tourism experiences in Zambia', *Journal of Ecotourism*, 6 (3): 184–209.

Jamal, T. and Hollinshead, K. (2001) 'Tourism and the forbidden zone: the underserved power of quality inquiry', *Tourism Management*, 22: 62–68.

Johnson, P. and Besselsen, D. (2002) 'Practical aspects of experimental design in animal research', *ILAR Journal*, 43 (4): 202–206.

Kearsley, G. and Shneiderman, B. (1998) 'Engagement theory: a framework for technology-based teaching and learning', *Educational Technology*, 38 (5): 20–23.

Kelle, U. (2001) 'Sociological explanations between micro and macro and the integration of qualitative and quantitative methods', *Forum Qualitative Social Research*, www.qualitative-research.net/index.php/fqs/article/view/966. [Accesssed 29 December 2011].

Lasso Communications (2009) *State of the Volunteer Travel Industry Survey: May 2009*, USA: Lasso Communications.

Laythorpe, K. (2009) *Sustainable Living in a Third World Country: Experiences of Long*

Term Volunteers in the Kilimanjaro Region of Tanzania, Best Education Network Think Tank – on the importance of values in Sustainable Tourism: First Symposium on volunteering and tourism, Singapore.

Lepp, A. (2008) 'Discovering self and discovering others through the Taita Discovery Centre Volunteer Tourism Programme, Kenya', in Lyons, K. and Wearing, S. (eds), *Journeys of Discovery in Volunteer Tourism: International Case Study Perspectives*. London: CABI Publishers, pp. 86–100.

Lincoln, Y. and Guba, E. (2000) 'Paradigmatic controversies, contradictions, and emerging influences', in Denzin, N. and Lincoln, Y. (eds), *Handbook of Qualitative Research* (2nd edition). California: Sage, pp. 163–213.

Lough, B., Moore McBride, A. and Sherraden, M. (2009a) *Perceived Effects of International Volunteering: Reports from Alumni*. CSD Research Report 09–10, Centre for Social Development, Washington University, St. Louis.

Lough, B., Moore McBride, A. and Sherraden, M. (2009b) *Measuring Volunteer Outcomes: Development of the International Volunteer Impacts Survey*. CSD Working Paper No. 09–31, Centre for Social Development, Washington University, St. Louis.

McCrae, R. and Costa, P. (2003) *Personality in Adulthood: A Five-Factor Theory Perspective* (2nd edition). New York: Guildford.

McGehee, N. (2012) 'Oppression, emancipation, and volunteer tourism: research propositions', *Annals of Tourism Research*, 39 (1):84–107.

McGehee, N. and Santos, C. (2005) 'Social change, discourse and volunteer tourism', *Annals of Tourism Research*, 32 (3): 760–779.

Machin, J. (2008) *The Impact of Returned International Volunteers: A Scoping Review*. United Kingdom: Institute for Volunteering Research.

McIntosh, A. and Zahra, A. (2007) 'A cultural encounter through volunteer tourism: reaching the ideals of sustainability?' *Journal of Sustainable Tourism*, 15 (5): 541–556.

Maddux, J. (2005) 'Self-efficacy: the power of believing you can', in Snyder, C. and Lopez, J. (eds), *Handbook of Positive Psychology*. New York: Oxford University Press, pp. 277–287.

Maslow, A. (1970) *Motivation and Personality* (2nd edition). New York: Viking Press.

Maslow, A. (1993) *The Farthest Reaches of Human Nature*. New York: Viking.

Mattero, M. (2008) 'Measuring the impact of youth voluntary service programs: summary and conclusions of the international experts, World Bank and innovations in civic participation', http://siteresources.worldbank.org/INTCY/Resources/395766–1187899515414/ ReportYouthServiceMeeting.pdf [Accessed 10 December 2009].

Meetoo, D. and Temple, B. (2003) 'Issues in multi-method research: constructing self-care', *International Journal of Qualitative Methods*, 2 (3): 1–21.

Moore, C. and Allen, P. (1996) 'The effects of volunteering on the young volunteer', *The Journal of Primary Prevention*, 17 (2): 231–258.

Morrow-Howell, N., Hinterlong, J., Rozario, P. and Tang, F. (2003) 'Effects of volunteering on the well being of older adults', *Journal of Gerontology: Social Sciences*, 58B (3): 137–145.

Mustonen, P. (2006) 'Volunteer tourism: postmodern pilgrimage?' *Journal of Tourism and Cultural Change*, 3 (3): 160–177.

Nakamura, J. and Csikszentmihalyi, M. (2005) 'The concept of flow', in Snyder, C. and Lopez, S. (eds), *Handbook of Positive Psychology*. New York: Oxford University Press, pp. 89–105.

Olsen, W. (2004) 'Triangulation in social research: qualitative and quantitative methods can really be mixed', in Holborn, N. (ed.), *Developments in Sociology 2004*. Ormskirk: Causeway Press, pp. 103–121.

Paine, A., Ockenden, N. and Machin, J. (2007) *Volunteers Can: Towards a Volunteering Strategy to Reduce Re-Offending*. Consultation Document, NOMS (National Offender Management Service), United Kingdom.

Patton, M. (1990) *Qualitative Evaluation and Research Methods*. London: Sage Publications.

Potter, J. and Wetherall, M. (1987) *Discourse and Social Psychology: Beyond Attitudes and Behaviour*. London: Sage Publications.

Ryckman, R. (2008) *Theories of Personality*. Belmont, CA: Thomas Wadsworth.

Ryff, C. and Singer, B. (2005) 'From social structure to biology: integrative science in pursuit of human health and well-being', in Snyder, C. and Lopez, J. (eds), *Handbook of Positive Psychology*. New York: Oxford University Press, pp. 541–555.

Schulman, M. (2005) 'The passion to know: a developmental perspective', in Snyder, C. and Lopez, J. (eds), *Handbook of Positive Psychology*. New York: Oxford University Press, pp. 313–326.

Sekaran, U. (2003) *Research Methods for Business: A Skill Building Approach* (4th edition). New York: John Wiley and Sons Inc.

Silverman, D. (1993) *Interpreting Qualitative Data, Methods of Analysing Talk, Text and Interaction*. London: Sage Publications.

Sin, H. (2009) 'Volunteer tourism: "involve me and I will learn"?' *Annals of Tourism Research*, 36 (3): 480–501.

Smith, J. and Osborn, M. (2004) 'Interpretative phenomenological analysis', in Blackwell, G. (ed.), *Doing Social Psychology Research*. Oxford: The British Psychological Society and Blackwell Publishing Ltd, pp. 229–254.

Stevens-Ratchford, R. (2005) 'Occupational engagement: motivation for older adult participation', *Topics in Geriatric Rehabilitation*, 21 (23): 171–181.

Stoddart, H. and Rogerson, C. (2004) 'Volunteer tourism: the case of habitat for humanity South Africa', *Geojournal*, 60: 311–318.

Wearing, S. (2001) *Volunteer Tourism: Experiences That Make a Difference*. Oxford: CABI Publishing.

Wickens, E. (2011) 'Journeys of the self: volunteer tourists in Nepal', in Benson, A. (ed.), *Volunteer Tourism: Theoretical Frameworks and Practical Applications*. Oxon: Routledge, pp. 42–52.

Williamson, G. (2005) 'Aging well', in Snyder, C. and Lopez, J. (eds), *Handbook of Positive Psychology*. New York: Oxford University Press, pp. 676–686.

Wilson, J. and Musick, M. (2000) 'The effects of volunteering on the volunteer', *Law and Contemporary Problems*, 62 (4): 141–168.

Zahra, A. and McIntosh, A. (2007) 'Volunteer tourism: evidence of cathartic tourist experiences', *Tourism Recreation Research*, 32 (1): 115–119.

Zahra, A. and Ryan, C. (2005) 'Reflections on the research process: the researcher as actor and audience in the world of regional tourist organisations', *Current Issues in Tourism*, 8 (1): 1–21.

Part III
Health and restoration

10 How does a vacation from work affect tourists' health and well-being?

Jessica de Bloom, Sabine Geurts and Michiel Kompier

Introduction

In the pyramid of Djoser, archaeologists discovered hieroglyphs roughly meaning 'Hadnachte and his brother Panachti have been here to make an excursion and enjoy Memphis' (Hachtmann, 2007). This ancient 'graffiti' dating from briefly before the birth of Christ is viewed as the first evidence of touristic activities and vacations. The etymologic origin of the word vacation dates back to the Roman Empire: 'vacatio' means 'leisure, a being free from duty' (Online Etymology Dictionary, 2008).

Whereas the need for recovery has long been acknowledged, scientific research on the effects of vacation on physical as well as mental well-being is scarce. A possible reason for this is the limited interaction and cross-fertilisation between the research fields of positive psychology and tourism (Uysal *et al.*, 2012). Only very recently, researchers have started to draw linkages between the two fields and combine the bodies of knowledge (Filep, 2012; Pearce, 2009; Nawijn, 2011).

An example for the relative independence of the fields is the definition of vacation. Whilst in tourism the focus is mostly on travel (e.g. World Tourism Organization, 1995), in psychology the emphasis is suspension of work (e.g. Eden, 2001). We try to combine both fields and define a vacation as 'a prolonged period of absence from work granted to an employee, used for rest, recreation or travel and lasting more than two days' (De Bloom, 2012; see also 'macrorecovery' in Sluiter *et al.*, 2000).

Whilst research on the psychological effects of vacation is still in its early stages, the detrimental effect of job stressors, which can be seen as the antithesis of recovery, has been well established (De Bloom *et al.*, 2009). Exposure to job stressors directly elicits physiological responses such as elevated levels of blood pressure, heart rate, catecholamines and cortisol (e.g. Hjortskov *et al.*, 2004). Particularly when these physiological responses prolong after demands and stressors have ended, health and well-being (H&W) are at risk (e.g. Vrijkotte *et al.*, 2000). Potential consequences of inadequate recovery are stress-related illnesses like burnout and severe sleep disturbances which are also prominent determinants of long-term sickness absence (Åkerstedt *et al.*, 2007).

Recent diary studies have revealed that workers often recover insufficiently during shorter respites like regular evening hours and weekends, for instance due to working overtime or ruminating about past stressors and worrying about present or future stressors (Fritz and Sonnentag, 2005). Therefore, a vacation as a long period of rest is presumably a prime opportunity to fully recover from work and a powerful weapon against work stress and its negative consequences (De Bloom et al., 2011).

In the following, we will present five theories that can explain why vacations may improve H&W. Thereafter, we will describe three longitudinal field studies in which we investigated four different types of holidays: long weekends, midweek breaks, winter sports vacations and summer vacations. After presenting the results of these studies and discussing the most important findings, we will conclude with directions for future research and practical implications of our studies.

Mechanisms through which vacations may contribute to recovery

Vacationing may contribute to recovery from work through a passive and an active mechanism, also referred to as the fulfilment of basic and growth needs respectively (e.g. Uysal et al., 2012). The passive mechanism reflects a direct release from daily exposure to job demands; that is a compensation for work stress. The active mechanism suggests that vacationing is more than stress relief. Vacations presumably enrich quality of life by offering the possibility to engage in valued, pleasant, self-chosen, non-work activities and to spend quality time with close others (De Bloom et al., 2010; Nawijn, 2011; Sirgy et al., 2011).

The passive recovery mechanism

The two most influential recovery theories, Effort-Recovery Theory (Meijman and Mulder, 1998) and Allostatic Load Theory (McEwen, 1998), merely presuppose the passive recovery mechanism. Both theories share the assumption that removal of demands previously put on the individual's psychobiological systems is a necessary prerequisite for recovery to occur (Sonnentag, 2001).

Effort-Recovery Theory (Meijman and Mulder, 1998): the basic idea of Effort-Recovery Theory is the necessity of mobilisation of capacities and resources to meet the demands of work. This effort expenditure at work is unavoidably associated with psycho-physiological costs or load reactions (e.g. fatigue). However, these acute load reactions will not have long-term negative health consequences as long as workers recover sufficiently after work. During time after work, effort is no longer expended and the psychobiological systems that were activated during work time will return to baseline (i.e. pre-demand) level. Recovery is correspondingly seen as a period of rest in which employees are relieved from the demands that are otherwise acting upon them. This absence of demands enables replenishment of resources.

Allostatic Load Theory (McEwen, 1998): as a physiological theory of stress, Allostatic Load Theory constitutes a model for the fluctuation of physiological systems within the body to meet stressful demands. The underlying principle is to achieve stability through change. This regulation process is called allostasis (Aronsson et al., 2003). Repeated or prolonged physiological activation may disturb an organism's precarious homeostatic (sympathetic-parasympathetic) balance. This disturbed balance and cumulative cost to the body, called allostatic load, will manifest itself in chronic overactivity or inactivity of crucial bodily systems (e.g. the immune system). Hence, allostatic load denotes the psychophysiological costs of chronic or repeated exposure to stress. Therefore, complete unwinding from load effects built up at work (i.e. recovery) is crucial for preserving H&W (Sonnentag and Geurts, 2009).

The active recovery mechanism

The active mechanism underlying vacation is best represented by three theories: Conservation of Resources Theory (Hobfoll, 1989), Self-Determination Theory (Ryan and Deci, 2000) and Broaden-and-Build Theory (Fredrickson, 2001). The starting point of these theories is the assumption that humans are 'masters of their own fate' who can actively and freely pursue their own interests and intentionally strive for desirable outcomes. Vacations form the breeding ground for self-fulfilment and energy replenishment. According to these theories, recovery occurs because vacationers are able to engage in self-chosen, pleasant activities and spend time with significant others.

Conservation of Resources Theory (Hobfoll, 1989): this theory claims that people strive to obtain, protect and build resources that have specific importance to them. Strain develops when these valued resources are threatened, lost or not gained after having invested in them. 'Resources' refer to a broad category including external objects and conditions such as relationships, as well as personal characteristics and energies. Vacation may constitute a possibility to replenish depleted resources and gain resources, because it is an excellent occasion to engage in freely chosen and energising activities such as the (re)connection with family and friends.

Self-Determination Theory (Ryan and Deci, 2000): regarding vacation effects, autonomy and relatedness are the most important elements of this theory. Autonomy and relatedness are considered fundamental human needs. Satisfaction of these needs elicits positive emotions, and its neglect leads to negative affect. Autonomy to initiate behaviour of one's own choice refers to volition and the experience of self-determined behaviour. Relatedness refers to the feeling of being closely connected to others. Earlier research has demonstrated that workers experience higher positive and lower negative affect during off-job time than during work periods due to satisfaction of the workers' need for autonomy and relatedness (Ryan et al., 2010; Reis et al., 2000). Following this reasoning, a vacation as a pre-eminent opportunity to engage in activities of one's own choice (autonomy) and to connect to close others (relatedness) may fulfil the basic needs of autonomy and relatedness, which should result in positive emotions and higher levels of H&W.

Broaden-and-Build Theory (Fredrickson, 2001): in this theory, positive emotions are considered crucial for H&W. According to Tugade and Fredrickson (2007), positive and negative emotions have complementary adaptive functions and effects. Whereas negative emotions evoke restricted and survival oriented behaviour, positive emotions are supposed to broaden people's thought-action repertoires, thereby encouraging varied, novel and exploratory thoughts and actions. Positive emotions can also rapidly undo the unfavourable cardiovascular arousal induced by negative emotions and have long-term beneficial effects by building enduring personal resources like coping capacity, psychological resilience, creativity and social support (Fredrickson *et al.*, 2000). These personal resources may also function as buffers for future stressors.

Research questions

Despite its assumed great recovery potential, vacation as a prototypical recovery opportunity has received relatively little scientific attention. Initially, a vacation was simply seen as a control occasion for the absence of stress (Eden, 2001). This means the major interest was not in vacation as such, but rather in demonstrating that on- and off-job situations differ in levels of psychological stress. Consequently, many studies on vacations applied a pre-post design in examining the effects of vacation. Pre-post changes in well-being were attributed to the in-between vacation period. In order to estimate the true contribution of vacation to well-being, however, reliable and valid on-vacation measurements are necessary. Accordingly, we defined a vacation effect as the difference in H&W before and during vacation. Research question 1 was:

Vacation effect: do health and well-being improve during vacation?

In case of an increase of H&W during vacation (i.e. a positive vacation effect), the next important question is how long this effect lasts after work resumption. As the vacation comes to an end and positive effects are assumed to fade out sooner or later after returning home and resuming work, the positive effect still persisting after vacation is labelled a vacation after-effect. Research question 2 was:

Vacation after-effect: how long do vacation effects last after work resumption?

Besides the mere absence of work, a vacation may positively influence H&W as it enables vacationers to spend time on valued free-time activities. A vacation may provide vacationers with the opportunity to go through unique and pleasant experiences. For that reason, vacation activities and the associated experiences may be core elements that promote or impede recovery processes during and after vacation. Consequently, research questions 3 and 4 were:

Vacation activities: how do vacation activities relate to changes in H&W during and after vacation?

Vacation experiences: how do vacation experiences relate to changes in H&W during and after vacation?

Method

In this chapter, we combined the evidence from three separate empirical studies that we conducted on four different types of holidays: long weekends (four days); midweek breaks (five days); winter sports vacations (nine days on average) and summer vacations (23 days on average).

Procedure

The studies conducted were longitudinal field studies covering a time span of at least three weeks. Every study included a minimum of six and maximum of ten repeated measurements within the same persons. Baseline levels of H&W were assessed two weeks prior to vacation. During vacation, we measured H&W two times in short vacations (i.e. long weekends and midweek breaks) and in winter sports vacations (on the second day after arrival and on the next to last day before departure). In summer vacations, H&W was measured four times: on the fourth, eighth, twelfth and sixteenth day of vacation. After resuming work, we measured H&W three times after short vacations: on the day of return, on the third workday and on the tenth workday. In winter sports vacations, H&W were assessed on Tuesday and Thursday during the first, second and fourth week after resuming work. In the study on summer vacations, returnees filled in digital questionnaires on their day of return and on Tuesdays during the first, second, third and fourth week after returning home. To calculate vacation (after-) effects, we averaged the scores during vacation (*Inter*) and in the first (*Post 1*), second (*Post 2*), third (*Post 3*) and fourth week (*Post 4*) after vacation.

In addition, three weeks before vacation, all participants filled in a general questionnaire including questions regarding demographics, basic job information and vacation characteristics. Before and after vacation, participants filled in online diaries. During winter sports and summer vacations, the participants were contacted for interviews on a mobile phone provided by the researchers. During short vacations, vacationers filled in paper-and-pencil questionnaires, to be returned in a postage-paid pre-addressed envelope.

To increase response rates, each participant received a tailor-made time schedule of measurement occasions, each measurement was preceded by two reminders (an email and a mobile phone text message) and we announced the possibility of winning a prize with higher chances of winning, the more questionnaires were returned.

Samples

Sample sizes were 52 (long weekends), 41 (midweek breaks), 96 (winter sports vacations) and 54 (summer vacations). Gender and level of education of the Dutch employees were generally evenly distributed. The participants worked in a variety of sectors and a substantial part (about one-third of each sample) worked in the commercial/service sector. Stress levels of the sample differed: part of the sample worked in demanding jobs (e.g. a self-employed entrepreneur who worked more than 50 hours a week), whereas some jobs can be considered routine jobs (e.g. a shop assistant who worked 24 hours a week). Weekly work hours ranged between 24 and 65 hours. On average, participants worked between 35 and 38 hours in the different studies. In all samples, a minority was self-employed (between 11 and 18 per cent) and between 30 and 47 per cent of the sample supervised at least three other employees. The mean age was 43 years in short and summer vacations and 44 years in winter sports vacations.

Measures

H&W: we measured basic H&W by six single items. Warr (1994) distinguished different forms of well-being: pleased versus displeased (represented as satisfaction in our study), depressed versus enthusiastic (represented as mood) and anxious versus comfortable (represented as tension). He further states that arousal should be assessed, which we measured in the form of energy level and fatigue. Moreover, we included a measure of physical well-being, namely health status. The answers were anchored according to the well-known Dutch grade notation system ranging from 1 (extremely low/negative) to 10 (extremely high/positive). We measured *health status* by the single-item measure: 'How healthy did you feel today?' (1 = 'very unhealthy', 10 = 'very healthy'). *Mood* was measured with the question: 'How was your mood today?' (1 = 'very bad', 10 = 'very good'). Levels of *fatigue* were assessed with the measure: 'How fatigued did you feel today?' (1 = 'not fatigued at all', 10 = 'very fatigued'). We measured *tension* with a single-item worded: 'How tense did you feel today?' (1 = 'very calm', 10 = 'very tense'). In addition, we asked respondents to indicate how *energetic* they felt ('How energetic did you feel today?' (1 = 'absolutely not energetic', 10 = 'very energetic'). Finally, respondents were asked to indicate day *satisfaction* on a single-item measure: 'How satisfied do you feel about this day?' by means of a report mark ranging from 1 ('absolutely not satisfied') to 10 ('very satisfied'). We combined the six indicators into one overall indicator of basic H&W. Exploratory factor analysis validated this approach and Cronbach's α for this basic H&W construct was higher than .80 in all studies.

Vacation activities: during short and winter sport vacations participants were asked to estimate the time (in hours) they had engaged in work-related, physical, social and passive activities. During summer vacations, participants were asked to indicate how many hours they had engaged in working. Regarding the other (i.e. physical, social and passive) activities during vacation, participants reported afterwards (on the first workday after vacation) the percentage of vacation time devoted to each activity.

Sleep: to assess *sleep quantity* during vacation, we asked the participants to indicate how many hours they slept on average during the previous four nights. To assess *sleep quality* we asked the participants: 'How did you generally sleep during the previous four nights?' (1 = 'very poorly', 10 = 'very well').

Pleasure from activities: participants were asked to rate the pleasure they derived from their vacation activities (1 = 'very unpleasant', 10 = 'very pleasant').

Recovery experiences were measured during all vacation types except winter sports vacations. To measure psychological detachment, relaxation and control over leisure time during vacation, we applied the validated Recovery Experience Questionnaire (Sonnentag and Fritz, 2007). Each construct was measured with three items that were adapted to the vacation context. Participants could respond on a 5-point Likert scale, ranging from '1 = strongly disagree' to '5 = strongly agree'. An example item for psychological detachment from work is: 'During this vacation, I don't think about work at all'. Relaxation was assessed with items like: 'During this vacation, I use the time to relax', and an example item for control is: 'During this vacation, I determine for myself how I will spend my time'.

Results

Vacation (after-) effects on health and well-being (Research question 1 and 2)

In the four types of vacations, average levels for basic H&W during vacation (*Inter*) were similarly high: between 7.7 for winter sports and midweek breaks and 7.9 for summer vacations on a 10-point scale (see Figure 10.1). The highest level of H&W was 8.2, reported on the eighth day during summer vacations. The increase in H&W from *Pre* to *Inter*, i.e. the vacation-effect, was substantial and significant in all vacations. Effect size Cohen *d* for the vacation-effect was medium in all vacations (0.55 in winter sports vacations, 0.56 in long weekends, 0.70 in midweek breaks and 0.73 in summer vacations).

After the vacation, once work was resumed, basic H&W rapidly decreased, rather independent from the type of vacation (see Figure 10.1). Although mean levels of H&W seem somewhat higher in the first week after work resumption, especially after summer vacations (i.e. effect size Cohen *d* was greater than 0.15 compared to baseline on all occasions after vacation), the difference between H&W *Pre* and H&W *Post* was non-significant. This means that basic H&W returned to baseline levels in the first week after returning home and resuming work in all four vacations.

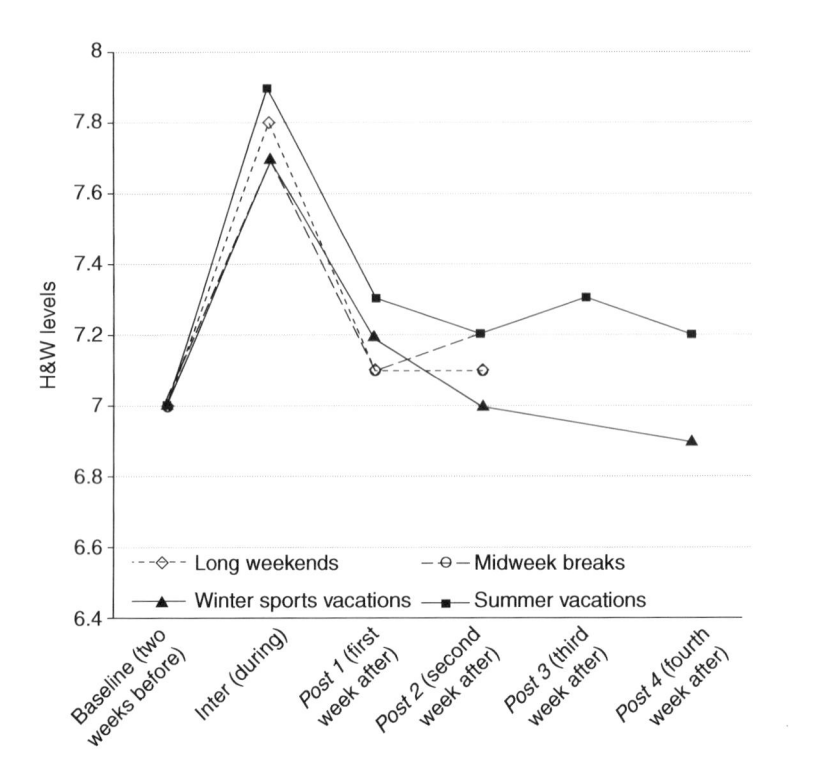

Figure 10.1 Mean levels of health and well-being across four types of vacations.

Vacation activities (Research question 3)

Work-related activities: in the different types of vacation, 10 per cent (during long weekends) to 28 per cent (during summer vacations) of the participants spent time on work-related activities during their holiday. Daily working time during vacation varied between 5 and 15 minutes for the whole sample (working and nonworking vacationers) and between 24 and 66 minutes for those who actually spent time on working during vacation. Work-related activities during vacation were linked to a decrease in H&W one week after midweek breaks and two weeks after long weekends. At other time points during or after short vacations, and in other types of vacations, work-related activities were unrelated to changes in H&W (Table 10.1).

Physical and social activities: in all types of holidays, vacationers engaged in physical activities. During winter sports vacations, vacationers were physically active for almost five hours a day and engagement in physical activities constituted 27 per cent of the total vacation time in summer vacations. Social activities were also frequently reported: at least 89 per cent of the samples devoted some time to these activities during holidays and vacationers reported at least two

Table 10.1 Partial correlations of health and well-being during (*Inter*) and after vacation (*Post 1, Post 2, Post 3, Post 4*) with vacation activities and experiences controlled for health and well-being before vacation (*Pre*)

Health and Well-being levels on

	Inter			Post 1				Post 2				Post 3		Post 4	
	LW	MW	WS	SV	LW	MW	WS	SV	LW	MW	WS	SV	SV	WS	SV
Activities
Work-related activities	.14	−.21	.06	.12	.18	−.52*	.11	.06	−.58*	−.33	−.06	−.10	−.10	−.15	−.00
Physical activities	.28	.17	.31*	−.03	.18	.06	.01	.04	−.04	−.06	.09	.27*	−.02	.19	.04
Social activities	.05	.29	.19	.29*	−.19	.18	.03	.15	.00	.04	−.16	−.05	.01	−.03	.19
Passive activities	.04	.20	−.27*	.43*	.07	.07	−.11	.41*	−.09	−.17	−.11	.38*	.23	−.15	.38*
Sleep time	.29	−.02	−.14	.38*	.16	−.11	.03	.24	−.07	−.27	−.02	.30*	.18	.23*	.14
Experiences
Sleep quality	.55*	.35*	.47*	.38*	.36*	.23	.37*	.23	.20	.30	.12	.27*	.11	.02	.16
Pleasure from activities	.38*	.44*	.49*	.67*	.37*	.16	.21	.41*	.14	.03	.15	.29*	.25	.19	.47*
Negative incidents	−.49*	−.03	−.41*	−.09	−.11	−.15	−.26*	−.13	−.00	−.03	−.15	−.24	−.11	−.10	−.17
Detachment	.32*	.35*	—	.14	.06	.33	—	.24	.65*	.24	—	.15	.07	—	.19
Relaxation	.37*	.53*	—	.65*	.30	.28	—	.49*	.13	.06	—	.37*	.40*	—	.35*
Control	.06	.55*	—	.43*	−.02	.34	—	.34*	−.19	−.02	—	.35*	.28*	—	.40*

Notes
* $p < .05$.
LW = Long weekends, MW = Midweek breaks, WS = Winter sports vacations, SV = summer vacations.

hours of social activities per day. In general, physical and social activities were rather weakly linked to increases in H&W during and after vacations (Table 10.1). More concretely, time spent on physical vacation activities was related to improved H&W during winter sports and two weeks after summer vacations. Time spent on social activities was related to improved H&W during summer vacations only.

Passive activities: most vacationers spent time on passive activities during vacations. In short vacations, about two hours per day were spent in passive activities. In summer vacations, passive activities constituted one-quarter of the total vacation time. During active winter sports vacations, passive activities were less frequently reported: half of the sample spent time on passive activities and the average time engaged in these activities was only 36 minutes. Passive activities showed a rather inconsistent pattern: time spent on passive activities was linked to H&W decreases during winter sports vacations and to H&W increases during and after summer vacations. In long weekend and midweek breaks no relationship between changes in H&W were found.

Sleep time: sleep time ranged between 7.4 (during summer vacations) and 8.9 hours (during midweek breaks) per night. Preliminary analyses showed that sleep time increased about one hour during holidays compared to baseline in all types of vacations. Although vacationers slept significantly more, sleep time was related to improved H&W in summer vacations only.

Vacation experiences (research question 4)

Sleep quality: sleep quality ranged between 7.0 (during short vacations) and 7.5 (during winter sports vacations). Sleep quality was associated with increases in H&W during all types of vacations. Moreover, sleep quality was related to H&W increases after long weekends, winter sports and summer vacations.

Pleasure derived from vacation activities: in all types of holidays, vacationers experienced high levels of pleasure from their vacation activities: mean scores of pleasure ranged between 7.9 (during short vacations) and 8.1 (during winter sports and summer vacations). Pleasure was strongly linked to increases in H&W during all vacations. After vacation, pleasure was also associated with improved H&W up to four weeks after summer vacation and during the first week after a long weekend.

Negative incidents: proportions of vacationers who experienced at least one negative incident ranged between 13 (midweek breaks) and 55 per cent (summer vacations). As chances on incidents are higher the longer the vacation lasts, the frequency of incidents was higher in longer vacations, i.e. winter sports and summer vacations. During short vacations, incidents were mostly related to illness (of oneself or a close other) or disturbances such as lost baggage and crowded swimming pools. During winter sports and summer vacations, sickness or injuries were the most frequently reported incidents. Bad weather was repeatedly complained about as well. A few vacationers were also burdened with travel stress, conflicts with travel companions or interruptions of their 'feeling of being away' due to work (e.g. ruminating about work, a phone call from the office). Negative incidents were related to decreases in H&W during long weekends and winter sports vacations. After returning home and resuming work, winter sports vacationers who experienced negative incidents during their holiday also experienced lower levels of H&W one week after vacation.

Recovery experiences: vacationers reported reasonable and comparable high levels of psychological detachment, relaxation and control in all vacations under study: at least 3.6 on a 5-point scale. Relaxation was strongly and consistently related to increases in H&W during all vacations and after summer vacations. Detaching psychologically from work was related to H&W improvements in long weekends and midweek breaks. Vacationers who exerted control over their vacation activities experienced increased H&W during midweek breaks and summer vacations and in the weeks after summer vacations (Table 10.1).

Discussion

Vacation (after-) effects on H&W (research question 1 and 2)

This research has shown that basic H&W rapidly improved during all types of vacations. The results from the long summer vacation suggest that H&W peak after eight days (for a detailed within-vacation analysis, see De Bloom *et al.*, in press; Nawijn, 2010). The increase in H&W during vacation supports the idea that the absence of work demands during vacation enables psychobiological systems to return to baseline, reduces work load effects and replenishes depleted resources, which in turn enhances basic H&W (McEwen, 1998; Hobfoll, 1989). Consequently, a holiday from work constitutes a powerful opportunity to recover from work demands.

However, the evidence from our studies also suggests that positive vacation effects on basic H&W are generally short-lived: they fade out within the first week after resuming work, independent from the type and duration of the holiday. Therefore, it seems plausible that the quality of a vacation is more important for the strength of the vacation effect than the sheer number of days away from work (Etzion, 2003). However, our studies also suggest that the longer the vacation period lasts, the longer the improved H&W status during vacation lasts.

An intriguing question in light of our results is: why should we keep going on vacation at all if the effects wash out so fast? First, apart from easily accessible resources that we daily use to meet every-day demands and that are relatively easily rechargeable, there may be a more basic resource (i.e. a reserve) that we in principle do not draw upon. It could be that only if the every-day resources are seriously depleted, this basic resource is called upon, which is associated with psychological and/or physical health damage. Regular vacations may prevent using up our basic resource that we urgently need to conserve.

Second, it is possible that although the direct vacation effects on H&W fade out fast, positive vacation memories may have the power to enhance mood and well-being, at least temporarily (Parrott and Sabini, 1990; Kemp et al., 2008). Accordingly, vacation memories may serve as a resource, especially in times of need (Larsen, 2007).

Third, vacationing may act as a bonding activity which creates a sense of relatedness, a fundamental human need (Ryan and Deci, 2000). Vacations may also help to put life in perspective, enhance meaning and coherence and make people realise that there is more to life than work. Although these factors may not raise basic H&W directly, they may assist in creating psychological resilience and in buffering future stress in line with the Broaden-and-Build Theory (Fredrickson, 2001).

Summing up, our studies suggest that recovery during vacation as an antagonist of work stress plays a crucial role in protecting employees' basic H&W (Geurts and Sonnentag, 2006), especially in light of the fact that not taking annual vacations is associated with a higher risk of morbidity and even premature mortality (Gump and Matthews, 2000; Eaker et al., 1992). Vacationing is an effective, natural way to boost well-being and is important for long-term health and vitality.

Vacation activities and experiences (research question 3 and 4)

In our longitudinal field studies, the time vacationers engaged in certain activities is weakly and sometimes inconsistently associated with changes in H&W during and after a holiday. The results suggest that engagement in self-chosen and valued vacation activities is more important for improvements in H&W than the type of activity per se. For example, passive activities relate to decreases in H&W during winter sport vacations and to increases in H&W during long summer vacations, suggesting that H&W increase mostly, if vacationers can do what they came for: that is to be physically active during winter sports and to relax during summer vacations. It is rather the experience associated with the activity and the degree to which an activity matches one's preferences that makes the difference which also corroborates earlier research (Pressman, et al., 2009; Tucker et al., 2008).

Vacation experiences are generally strongly linked to vacation (after-) effects on H&W. Of the investigated experiences, pleasure derived from vacation activities and relaxation seems to be most consistently and strongly related to improvements in H&W during and after vacation. Negative incidents, psychological detachment from work and control were also related to H&W in some vacations.

Regarding sleep, our study showed that vacations enable employees to sleep longer than during working times. However, it was sleep quality rather than sleep quantity that was linked to improvements in H&W in all vacations.

To summarise, the evidence from this research suggests that vacationing affects employee' H&W not only by removing work strain. Vacation activities and especially the associated experiences of pleasure and relaxation are consistently related to improvements in H&W. Therefore, this research indicates that a holiday is more than the sheer liberation from work demands. A vacation seems to constitute an excellent opportunity to fulfil the fundamental human needs of relatedness and autonomy, rendering support for Self-Determination Theory (Ryan and Deci, 2000).

Strengths and limitations

This chapter makes several noteworthy contributions to methodology for examining recovery in general and vacations in particular. First, we applied multiple on-vacation measurements to assess well-being, activities and experiences repeatedly while people were actually on vacation. In doing this, we drastically reduced retrospective biases and increased the validity of our findings. The use of these measures also enabled us to define the vacation effect as the difference between H&W before and during vacation, which constitutes the most direct effect of vacationing, as every measurement after vacation is affected by work resumption.

Second, despite conducting multiple measurements across a vacation period, we succeeded in keeping the measurements minimally invasive for the vacationers. For example, we reduced the effort investment of participants by applying one-item measures, which also turned out to be reliable measures of the concept H&W.

Third, we applied solid baseline measures of H&W two weeks before vacation. Baseline measures before vacation may be biased by pre-vacation stress or looking forward to the vacation (DeFrank et al., 2000; Gilbert and Abdullah, 2002; Westman, 2005).

A limitation of our field studies lies in the fact that our samples were not very large and perhaps also selective. This may limit the external validity of our findings.

A second source of weakness in our field studies is the difficulty to establish causality. With regards to vacation activities and experiences, co-varying levels of H&W do not necessarily mean that the variables are causally related. For example, increases in H&W may be a precursor as well as an outcome of relaxation, pleasure or detachment.

Third, vacation (after-) effects partly depend on baseline levels of H&W. However, the danger of regression fallacy (i.e. erroneously attributing change to an intervention rather than statistical regression, see Gilovich, 1991; Thorndike, 1924) is notably smaller in our studies. Baseline measures immediately before vacation may be biased by pre-vacation stress or looking forward to the vacation, leading to under- or overestimations of normal H&W levels during working time (DeFrank et al., 2000; Gilbert and Abdullah, 2002; Westman, 2005). However, we cannot completely rule out that these effects may have coloured our results.

Fourth, our studies focused on vacation (after-) effects on rather fundamental aspects of well-being which we termed basic H&W. Future studies could investigate effects on the broader concept of well-being embracing for instance interpersonal relationships, personal development (Schalock *et al.*, 2002) and psychological capital (Luthans *et al.*, 2007) including self-efficacy, optimism (Seligman, 1998), hope (Snyder, 2000), resilience and flourishing (Keyes, 2002).

Reactance is another problem since repeatedly filling in comparable questionnaires could alter behaviour, thoughts and feelings of respondents. In future studies, data triangulation of self-report questionnaires with additional measures such as physiological indices of well-being and supervisor or partner ratings would be a means to further improve vacation research and to generate valid and reliable results.

Directions for future research

Vacations may affect outcome variables which have not yet been investigated. For example, we could investigate physiological adaptation processes during and after vacation. Cardiovascular (e.g. blood pressure, heart rate, heart rate variability) or neuroendocrine indicators (e.g. cortisol) could be applied as indices for physical restoration (see Sluiter *et al.*,1998; Strauss-Blasche *et al.*, 2005). In addition, upcoming vacation studies could investigate the effect of vacation on work performance, including creative problem solving, productivity, extra role behaviour and work engagement (Bakker and Schaufeli, 2008).

Regarding potential determinants that may affect changes in H&W during and after vacations, more studies on the role of work-related activities during vacation are highly needed. Due to our small sample sizes and the small percentage of vacationers spending time on work tasks, the influence of working during holidays on recovery processes deserves further research attention. In this regard, freedom of choice to work, rumination and negative work reflection may play a crucial role (see for example Fritz and Sonnentag, 2006).

Research on factors that accelerate or decelerate the fade-out process would also be useful. In this regard, increased work load before or after vacations (Kühnel and Sonnentag, 2011), homeload (e.g. washing clothes, unpacking, social obligations) and the structure of return (e.g. resuming work on Monday or Wednesday; Strauss-Blasche *et al.*, 2004) seem to be prime candidates affecting changes in well-being after vacation. Moreover, we could investigate the value of autobiographical vacation memories. Experimental designs in which, for example, after stress exposure vacation photographs are shown to induce positive mood states could help us in answering the question of whether positive vacations memories may down-regulate the stress response and act as a buffer against future stressors.

Practical suggestions

For employees, our results suggest that regularly scheduled getaways may be more beneficial to preserve H&W in the long run than only one long vacation across a working year. In addition, a recent study on pre-vacation time (Nawijn *et al.*, in press) showed that H&W deteriorated prior to vacation and that this decrease was related to pre-vacation workload. It seems plausible that longer vacations (i.e. longer absences from work) might go hand in hand with higher pre-vacation workload. Moreover, occasional negative incidents (e.g. illness) might spoil a vacation. Consequently, vacationers are advised not to 'put all eggs in one basket' and to take regular vacations instead of one long vacation only.

In addition, our research cautiously suggests that employees may need a couple of days to fully recover from work and reach highest levels of H&W. Therefore, a vacation should also be long enough to attain peak levels of H&W. Moreover, two weeks of high well-being are in itself better than one week, regardless of the persistence of these effects after work resumption. Employees should therefore try to schedule at least one longer vacation across a work year.

Regarding vacation activities and experiences, it seems crucial to engage in activities that are valued and that match one's preferences. It is important that employees are 'in control' and freely decide whether, when and how long they work and which work-related activity they pursue. Although the causal direction between sleep quality and H&W is yet unclear, it seems reasonable for vacationers to pay special attention to a proper sleep environment which enables a good night's sleep (e.g. a dark, well-tempered, quiet bedroom).

Employers should encourage vacationing as it assures long-term work ability and productivity. They could achieve this aim by adopting a policy that prohibits selling and hoarding up vacation days. For example, in Europe, a minimum period of annual leave (20 days) may not be replaced by an allowance in lieu (EC of the European Parliament and the Council, 1993). Further, employers may discourage carrying over vacation days to the next work year. Employers should also permit employees to schedule vacations at a point in time when they need them, because vacations could serve as way to undo stress and to promote and conserve well-being (Westman and Etzion, 2001). In addition, frequent (short) vacations across a work year should be especially promoted, but employers should encourage longer vacations as well. During longer vacations, peak levels of well-being can be achieved and possibly maintained a bit longer. Employees may especially value these holidays because longer vacations can provide more opportunities to engage in self-chosen activities which are experienced as pleasant and relaxing.

References

Åkerstedt, T., Kecklund, G., Alfredsson, L. and Selen, J. (2007) 'Predicting long term sickness absence from sleep and fatigue', *European Sleep Research Society*, 16: 341–345.

Aronsson, G., Svensson, L. and Gustafsson, K. (2003) 'Unwinding, recuperation, and health among compulsory school and high school teachers in Sweden', *International Journal of Stress Management*, 3: 217–234.

Bakker, A.B. and Schaufeli, W.B. (2008) 'Positive organizational behavior: engaged employees in flourishing organizations', *Journal of Organizational Behavior*, 29: 147–154.

De Bloom, J. (2012) *How do Vacations Affect Workers' Health and Well-Being? Vacation (After-) Effects and the Role of Vacation Activities and Experiences*. Doctoral dissertation, Radboud University (the Netherlands).

De Bloom, J., Geurts, S. and Kompier, M. (2010) 'Vacation from work as prototypical recovery opportunity', *Gedrag & Organisatie*, 23: 333–349.

De Bloom, J., Geurts, S.A.E. and Kompier, M.A.J. (in press) 'Vacation (after-) effects on employee health and well-being, and the role of vacation activities, experiences and sleep', *Journal of Happiness Studies*.

De Bloom, J., Geurts, S.A.E., Sonnentag, S., Taris, T., De Weerth, C. and Kompier, M.A.J. (2011) 'How does a vacation from work affect employee health and well-being?' *Psychology & Health*, 26: 1606–1622.

De Bloom, J., Kompier, M., Geurts, S., De Weerth, C., Taris, T. and Sonnentag, S. (2009) 'Do we recover from vacation? Meta-analysis of vacation effects on health and well-being', *Journal of Occupational Health*, 51: 13–25.

DeFrank, R.S., Konopaske, R. and Ivancevich, J.M. (2000) 'Executive travel stress: perils of the road warrior', *The Academy of Management Executive*, 14: 58–71.

Eaker, E.D., Pinsky, J. and Catelli, W.P. (1992) 'Myocardial infarction and coronary death among women: psychosocial predictors from a 20-year follow-up of women in the Framingham Heart Study', *American Journal of Epidemiology*, 135: 854–864.

EC of the European Parliament and of the Council (1993) Directive 93/104/EC of the European Parliament and of the Council of 23 November 1993 concerning certain aspects of the organisation of working time. http://eurlex.europa.eu/smartapi/cgi/sga_d oc?smartapi!celexapi!prod!CELEXnumdoc&lg=EN&numdoc=31993L0104&model=g uichett. [Accessed 21 June 2011].

Eden, D. (2001) 'Vacations and other respites: studying stress on and off the job', in Cooper, C. and Robertson, I.T. (eds), *Well-Being in Organizations*. West Sussex: John Wiley & Sons Ltd, pp. 305–330.

Etzion, D. (2003) 'Annual vacation: duration of relief from job stressors and burnout', *Anxiety, Stress, and Coping*, 16: 213–226.

Filep, S. (2012) 'Positive psychology and tourism', in Uysal, M., Perdue, R. and Sirgy, J. (eds), *The Handbook of Tourism and Quality-of-Life: The Missing Links*. Dordrecht: Springer, pp. 31–50.

Fredrickson, B.L. (2001) 'The role of positive emotions in positive psychology: the Broaden-and-Build Theory of positive emotions', *American Psychologist*, 56: 218–226.

Fredrickson, B.L., Mancuso, R.A., Branigan, C. and Tugade, M.M. (2000) 'The undoing effect of positive emotions', *Motivation and Emotion*, 24: 237–258.

Fritz, C. and Sonnentag, S. (2005) 'Recovery, health, and job performance: effects of weekend experiences', *Journal of Occupational Health Psychology*, 10: 187–199.

Fritz, C. and Sonnentag, S. (2006) 'Recovery, well-being, and performance related outcomes: the role of workload and vacation experiences', *Journal of Applied Psychology*, 91: 936–994.

Geurts, S.A.E. and Sonnentag, S. (2006) 'Recovery as an explanatory mechanism in the relation between acute stress reactions and chronic health impairment', *Scandinavian Journal of Work, Environment & Health*, 32: 482–492.

Gilbert, D. and Abdullah, J. (2002) 'A study of the impact of the expectation of a holiday on an individual's sense of well-being', *Journal of Vacation Marketing*, 8: 352–361.

Gilovich, T. (1991) *How We Know What Isn't So: The Fallibility of Human Reason in Everyday Life*. New York: The Free Press.

Gump, B.B. and Matthews, K.A. (2000) 'Are vacations good for your health? The 9-year mortality experience after the multiple risk factor intervention trial', *Psychosomatic Medicine*, 62: 608–612.

Hachtmann, R. (2007) *Tourismus-Geschichte*. Göttingen: Vandenhoek and Ruprecht.

Hjortskov, N., Rissen, D., Blangsted, A.K., Fallentin, N., Lundberg, U. and Sogaard, K. (2004) 'The effect of mental stress on heart rate variability and blood pressure during computer work', *European Journal of Applied Physiology*, 92: 84–89.

Hobfoll, S.E. (1989) 'Conservation of resources: a new attempt at conceptualizing stress', *American Psychologist*, 44: 513–524.

Kemp, S., Burt, C.D.B. and Furneaux, L. (2008) 'A test of the peak-end rule with extended autobiographical events', *Memory & Cognition*, 36: 132–138.

Keyes, C.L.M. (2002) 'The mental health continuum: from languishing to flourishing in life', *Journal of Health and Social Behavior*, 43: 207–222.

Kühnel, J. and Sonnentag, S. (2011) 'How long do you benefit from vacation? A closer look at the fade-out of vacation effects', *Journal of Organizational Behavior*, 32: 125–143.

Larsen, S. (2007) 'Aspects of a psychology of the tourist experience', *Scandinavian Journal of Hospitality and Tourism*, 7: 7–18.

Luthans, F., Youssef, C.M. and Avolio, B.J. (2007) *Psychological Capital: Developing the Human Competitive Edge*. Oxford: Oxford University Press.

McEwen, B.S. (1998) 'Stress, adaptation, and disease: allostasis and allostatic load', *Annals of the New York Academy of Sciences*, 840: 33–44.

Meijman, T.F. and Mulder, G. (1998) 'Psychological aspects of workload', in Drenth, P.J.D., Thierry, H. and de Wolff, C.J. (eds), *Handbook of Work and Organizational Psychology. Vol. 2 Work Psychology* (2nd edition). Hove: Psychology Press, pp. 5–33.

Nawijn, J. (2010) 'The holiday happiness curve: a preliminary investigation into mood during a holiday abroad', *International Journal of Tourism Research*, 12: 281–290.

Nawijn, J. (2011) 'Happiness through vacationing: just a temporary boost or long-term benefits?' *Journal of Happiness Studies*, 12: 651–665.

Nawijn, J., De Bloom, J. and Geurts, S. (in press) 'Pre-vacation time: blessing or burden?' *Leisure Sciences*.

Online Etymology Dictionary (2008) www.etymonline.com/index.php?allowed_in_frame =0&search=vacation&searchmode=none. [Accessed 31 July 2012].

Parrott, W.G. and Sabini, J. (1990) 'Mood and memory under natural conditions: evidence for mood incongruent recall', *Journal of Personality and Social Psychology*, 59: 321–336.

Pearce, P.L. (2009) 'The relationship between positive psychology and tourist behaviour studies', *Tourism Analysis*, 14: 37–48.

Pressman, S.D., Matthews, K.A., Cohen, S., Martire, L.M., Scheier, A. and Baum, A. (2009) 'Association of enjoyable leisure activities with psychological and physical well-being', *Psychosomatic Medicine*, 71: 725–732.

Reis, H.T., Sheldon, K.M., Gable, S.L., Roscoe, J. and Ryan, R.M. (2000) 'Daily well-being: the role of autonomy, competence, and relatedness', *Personality and Social Psychology Bulletin*, 26: 419–435.

Ryan, R.M. and Deci, E.L. (2000) 'Self-Determination Theory and the facilitation of intrinsic motivation, social development, and well-being', *American Psychologist*, 55: 68–78.

Ryan, R.M., Bernstein, J.H. and Brown, K.W. (2010) 'Weekends, work, and well-being: psychological need satisfactions and day of the week effects on mood, vitality, and physical symptoms', *Journal of Social and Clinical Psychology*, 29: 95–122.

Schalock, R.L., Alonso, M.A.V. and Braddock, D.L. (2002) *Handbook on Quality of Life for Human Service Practitioners*. Washington, DC: American Association on Mental Retardation.

Seligman, M.E.P. (1998) *Learned Optimism*. New York: Pocket Books.

Sirgy, M.J., Kruger, S.P., Lee, D.J. and Yu, G.B. (2011) 'How does a travel trip affect tourists' life satisfaction?' *Journal of Travel Research*, 50: 261–275.

Sluiter, J.K., Van der Beek, A.J. and Frings-Dresen, M.H.W. (1998) 'Work stress and recovery measured by urinary catecholamines and cortisol excretion in long distance coach drivers', *Occupational and Environmental Medicine*, 55: 407–413.

Sluiter, J.K., Frings-Dresen, M.H.W. and Meijman, T.F. (2000) 'Reactivity and recovery from different types of work measured by catecholamines and cortisol: a systematic literature overview', *Occupational Environmental Medicine*, 57: 298–315.

Snyder, C.R. (2000) *Handbook of Hope*. San Diego: Academic Press.

Sonnentag, S. (2001) 'Work, recovery activities, and individual well-being: a diary study', *Journal of Occupational Health Psychology*, 16: 196–210.

Sonnentag, S. and Fritz, C. (2007) 'The recovery experience questionnaire: development and validation of a measure for assessing recuperation and unwinding from work', *Journal of Occupational Health Psychology*, 12: 204–221.

Sonnentag, S. and Geurts, S.A.E. (2009) 'Methodological issues in recovery research', in Sonnentag, S., Perrewe, P.L. and Ganster, D.C. (eds), *Current Perspectives on Job-Stress Recovery*. Bingley: Esmeralda Group Publishing Ltd, pp. 1–36.

Strauss-Blasche, G., Muhry, F., Lehofer, M., Moser, M. and Marktl, W. (2004) 'Time course of well-being after a three-week resort-based respite from occupational and domestic demands: carry-over, contrast and situation effects', *Journal of Leisure Research*, 36: 293–309.

Strauss-Blasche, G., Reithofer, B., Schobersberger, W., Ekmekcioglu, C. and Marktl, W. (2005) 'Effect of vacation on health: moderating factors of vacation outcome', *Journal of Travel Medicine*, 12: 94–101.

Thorndike, E.L. (1924) 'The influence of chance imperfections of measures upon the relation of initial score to gain or loss', *Journal of Experimental Psychology*, 7: 225–232.

Tucker, P., Dahlgren, A., Akerstedt, T. and Waterhouse, J. (2008) 'The impact of free-time activities on sleep, recovery and well-being', *Applied Ergonomics*, 39: 653–662.

Tugade, M.M. and Fredrickson, B.L. (2007) 'Regulation of positive emotions: emotion regulation strategies that promote resilience', *Journal of Happiness Studies*, 8: 311–333.

Uysal, M., Perdue, R. and Sirgy, M.S. (2012) 'Prologue: tourism and quality-of-life. Research: the missing links', in Uysal, M., Perdue, R. and Sirgy, J. (eds), *The Handbook of Tourism and Quality-of-Life: The Missing Links*. Dordrecht: Springer, pp. 31–50.

Vrijkotte, T.G.M., van Doornen, L.J.P. and de Geus, E.J.C. (2000) 'Effects of work stress on ambulatory blood pressure, heart rate and heart rate variability', *Hypertension*, 35: 880–886.

Warr, P. (1994) 'A conceptual framework for the study of work and mental health', *Work & Stress*, 8: 84–97.

Westman, M. (2005) 'Strategies for coping with business trips: a qualitative exploratory study', *International Journal of Stress Management*, 11: 167–176.

Westman, M. and Etzion, D. (2001) 'The impact of vacation and job stress on burnout and absenteeism', *Psychology and Health*, 16: 95–106.

World Tourism Organization (1995) *UNWTO Technical Manual: Collection of Tourism Expenditure Statistics.* http://pub.unwto.org/WebRoot/Store/Shops/Infoshop/Products/1034/1034-1.pdf. [Accessed 31 October 2011].

11 Anticipating a flourishing future with tourism experiences

Christina Hagger and Duncan Murray

Introduction

The pace of ageing in Australia is increasing as the largest wave of ageing people ever known, the baby boomer generation, heads towards retirement (Hugo, 2003). The first of the baby boomers turned 60 in 2006, the rest will reach that benchmark over the next two decades (Australian Bureau of Statistics (ABS), 2006a) and, as a group, they are expected to contribute significantly to increased spending on health care over the next 40 years (ABS, 2011). They carry the critical mass of numbers to be a key area for policy concern at all levels of government (ABS, 2006b) and provide associated opportunities as well as challenges in policy, planning and service provision (Hugo, 2003).[1]

In addition, advances in health care, combined with reductions in some risk factors, are resulting in people living longer (ABS, 2006b). People may now live for 20 years or more as retirees and, for some, the period of post retirement life may be longer than their working lives (Patrickson and Ranzijn, 2004). It is important that such years are meaningful (Ranzijn, 2002). The importance of sustaining meaning is underscored by research which indicates that one's purpose in life could be a protective factor against heart disease (Kim, *et al.* 2012). Studies from Japan suggest that *ikigai*, (a sense of purpose for a life worth living) is associated with reduced heart disease (Koizumi *et al.*, 2008). Likewise, recent studies have found that a satisfying life or positive psychological well-being may be a buffer against coronary heart disease (Boehm *et al.*, 2011a and b).

However, retaining one's meaning in life after retirement is not necessarily simple. Retirement can mean the loss of work/life satisfaction, as work is central to the lives of many (Pocock, 2003, 2006). It provides significant non-monetary benefits such as 'a structure for the day, social contact, a means of achieving respect, and a source of engagement, challenge and meaning' (Diener and Seligman, 2004, p. 11). The workplace can be, for many, a sustaining network, almost a 'family', where people have 'laughs, fun and social life' (Pocock, 2003, p. 52).

So when people retire, they leave this network behind. They enter a new world in which they need to develop – and evolve – new roles and new life scripts, or at least adapt existing ones (Wells and Kendig, 1999) in order to maintain their well-being and health.

Retirees and engagement with life

So what roles are available for retirees? Volunteering, caring for grandchildren and bridging employment are commonly seen as the usual options. Yet such roles may not necessarily be chosen by the individual or valued by society (IPSOS, 2005) and therefore may fail to offer a sense of engagement. Such externally determined goals are likely to fade over time (Judge *et al.*, 2005) and are less likely to assist an individual in their search for meaning or fulfilment and engagement in life. By contrast, self-concordant or freely selected goals are typically more satisfying and attainable (Judge *et al.*, 2005).

The importance of engagement with life is central to the field of positive psychology suggesting that well-being (comprising positive emotion, engagement, purpose, positive relationships and positive accomplishment) may be one of the 'best weapons against mental disorder' (Seligman, 2008, p. 5). These five elements encapsulate the multi-dimensional aspects and active, indeed intentional, processes that underpin individual human flourishing (Forgeard *et al.*, 2011).

Clearly this has implications also for broader society. System level recognition of the importance of meaning and well-being for retirees is reflected in calls for effective public policy to promote healthy ageing from middle age onwards (Bowling and Dieppe, 2005). In their article, 'Beyond money: toward an economy of well-being', Diener and Seligman (2004) observe that well-being can powerfully predict future health and longevity and therefore has major implications for health, and health care costs.

Therefore, both for the individual and wider society, it is important to encourage active, intentional strategies that support retirees to flourish. Retirees need to discover alternate sources of the meaning, significance and life satisfaction they once gained from employment. Self-concordant goal setting that reflects their personal constructs and inner values may therefore be an essential part of this quest or search to retain, or even expand, meaning and quality of life in retirement.

It is suggested that the goal setting, anticipation and savouring associated with tourism, particularly multiple tourism events, can play a role here. Research indicates that even single tourism experiences can make a significant contribution to quality of life (Pearce, 2005; Dolnicar *et al.*, 2012) and life satisfaction (Neal *et al.*, 1999; Sirgy *et al.*, 2011). There is some evidence that vacations can provide a protective health function (Gump and Matthews, 2000) while Hunter-Jones (2003, 2005) maintains that leisure travel makes an important contribution to the well-being of cancer patients. Travel can be a 'metaphor for recovery' for people with an acquired disability in which the sense of purpose and meaning associated with travel can build self-confidence and also demonstrate to self, as well as others, a recovery of control over individual destiny (Yau *et al.*, 2004, p. 958).

It is evident that there are clear benefits to be gained from even one tourism experience. This study extends the debate to suggest that multiple cycles of tourism experiences have the potential to offer benefits beyond that of a single holiday.

The tourism experience

A tourism experience may be seen as a significant life event which extends far beyond the actual core of the activity. It absorbs a major investment of time and personal energy prior to and post the experience (Clawson and Knetsch, 1966; Larsen, 2007). This phased process can extend over months, even years. Most importantly, recollection can enter long-term memory and be savoured as an extended lifetime experience. It follows that the real length of a tourism experience is created by the individual, incorporating all phases of the experience and the memory becomes their personal intellectual property (Hagger, 2009). As Pearce (2005, p. 10) notes, the reflection phase of tourist experiences can last for years after the event and, in this sense, the experienced product never actually 'wears out' and can even be augmented by subsequent visits or ongoing information. Individuals can use story-telling to revisit tourist experiences and thus 'prolong or rekindle' the positive feelings associated with such an event and such savouring indicates a strong association with enhanced well-being (Bryant, 2003, p. 177).

These memories may be more positive than the actual experience itself. Research into the 'rosy glow' phenomenon suggests that people's anticipation and recollection of positively anticipated personal events is typically found to be more positive than the actual experience (Mitchell *et al.*, 1997). People may choose to travel on a holiday knowing they will enjoy the anticipation and memory for a period far longer than the activity itself.

Likewise, the duration of the actual core tourism activity need not be particularly long. The peak-and-end rule (Fredrickson, 2000; Larsen, 2006) argues that an individual's global evaluation of an event (and their subsequent choices) may be predicted by the affect experience at just two key moments: the peak moment and the ending. Accordingly, the length of a holiday may well be less important to the memory than these key moments. This is important as contemporary retirement can be dogged by either time and/or financial constraints that restrict the ability of many people to have an extended holiday.

Multiple cycles of tourism experiences: anticipation through to memory

The central purpose of this study is to investigate the sense of purpose and meaning that can be created through multiple cycles of tourism experiences. It is argued that the progress towards personally valued goals gained through multiple cycles of tourism experiences can deliver, and possibly exceed, the well-being benefits associated with one extended or epic tourism event such as long-term travel (i.e. Grey Nomads or Snowbirds) undertaken by retirees (Onyx and Leonard, 2005). The five main premises which support this argument for the benefits of multiple tourism experiences are briefly outlined below.

Progress toward personally valid goals

First, the cycles of anticipation and recollection (Larsen, 2006) associated with multiple tourism events ensure ongoing progress towards personally valid or self-concordant goals. Such freely chosen goals are more likely to assist an individual in their search for fulfilment, meaning and life satisfaction (Judge *et al.*, 2005; Sheldon and Elliot, 1999).[2]

Multiple cycles of anticipation and memory

Second, multiple cycles of tourism experiences support multiple cycles of anticipation as well as memory. These cycles can be savoured or relished, and such savouring is strongly associated with individual well-being founded on perceived personal or internal locus of control (Bryant, 2003) and the principles of positive psychology (Seligman and Csikszentmihalyi, 2000). The anticipation of a holiday offers engagement and purpose while the memory offers a sense of positive accomplishments, both of which are key in positive mental health (Seligman, 2008). The desired aspects of a single holiday can generate happiness (Pearce *et al.*, 2011). Furthermore, it appears that repetitive, cyclical thoughts about positive, happy experiences (such as multiple holidays) maintain positive emotions and can be associated with personal growth and health (Lyubomirsky *et al.*, 2006).

The central importance of anticipation is demonstrated in Kelly's personal construct theory (1955, 1991) where it is argued that an individual's processes are psychologically channelled by the manner of anticipation rather than actual past or future events. Similar to Seligman (2012), the argument views the anticipation of events as the basic theme of human life. Such anticipation, of course, can be positive or negative. The value of positive anticipation in tourism is reflected in a study which suggests that anticipation is of greater benefit than memory and that people derive greater happiness from anticipating two or more breaks spread over a year rather than one longer holiday period (Nawijn *et al.*, 2010)

Opportunities for personal reconstruction

Third, multiple cycles of planned and savoured tourism experiences offer individuals repeated potential opportunities to reconstruct their personal world. This notion is based on Kelly's (1955, 1991) theory of personal constructs, which is grounded in personal inquiry for meaning and charts individual changes in self-construction as people develop an understanding of the world, the people around them and themselves. Each of us lives in a 'fragile, self-constructed world' and it is suggested that tourism experiences, by taking people away from their home place, requires them to 'rejig', drop and elaborate their perspectives, and, in return, offers individuals the potential to reconstruct their personal worlds (Botterill, 1989, pp. 291–292). Each cycle of tourism experience facilitates a 'sense of personal discovery and progress' (Botterill, 1989, p. 293) for the individual who finds their existing level of personal construction either useful or inadequate when it comes to understanding this new vacation space. This discovery leads to personal reconstruction (Botteril and Crompton, 2006). It is significant that the role of the tourist cannot be delegated and there is no 'understudy' (Hagger, 2009, p. 54) so each individual has the opportunity to benefit from engagement with new perspectives and outlooks on life. As Lawrence Durrell wrote in his opening lines of his novel *Bitter Lemons* (1970, p. 15),

> The best [of journeys] lead us not only outwards in space, but inwards as well. Travel can be one of the most rewarding forms of introspection.

Aggregate of consumer satisfaction

Fourth, drawing on consumer satisfaction research, it follows that a repetition of multiple tourism experiences allows the development of an accumulated or aggregate fulfilment of satisfaction in which future 'expectations of satisfaction' formed as 'post-consumption states become pre-consumption states for the next purchase round' (Oliver, 1997, p. 387). In other words, the consumption satisfaction cycle of the individual tourist reflects their own personal, unique lens which combines satisfaction with their previous holiday, as part of their purchase plans for the next. The resulting 'halo effect' of satisfaction with multiple holidays may make an aggregate contribution to life satisfaction. Significantly, by contrast, one-off encounters, such as the so called 'holiday of a lifetime', stand in isolation as the consumer satisfaction assessment can be based only on this singular event. There is no ongoing aggregate of consumer satisfaction to contribute to maintenance, let alone, enhancement of well-being.

Identity as 'serious' traveller

Finally, it is suggested that multiple cycles of tourism events may lead to the 'deeply satisfying' rewards normally associated with serious leisure: fulfilment, self-expression, development of a valued identity and extended social relationships (Stebbins, 2001, p. 54) without, however, demanding in return the usual rigour of extensive training, knowledge and skill. A retiree may choose to develop a 'valued identity' or even career as a 'serious' or dedicated traveller which may, at least partially, replace their former working role identity. As noted previously, retirement is a major transition time that requires the renegotiation of identity, construction of a new autobiography and setting of new life trajectories (Desforges, 2000, p. 932; Kendig, 2004). Travel decisions at this time may construct (and also signal to others) a new or subsidiary identity that reflects a choice towards generativity or engagement with life as retirees move towards the penultimate stage of the life-span.

It is worth noting that such a valued identity can be developed within a framework of domestic tourism. Authentic experiences can arise from the local 'other' as readily as from more exotic or international alternatives (Lengkeek, 2001, pp. 176, 177) as the key to a holiday is that it is a temporary departure, at 'a distance from the normal home environment' to any one of an 'infinite number and several types of possible centres-out-there'. As MacCannell (2001, p. 390) suggests, the 'other' need not be 'half a world away but only a few miles, or blocks or inches'. All tourists, whether seeking adventure or the safety of a package tour, are capable of experiencing the 'other' world of the holiday destination and the associated possibilities of reconstruction (Botterill and Crompton, 2006). A holiday does not have to be an extended journey in an exotic location before it can provide the individual with the opportunity to re-focus and develop new channels, even new trajectories in life. In summary, through their engagement in multiple tourism experiences, retirees are able to pursue aspects of the engaged, the pleasant and the meaningful life (Seligman, 2008) that can assist them to maintain, and possibly even enhance their well-being.

The study

This study aimed to investigate whether multiple tourism experiences have the potential to maintain life satisfaction in retirees. It drew on the literature to suggest that such experiences could deliver: multiple opportunities to progress toward personally valid goals; multiple cycles of anticipation and memory; multiple opportunities for personal reconstruction; and, allow development of an aggregate of consumer satisfaction as well as foster the growth of a new 'career' as a serious traveller.

A sequential mixed method was employed. Quantitative data were collected from two samples, (a) 159 University employees attending pre-retirement sessions arranged by UniSuper (an Australian superannuation fund) and (b) 134 members of the South Australian Council on Ageing (SACOTA). These data were enriched with qualitative material. The construct of life satisfaction was used as one measure of well-being (Forgeard et al., 2011).

The optimal survey method for each group was agreed with representatives of each organisation. A random computer generated mail survey was selected as the most representative response of the SACOTA membership. A total of 600 questionnaires were mailed out, with a response rate of 24 per cent. In contrast, the optimal survey method for the UniSuper group was for the researcher to attend each pre-retirement session and distribute questionnaires to attendees resulting in a response rate of 58 per cent.

Respondents from each group were able to indicate their interest in participating in a subsequent focus group with nine people volunteering. This allowed the 'holiday-makers to speak of their own experiences in their own words' (Ryan, 1995, p. 214).

Limitations of the sample

A number of potential limitations of the sample were apparent. First, the study was restricted predominantly to a metropolitan sample in Australia. Rural or regional retirees may face a unique host of potential impediments to their tourism choices which differ from people in metropolitan locations. A second limitation was that, while the UniSuper sample included a diverse range of employment categories, including technical and clerical staff as well as academic, nonetheless, it was weighted more towards white collar groupings than the population in general.

Overall this study was restricted predominantly to a culturally Western sample, characterised by an individualistic culture emphasising the independence of the individual, freedom of choice and individual needs (Schimmack *et al.*, 2002). This culture is supportive of personal tourism, so that an individual's tourism goals are more likely to be valued by peers, friends and family. As Diener and colleagues (1999) note, cultural support can influence the goals that people choose – as well as their commitment to achieving them. However, a recent study of senior travellers in Beijing and Shanghai (Hsu *et al.*, 2007, p. 1271) reports a 'phenomenal growth' in both domestic and outbound tourism. Similarly Patterson (2006) suggests that the market for senior tourism is set to expand dramatically in countries as diverse as Germany, Israel, Japan and the UK. Such research suggests senior tourism may be unfolding as a cross cultural force.

Demographics of sample

A total of 34.9 per cent of respondents were aged 59 years or under; 30.3 per cent were aged between 60 and 69; 18.4 per cent were aged between 70 and 79 while 16.4 per cent were aged 80 years or older. The majority (46.3 per cent) of respondents were from the Baby Boomer Generation (born 1945–1965) while just over a quarter (26.9 per cent) were from the Silent Generation (born 1933–1945) and a further 20.1 per cent from the GI Generation (born 1901–1932).

An analysis of total income shows that overall 23.2 per cent had an income of $31,199 per annum ($600 per week) or less while only 5.8 per cent had an income of $104,000 per annum ($2000 per week) or more. The ABS (2006c) defines low income households as those with a gross weekly income of less than $500 while high income households are defined as those with a gross weekly income of $2,500 or more. As a counter-claim to stereotypes of 'cashed-up' retirees, less than 6 per cent of respondents were in the high income bracket, around 70 per cent were on an average income, and almost a quarter were on between low and average incomes.

The percentage of female respondents across both samples was 54.1 per cent, with the percentage of males 45.9 per cent. Respondents who were married/de facto accounted for 62.6 per cent of the sample, whilst divorced/separated respondents comprised 16 per cent of the sample, compared to widowed respondents (11.6 per cent) and respondents who were never married (8.8 per cent). The majority of respondents (75.9 per cent) reported their health as either very good (30.3 per cent) or good (45.6 per cent) while 6.8 per cent reported their health as poor.

The analysis of the survey findings was enriched with the personal accounts of respondents who provided comments in the final section of the questionnaire and/or who participated in a focus group.

Findings

The contribution of multiple tourism experiences to life satisfaction was evident in the findings. Results of the statistical analysis indicated that respondents who have travelled over the past five years have a significantly higher overall life satisfaction ($M=17.76$) compared to those who have not travelled ($M=15.71$). The difference in life satisfaction was found to be statistically significant ($F=11.31$, $df=1,281$; $p<.05$. Furthermore, there was a significant increase in life satisfaction based on increases in the number of tourism experiences. Respondents who travelled 11 or more times over the previous five years recorded a higher life satisfaction ($M=18.98$) than those who travelled either 6–10 times ($M=17.93$) or 1–5 times ($M=17.34$). It is noteworthy that respondents who did not travel at all during this period recorded the lowest life satisfaction ($M=15.55$). These differences were found to be statistically significant ($F=8.84$, $df=3,277$; $p<.001$).

A number of other factors may influence the frequency of tourism experiences for an individual that may also influence their life satisfaction. Most notable of these are income and perceived health. Restricted income and health limitations may constrain travel opportunities (Nimrod, 2007). In order to determine whether the difference in life satisfaction could be solely attributed to tourism experiences, a series of calculations were undertaken to investigate the interaction effects of perceived health and income. No significant interaction effects between tourism experiences and either income ($F=0.63$, $df=4,273$: $p=.645$) or perceived health ($F=1.12$, $df=3,273$; $p=.001$) were found, indicating that tourism experiences have a unique effect on increased life satisfaction, irrespective of the health or income status of the participant.

Significant association between anticipation of holidays and life satisfaction

The next step was to investigate whether, beyond the holiday event itself, there is an interaction between the anticipation of tourism experiences and life satisfaction. Respondents who were anticipating travel had a higher overall life satisfaction ($M=17.60$) than those who were not anticipating travel ($M=15.93$). The difference in life satisfaction based on anticipation of future tourism experiences was statistically significant ($F=8.36$, $df=1,288$: $p=.004$). Again, potential interaction effects with income and health were examined with once again no significant interaction effects evident with either income ($F=2.08$, $df=4,288$; $p=0.84$) or health ($F=1.67$, $df=3,288$; $p=.173$). The real significance of anticipation was indicated in the following comments from respondents:

> Importance of anticipation – certainly for bush-walking – it makes it easier to stay motivated and stay fit. Could be a chore staying fit if doing it for the sake of staying fit. Much easier to stay motivated if you have real goals.
>
> (Female, age not given)

> Locking in plans ahead of time with friends is part of the fun of travelling.
>
> (Female, age not given)

The importance of the full cycle of anticipation, the holiday itself and the memories was reflected as follows:

> I find the 'tourism experiences' can add a lot to normal life experience. The planning phase, the trip itself and memories afterwards all enhance one's working and home life.
>
> (Male, age 64)

> The experience has given us memories we'll really treasure for the rest of our lives.
>
> (Female, age not given)

The sense of freedom arising from the pursuit of self-concordant goals was also evident:

> Holidays ... allow complete control of your surroundings and your self – and it's voluntary. Time doesn't mean that much.
>
> (Female, age 63)

> I found my wife again – memories – sense of the warmth of interaction. Climbing a mountain, doing this with my wife. Driving through a winter wonderland, heater on and talking to my wife. Freedom. No pressure to be, anything, anywhere, these are the things I cherish most.
>
> (Male, age not given)

The potential for personal reconstruction was also evident. One respondent observed that multiple cycles of tourism experiences allowed her husband (a former lawyer) to blossom in retirement. She commented as follows:

> Other parts of your life can blossom that you don't know are there. My husband was seen as a lawyer and felt the loss of this identity. I suggested to him that you are still a lawyer, no-one can take that away from you, however there are still all the other parts of your being. The lawyer part is still real, it is still part of your identity, but people aren't that one-dimensional.
>
> (Female, age not given)

> Keep travelling to contribute good experiences as deposits in the life bank.
>
> (Female, age not given)

The personal reconstruction aspects were evident also in the following comments:

> Travelling does enormous amounts for you, broadens horizons, more aware of how other people live. It doesn't matter where you go. When you have been to a place you feel connected to it, breathing the air, drinking the water (even if bottled) – there is a physical and emotional connection. If you travel, you start to feel like a citizen of the world, mentally and spiritually, it becomes part of you for the rest of your life because of the memories. How can you appreciate what you have, if you do not have another perspective?
> (Female, age not given)

> Travelling can step right outside your role (working or retired) because no one has any expectations of you because they don't know what you do in your normal life. It is very liberating, there are other aspects to you! No-one has any expectation of you from your profession, your relationships, you can really be you. You can have simple, free, spontaneous fun. It is a chance to get free of the expectations of your role. Be totally new to these experiences and just absorb them and react – the real you. This is something big about travel.
> (Female, retired age not given)

A supplementary research theme was the potentially strong relationship between life satisfaction and tourism satisfaction resulting solely from domestic tourism. Analysis of the data found no significant difference in life satisfaction across people regardless of their tourism destination, be it predominantly local ($M=17.25$); national ($M=17.48$) or international ($M=16.96$). No statistical difference was found in life satisfaction across the three travel destination groups ($F=0.34$, $df=2,288$; $p>0.5$).

The enthusiasm for domestic travel was shown in the following comments:

> Travelling in Australia is an experience all should have!
> (Male, age 61)

> In this day I would not put up with the hassle of airports, customs, buses, trains, ships etc. My travelling would be in Oz and bicycle and/or hitchhiking.
> (Male, age 80)

Extending the domestic aspect of holidays, another respondent noted that the length of the holiday was unimportant and suggested it was more important just to go somewhere, even if only for a week:

> It is a mistake to wait. Go – even if only for somewhere for a week. Go somewhere – not even for long chunks of time – it tends to start snowballing as horizons broaden.
> (Female, age not given)

Integration of tourism policy with health and ageing portfolios

The findings of this study support the potential for multiple, short, local tourism experiences to contribute to well-being, particularly for retired people who may have restrictions on their time and finances. It is recommended that aspects of tourism policy be re-positioned to focus on the psychological health benefits of local tourism for retirees. Such a reorganisation would require integration of aspects of the portfolios of health, ageing and tourism. It is anticipated the benefits of such a strategy could flow into health budget savings. As Dann (2001, p. 12) observes:

> If vacations really do benefit the physical and mental health of the elderly, the subsidisation of such trips could not only remove one of the most commonly identified barriers to travel, but might also represent significant savings to the provision of health services for seniors in the home society.

Such a policy redirection would recall the message of the World Tourism Organization *Manila Declaration* (1980) which states that tourism has social, health, community and personal returns which are worth far more than simply the economic returns it generates. As Higgins-Desbiolles (2006, p. 1204) writes:

> I view tourism as a similar sector to health and education.... We somehow know instinctively that education and health are 'invaluable' as they concern people and the public good.... I would advocate a similar attitude to tourism.

There is scope to consider the introduction of the European concept of social tourism into the Australian context. Social tourism supports groups in society who are excluded from taking holidays for economic or health reasons (McCabe *et al.*, 2012). It is an emerging area of policy and practice in Europe where its role in the welfare sector is increasingly seen as 'an investment in the well-being and fabric of society' and one that justifies an investment in stimulus funding (McCabe *et al.*, 2012, p. 186). As Minnaert and colleagues (2011) observe, visitor-related social tourism has a valued role to play in governments' increasing search for flexible, alternate strategies to deliver welfare results.

In the Australian context, an adapted version of social tourism could see the introduction of a voucher system, petrol subsidy or health insurance rebate to encourage short, local holidays for retirees. As one respondent in one of the focus groups in the study observed:

> Over 60s should have subsidised holidays – it would pay in saving to the national health service – just give us a discount in fuel taxes – take off diesel tax.
>
> (Male, retired age not given)

The prerequisite policy models are in place. In 2004 the Australian Labour Party (ALP, 2004; Higgins-Desbiolles, 2006) included social tourism for high school students as part of its policy platform for a Federal election campaign. In a similar vein, although with a direct economic intent, the domestic tourism industry lobbied the Federal Government to mitigate the effects of the global financial crisis by offering tax rebates for Australians to take their leave at home (Rubinsztein-Dunlop, 2009). It is important in any such policy approach that individuals retain some freedom to make their individual tourism choices as a degree of personal control is fundamental to the generation of well-being and any associated welfare benefits (Hall and Brown, 2012).

Other policy options could include the introduction of tourism education for retirees who have limited tourism experience or do not travel at all and are unaware of the psychological benefits travel can offer to maintain, or supplement their well-being. As De Botton (2003, p. 9) observes, 'we are inundated with advice on *where* to travel to, but we hear little of *why* and *how* we should go'.

Conclusions

This study indicates that tourism satisfaction is a significant indicator of life satisfaction and that, importantly, respondents indicate a higher overall level of life satisfaction if they are anticipating holidays. Multiple holidays increase the level of life satisfaction and this finding is independent of both income and perceived health. It is significant that holidays do not have to be extended, international or even national in order for them to contribute to life satisfaction. The potential for multiple cycles of short-term domestic tourism to contribute to well-being has implications for both health and tourism government policy.

It follows that people who do not travel may be limiting their options to maintain their life satisfaction and well-being. This is particularly significant for positive ageing as satisfaction with life, both past and present, is central to any definition of ageing well (Bowling and Dieppe, 2005) and clearly has implications for both psychological as well as physical health (Diener and Seligman, 2004). As the deputy editor of the *British Medical Journal* has written 'Happiness therefore seems to add years to life as well as life to years' (Delamothe, 2005, p. 1490).

The authors do not imply that tourism is the only strategy to maintain well being and encourage flourishing in retirement – indeed research indicates that satisfaction in different life domains combine to predict or promote an overall sense of life satisfaction (Lent *et al.*, 2005). However it is important to find positive reasons for living (Seligman and Csikszentmihalyi, 2000) at all ages and, as humans, we have the capacity to anticipate and to daydream (Seligman, 2012), and tourism offers opportunities to dream and select options from an array of possible futures. As such it allows control over futures and immunisation of our psychological well-being (Seligman, 2012).

As a closing thought, in a contribution to the *British Medical Journal*, one author wrote of the complexities of the (admittedly) final stages of life of an elderly patient with multiple co-morbidities whose main interest was to see her son in Australia before she died (Smith, 2008). Using a telling choice of phrase he wrote:

> She needs a travel agent, not five doctors, but doctors are supplied on the NHS [National Health Service] and travel agents aren't.

Notes

1 The Australian Bureau of Statistics (2006b) refers to people born between 1946 and 1965 as baby boomers.
2 It is acknowledged that people on holiday may be under 'agreeable' obligations such as a partner's choice of destination, however, consistent with the work of Stebbins (2000), it is argued, that, in the main, people on holiday are allowed the essential freedom of choice in how they spend their time away from the habitual patterns of their daily routine.

References

Australian Bureau of Statistics (2006a) *Media Release: First Australian Boomers Reach 60*, www.abs.gov.au [Accessed 16 April 2007].
Australian Bureau of Statistics (2006b) *Australian Social Trends*, cat. no. 4102.0, ABS, Canberra.
Australian Bureau of Statistics (2006c) *Census Data by Topic (Income: Personal, Family and Household)*, www.censusdata.abs.gov.au [Accessed 5 March 2008].
Australian Bureau of Statistics (2011) *Australian Social Trends, Life Expectancy Trends – Australia*, cat. no. 4102.0, ABS, Canberra.
Australian Labour Party Policy Document (2004) *Creating Opportunities for Australian Tourism*, Canberra.
Boehm, J.K., Peterson, C., Kivimaki, M. and Kubzansky, L. (2011a) 'A prospective study of positive psychological well-being and coronary heart disease', *Health Psychology*, 30 (3): 259–267.
Boehm, J.K., Peterson, C., Kivimaki, M. and Kubzansky, L.D. (2011b) 'Heart health when life is satisfying: evidence from the Whitehall II cohort study', *European Heart Journal*, 32: 2672–2677.
Botterill, T.D. (1989) 'Humanistic tourism? Personal constructions of a tourist: Sam visits Japan', *Leisure Studies*, 8 (3): 281–293.
Botterill, T.D. and Crompton, J.L. (2006) 'Two case studies exploring the nature of the tourist's experience', *Journal of Leisure Research*, 28 (1): 57–82.
Bowling, A. and Dieppe, P. (2005) 'What is successful ageing and who should define it?' *British Medical Journal*, 331: 1548–1551.
Bryant, F.B. (2003) 'Savoring beliefs inventory (SBI): a scale for measuring beliefs about savoring', *Journal of Mental Health*, 12 (2): 175–196.
Clawson, M. and Knetsch, J. (1966) *Economics of Outdoor Recreation*. Baltimore: John Hopkins Press.
Dann, G.M.S. (2001) 'Senior tourism and the quality of life', *Journal of Hospitality and Leisure Marketing*, 9 (1–2): 5–19.
De Botton, A. (2003) *The Art of Travel*. London: Penguin.
Delamothe, T. (2005) 'Happiness', *British Medical Journal*, 3331: 1489–1490.

Desforges, L. (2000) 'Traveling the world: identity and travel biography', *Annals of Tourism Research*, 27 (4): 926–945.

Diener, E. and Seligman, M.E.P. (2004) 'Beyond money: toward an economy of well-being', *Psychological Science in the Public Interest*, 5 (1): 1–31.

Diener, E., Suh, E.M., Lucas, R.E. and Smith, H.L. (1999) 'Subjective well-being: three decades of progress', *Psychological Bulletin*, 125 (2): 267–302.

Dolnicar, S., Yanamandram, V. and Cliff, K. (2012) 'The contribution of vacations to quality of life', *Annals of Tourism Research*, 39 (1): 59–83.

Durrell, L. (1970) *Bitter Lemons*. London: Faber.

Forgeard, M.J.C., Jayawickreme, E., Kern, M.L. and Seligman, M.E.P. (2011) 'Doing the right thing: measuring well-being for public policy', *International Journal of Wellbeing*, 1 (1): 79–106.

Fredrickson, B.L. (2000) 'Extracting meaning from past affective experiences: the importance of peaks, ends, and specific emotions', *Cognition and Emotion*, 14 (4): 577–606.

Gump, B.B. and Matthews, K.A. (2000) 'Are vacations good for your health? The 9-year mortality experience after the multiple risk factor intervention trial', *Psychosomatic Medicine*, 62 (5): 608–612.

Hagger, J.C. (2009) 'The impact of tourism experiences on post retirement life satisfaction', PhD thesis, University of South Australia, Adelaide, Australia.

Hall, D. and Brown, F. (2012) 'The welfare society and tourism: European perspectives', in McCabe, S., Minnaert, L. and Diekmann, A. (eds), *Social Tourism in Europe: Theory and Practice*. Bristol: Channel View Publications, pp. 108–118.

Higgins-Desbiolles, F. (2006) 'More than an "industry": the forgotten power of tourism as a social force', *Tourism Management*, 27 (6): 1192–1208.

Hsu, C.H.C., Cai, L.A. and Wong, K.K.F. (2007) 'A model of senior tourism motivations: anecdotes from Beijing and Shanghai', *Tourism Management*, 28 (5): 1262–1273.

Hugo, G. (2003) 'Australia's ageing population', *Australian Planner*, 40 (2): 109–118.

Hunter-Jones, P. (2003) 'The perceived effects of holiday-taking upon the health and well-being of patients treated for cancer', *International Journal of Tourism Research*, 32 (1): 70–92.

Hunter-Jones, P. (2005) 'Cancer and tourism', *Annals of Tourism Research*, 32 (1): 70–92.

IPSOS Mackay Report (2005) *Whither the Boomers?* Report No. 117, North Sydney, Ipsos Australia, NSW.

Judge, T.A., Bono, J.E., Erez, A. and Locke, E.A. (2005) 'Core self-evaluations and job and life satisfaction: the role of self-concordance and goal attainment', *Journal of Applied Psychology*, 90 (2): 257–268.

Kelly, G.A. (1955) *The Psychology of Personal Constructs*. New York: Norton.

Kelly, G.A. (1991) *The Psychology of Personal Constructs, Volume One: a Theory of Personality*. London: Routledge.

Kendig, H. (2004) 'Keynote session: the social sciences and successful aging – issues for Asia-Oceania', *Geriatrics and Gerontology International*, 4 (1): S6–S11.

Kim, E.S., Sun, J.K., Park, N., Kubzansky, L.D. and Peterson, C. (2012) 'Purpose in life and reduced risk of myocardial infarction among older US adults with coronary heart disease: a two-year follow-up', *Journal of Behavioral Medicine*, published online 23 February 2012 (online Springer).

Koizumi, M., Ito, H., Kaneko, Y. and Motohashi, Y. (2008) 'Effect of having a sense of purpose in life on the risk of death from cardiovascular diseases', *Journal of Epidemiology*, 18 (5): 191–196.

Larsen, S. (2006) 'The psychology of the tourist experience: expectations, events and memories', paper presented to 16th Council of Australian University Tourism and Hospitality Education (CAUTHE) Conference, Melbourne, 1499–1506.

Larsen, S. (2007) 'Aspects of a psychology of the tourist experience', *Scandinavian Journal of Hospitality and Tourism*, 7 (1): 7–18.

Lengkeek, J. (2001) 'Leisure experiences and imagination: rethinking Cohen's models of tourist experience', *International Sociology*, 165 (2): 173–184.

Lent, R.W., Singley, D., Sheu, H., Gainor, K.A., Brenner, B.R., Triestman, D. and Ades, L. (2005) 'Social cognitive predictors of domain and life satisfaction: exploring the theoretical precursors of subjective well-being', *Journal of Counselling Psychology*, 53 (3): 429–442.

Lyubomirsky, S., Sousa, L. and Dickerhoof, R. (2006) 'The costs and benefits of writing, talking and thinking about life's triumphs and defeats', *Journal of Personality and Social Psychology*, 90 (4): 692–708.

McCabe, S., Minnaert, L. and Diekmann, A. (2012) *Social Tourism in Europe: Theory and Practice*. Bristol: Channel View Publications.

MacCannell, D. (2001) 'Remarks on the commodification of cultures', in Smith, V.L. and Brent, M. (eds), *Hosts and Guests Revisited: Tourism Issues of the 21st Century*. New York: Cognizant Communications Corporation, pp. 380–390.

Minnaert, L., Maitland, R. and Miller, G. (2011) 'What is social tourism?' *Current Issues in Tourism*, 14 (5): 403–415.

Mitchell, T.R., Thompson, L., Peterson, E. and Cronk, R. (1997) 'Temporal adjustments in the evaluation of events: the "Rosy View"', *Journal of Experimental Social Psychology*, 33 (4): 421–448.

Nawijn, J., Marchand, M.A., Veenhoven, R. and Vingerhoets, A.J. (2010) 'Vacationers happier, but most not happier after a holiday', *Applied Research Quality Life*, 5: 35–47.

Neal, J.D., Sirgy, M.J. and Ulysal, M. (1999) 'The role of satisfaction with leisure travel/tourism services and experiences in satisfaction with leisure life and overall life', *Journal of Business Research*, 44 (3): 153–163.

Nimrod, G. (2007) 'Retirees' leisure: activities, benefits and their contribution to life satisfaction', *Leisure Studies*, 26 (1): 65–80.

Oliver, R.L. (1997) *Satisfaction: A Behavioural Perspective on the Consumer*. New York: McGraw Hill.

Onyx, J. and Leonard, R. (2005) 'Australian grey nomads and American snowbirds: similarities and differences', *The Journal of Tourism Studies*, 16 (1): 61–68.

Patrickson, M. and Ranzijn, R. (2004) 'Bounded choices in work and retirement in Australia', *Employee Relations*, 26 (4): 422–432.

Patterson, I. (2006) *Growing Older: Tourism and Leisure Behaviour of Older Adults*. Cambridge, MA: CABI International.

Pearce, P.L. (2005) *Tourist Behaviour: Themes and Conceptual Schemes*. Clevedon: Channel View Publications.

Pearce, P., Filep, S. and Ross, G. (2011) *Tourists, Tourism and the Good Life*. New York: Routledge.

Pocock, B. (2003) *The Work/Life Collision*. Annadale: The Federation Press.

Pocock, B. (2006) *The Labour Market Ate my Babies: Work, Children and a Sustainable Future*. Annadale: The Federation Press.

Ranzijn, R. (2002) 'Towards a positive psychology of ageing: potentials and barriers', *Australian Psychologist*, 37 (2): 79–85.

Rubinsztein-Dunlop, S. (2009) *Pay Aussies to Holiday at Home: Tourism Groups*, ABC,

Media Release, 12 January, www.abc.net.au/news/stories/2009 [Accessed 14 January 2009].
Ryan, C. (1995) 'Learning about tourists from conversations: the over 55s in Majorca', *Tourism Management*, 16 (3): 207–215.
Schimmack, U., Radhakrishnan, P., Oishi, S. and Dzokoto, V. (2002) 'Culture, personality, and subjective well-being: integrating process models of life satisfaction', *Journal of Personality and Social Psychology*, 82 (4): 582–593.
Seligman, M.E.P. (2008) 'Positive health', *Applied Psychology: An International Review*, 57: 3–18.
Seligman, M.E.P. (2012) 'The science of wellbeing – more than the absence of illness', Key note address presented at the Adelaide Thinker in Residence Conference, Adelaide, 24 February.
Seligman, M.E.P. and Csikszentmihalyi, M. (2000) 'Positive psychology: an introduction', *American Psychologist*, 55 (1): 5–14.
Sheldon, K.M. and Elliot, A.J. (1999) 'Goal striving, need satisfaction and longitudinal well-being: the self-concordance model', *Journal of Personality and Social Psychology*, 76 (3): 482–497.
Sirgy, M.J., Kruger, P.S., Lee, D. and Yu, G.B. (2011) 'How does a travel trip affect tourists' life satisfaction?', *Journal of Travel Research*, 50 (3): 261–275.
Smith, R. (2008) 'The end of disease and the beginning of health', *British Medical Journal Blogs*, 8 July 2008 [Accessed 19 September 2011].
Stebbins, R.A. (2000) 'Obligation as an aspect of leisure experience', *Journal of Leisure Research*, 32 (1): 152–155.
Stebbins, R.A. (2001) 'Serious leisure', *Society*, 38 (4): 53–57.
Wells, Y.D. and Kendig, H.L. (1999) 'Psychological resources and successful retirement', *Australian Psychologist*, 34 (2): 111–115.
World Tourism Organization (1980) *Manila Declaration on World Tourism*, www.world-tourism.org [Accessed 15 December 2008].
Yau, M.K., McKercher, B. and Packer, T.L. (2004) 'Travelling with a disability: more than an access issue', *Annals of Tourism Research*, 31 (4): 946–960.

12 Visitors' restorative experiences in museum and botanic garden environments

Jan Packer

Introduction to the concept of restoration

The concept of restoration has received considerable attention in the environmental psychology literature, although its roots can be traced to early psychological theories of attention, and clinical neurological studies of mental functioning (Kaplan, 1995). It focuses on the human need for rest and recuperation, recovery from mental fatigue and renewal of diminished capabilities (Hartig, 2004; Kaplan *et al.*, 1998). Restorative experiences are those that facilitate recovery from mental fatigue and help us continue to meet the demands of everyday life. Such experiences, many of which take place within the context of tourism and leisure, have the potential to contribute to the well-being and satisfaction of those who engage in them. The study of such experiences is thus highly relevant to the field of positive psychology. Indeed, restorative experiences have been shown to lead to improved emotional and cognitive functioning (Hartig *et al.*, 2003), and thus to mental health and well-being benefits for both individuals and communities.

Most of the existing research in this area has been conducted within the framework of Attention Restoration Theory (Kaplan, 1995; Kaplan and Kaplan, 1989). According to this theory, the capacity to continually focus attention on a particular activity can be reduced or lost through mental exhaustion. This state, referred to as 'directed attention fatigue', can result in irritability, anxiety, anger, frustration, mental and physical fatigue, diminished ability to perform cognitive tasks, and increased likelihood of errors in performance. In order to fully recover from directed attention fatigue, it is important that the individual's attention is engaged involuntarily or effortlessly, rather than intentionally. While the individual is engaged in involuntary attention or 'fascination', the effort involved in inhibiting distractions can be relaxed, and directed attention can be rested (Kaplan, 1995). Fascination (being engaged without effort) is thus one of four components that have been identified as integral to a restorative experience. The other three components are a sense of being away (being physically or mentally removed from one's everyday environment); the perception of extent (the environment provides enough to see, experience and think about to sufficiently engage the mind); and compatibility (providing a good fit with one's purposes or inclinations) (Kaplan and Kaplan, 1989; Kaplan, 1995). Research suggests that even short periods of time spent in a restorative environment can have significant effects on both cognitive capacity and quality of life (Cimprich, 1993).

Research on mental restoration has concentrated primarily on natural environments, which are generally perceived and experienced as more restorative than urban environments (Hartig and Staats, 2003; Kaplan, 1995; Ulrich, 1979, 1984). Despite the predominance of research in natural settings, however, there is evidence that some urban or built environments provide the attributes necessary for a restorative experience, and thus have the ability to 'create a sense of peace and calm that enables people to recover their cognitive and emotional effectiveness' (Kaplan *et al.*, 1993, p. 726).

The role of tourism and leisure in contributing to restorative experiences

Previous research suggests that the need or desire for restoration is an important motivation underlying engagement in tourism and leisure experiences (Iso-Ahola, 1980; Packer and Ballantyne, 2002; Pearce and Lee, 2005; Snepenger *et al.*, 2006). Early studies of tourism motivation (e.g. Hill, 1965; Crompton, 1979) identified the need for restoration or replenishment as an underlying motive for going on a vacation. When a vacation is not possible, this need may also be met in other kinds of activities. For example, according to Scopelliti and Giuliani (2004), visiting a museum and taking a walk in a park are among a range of activities people undertake in order to regain well-being and effectiveness in their everyday activities. Packer and Bond (2010) explored the restorative qualities and benefits of four types of tourism and leisure environments – a history museum, an art museum, an aquarium and a botanic garden – using quantitative measures drawn from Attention Restoration Theory literature (Laumann *et al.*, 2001; Staats *et al.*, 2003; Ouellette *et al.*, 2005). They found that, although visitors generally considered the history museum the least restorative, and the botanic garden the most restorative, each site attracted some people who visited predominantly for its restorative value.

Studies by Korpela and colleagues (Korpela and Hartig, 1996; Korpela *et al.*, 2008) suggest that many people have favourite places to which they become particularly attached, and to which they go to relax, calm down or clear their minds. These places include nature areas, waterside environments, green spaces and exercise areas, and are often perceived as being high in restorative attributes. Frequent visitors to particular types of sites, including natural environments, parks and gardens, museums and galleries, are more likely than infrequent visitors to consider these sites restorative (Packer and Bond, 2010). This has implications for tourism and leisure providers. By understanding and managing the environmental factors that support or encourage restorative experiences, tourism and leisure providers can better ensure that these needs are met, not only for local visitors but also for tourists. Tourists who maintain a hectic pace of visitation and rush from site to site trying to 'see it all', may well benefit from an attraction that enables them to slow down and recover their capacity for directed attention, while also qualifying as one of the destination's 'must see' tourism experiences. Museums, galleries and botanic gardens often provide such opportunities. When tourism and leisure providers consider visitors' needs in this way and attend to the details that result in visitor satisfaction, they are likely to add value to the 'total customer experience' (Schmitt, 2003).

Restorative experiences in museums and botanic gardens: a qualitative analysis

Previous research has demonstrated that museums, galleries and gardens are places where you can be engaged without effort, become absorbed in your surroundings, forget about the everyday stresses and strains of life and experience restorative outcomes such as feeling calm or peaceful, and renewing the ability to deal positively with life (Kaplan *et al.*, 1993; Packer, 2006, 2008; Packer and Bond, 2010). This chapter further explores restorative experiences at a history museum and botanic garden, using qualitative analyses of semi-structured interviews. The aim was to identify, from the visitors' perspective, the circumstances that facilitate and enhance restorative experiences in these contexts, and the ways in which visitors experience the restorative processes identified in other literature.

A total of 40 interviews were conducted with visitors to the Queensland Museum and Mt Coot-tha Botanic Gardens, both of which are located in Brisbane, Australia. Interviews of approximately 10–20 minutes were conducted, on both weekdays and weekends, with either individuals (ten at the museum and nine at the gardens) or couples who had visited together (nine at the museum and 12 at the gardens). Table 12.1 illustrates the kinds of questions

Table 12.1 Semi-structured interview questions

1	What was your main reason for coming today: to learn and discover something new; to spend time with friends or family; to relax and recover from the stresses of life; or to have something enjoyable to do?
2	Do you often visit museums/botanic gardens?
3	Did you find this visit relaxing? What was it about the visit that helped you to relax and/or recover? For example, is there something about the physical environment, or about other people, or something else about coming here for a visit?
4	Did you have a feeling of peace or calm during the visit? What parts of your visit helped you to feel calm or peaceful?
5	Were there things here that really drew you in, or captured your attention?
6	Did you feel like you were able to lose yourself in another world?
7	Did the visit help to make you more thoughtful or reflective about things? What parts of your visit helped you to be thoughtful or reflective?
8	Do you now feel refreshed and better able to concentrate on things? What parts of your visit helped you to feel refreshed and better able to concentrate?
9	Think of a place that really helps you to relax and unwind. What would your ideal place be? How does this place compare to your ideal?

that were asked, although it should be noted that points of interest introduced by the respondents were followed up in greater depth as they arose, and thus the interviews did not all follow exactly the same pattern. Aspects contributing to restorative experiences were extracted by thematic analysis of responses to questions 3–8. These analyses were conducted separately for museum and gardens visitors, but were integrated at the reporting stage to enable the similarities and differences between sites to be identified. Excerpts from individual interviewees are identified using *M* for museum visitors and *G* for gardens visitors. Wherever possible, excerpts from both tourists and local residents are provided.

Previous quantitative research suggests that botanic gardens visitors are more likely to visit specifically for the purpose of restoration than museum visitors (Ballantyne *et al.*, 2008), and the interview responses confirmed this trend. 'To relax and recover' was selected as the main reason for visiting in 16 per cent of museum interviews and 43 per cent of gardens interviews. Interviewees at both sites included a mixture of frequent and occasional visitors, and a mixture of local visitors and tourists. Botanic gardens visitors were more likely to be frequent visitors who lived locally while museum visitors were more likely to be tourists. However at both sites, the majority of respondents indicated that they liked to visit museums/botanic gardens whenever they travelled away from home.

Most interviewees agreed that their visit had been relaxing and identified a range of environmental features that they felt had contributed to (or in some cases detracted from) their ability to experience various aspects of restoration, including feeling relaxed, calm, engaged, absorbed and refreshed. The following presentation of the results of the qualitative analysis explores: (1) the environmental features that visitors identified as supporting restoration, under the headings Physical environment, Sensory environment, Social environment, Cognitive environment and Temporal environment; (2) the ways in which processes of fascination, being away, extent and compatibility are embedded within museum and botanic gardens environments; and (3) visitors' accounts of the restoration outcomes they experienced (see Figure 12.1).

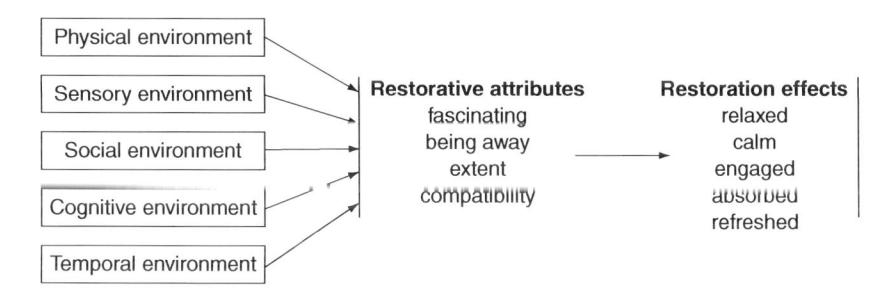

Figure 12.1 Environments, restorative attributes and restorative effects.

Environmental features that support restoration

Physical environment

Most respondents, in both the museum and botanic gardens, identified features of the physical environment that had enhanced their ability to relax and recover. Museum visitors often described features that averted negative responses by helping them not to feel confined, confused, cluttered, busy or over-stimulated, while gardens visitors focused more on features that created a positive sense of calm. In both the museum and the gardens, it seemed important to have a balance between open spaces and more private or secluded areas that visitors could escape to. This is consistent with the environmental preferences literature (e.g. Kaplan, 1987), which points to the human need for both understanding (being able to make sense of the scene) and exploration (being attracted by something complex or mysterious); for both prospect (having an overview of the landscape) and refuge (having a safe place to hide). Visitors' comments provide some evidence of these underlying preferences. The need for the physical environment to support both rest and low levels of activity was also noted.

An open or spacious environment averts feelings of confinement:

> We were just commenting on how relaxing it is, you know, that exhibits are quite large so you don't feel you're confined ... it's very wide, very open, there isn't a sense of clutter. There's good space between the exhibits ... I think the environment is very important ... it's spacious, it's airy, you don't feel hemmed in, you have no sense of claustrophobia within it, you know, it's extremely relaxing.
>
> (M17, tourist)

> Outside it's not claustrophobic, you've plenty of space.
>
> (G4, tourist)

A layout that provides areas of escape reduces noise, creates a sense of being away and suggests that there are interesting spaces to explore:

> I like how there are separate rooms for everything where you can go and that is a little bit quieter. Away from the mainstream of where everyone is. Which is really nice and it does make it more relaxing ... it takes you away from the busy mainstream corridors, which is nice because it tones the noise level down and you can actually relax and enjoy what you are looking at.
>
> (M1, local resident visiting alone)

> I thought that the layout and the design of the exhibits was very interesting because ... they enclosed you so that when you were in that place, there was nothing else that you were kind of looking at and wondering should I go here ... even though you were enclosed, you were spaced.
>
> (M17, tourist)

I also like the rainforest and the really big trees and lots of hiding places. Some open spaces but then again some hiding places ... where children in particular, but anyone can just go and sort of dive into a little cave somewhere.

(G11, local resident)

Visitors appreciated the provision of rest areas:

The little seated areas outside of the actual exhibits were a very good idea ... the fact that you had somewhere to sit down was quite relaxing.

(M17, tourist)

To feel welcome, having chairs there so you can sit, feeling like you don't have to be there just to see the things and get out, you know ... having couches and cushions there is great.

(M19, local resident)

Just being able to sit down on the grass and watch the day go by and watch what everyone else is doing and all the animals.

(G4, tourist)

As visitors considered walking to be conducive to relaxation, an environment that facilitated ease of movement and way-finding was most likely to be compatible with visitors' needs:

You didn't really have to think about where you were going next because it is laid out quite well.

(M9, tourist)

There's all these native plants and trees up there so we'll go walking in there and it's just a time to wind down, I suppose.

(G11, local resident)

Sensory environment

Both museum and gardens visitors referred to aspects of aesthetics, colours, sounds, lighting and motion as contributors to the restorative experience. In this regard, there were strong similarities between the two sites, although again there was a tendency for museum visitors to talk about the lack or amelioration of negative influences and for gardens visitors to talk about the presence of calming influences. To create a relaxing sensory environment, visitors seem to prefer low levels of noise, light and motion. Of course, designers often intentionally use light, sound and colour to create specific effects for their own purposes. However in doing so, they need to be aware that they may be spoiling the experience for some visitors who have a totally different agenda for their visit.

Aesthetic elements were often associated with restorative experiences:

> We often say when you sit somewhere that's beautiful, it's good for your mental well-being.
>
> (G3, tourist)

> I like the simplicity and just the tranquillity of all this, but particularly the Japanese section ... it's just beautiful. Relaxing, calm and they've got an elegance about their design, it's simple and effective I think ... a lot of thought goes into their design ... they design it to be relaxing and it works for me.
>
> (G14, local resident)

Visitors commented on the influence of colour on their feelings of relaxation:

> I felt very relaxed in there, just that sort of feeling of, you know, the jellyfish sort of floating in the water. I thought that was nice ... the colours, the blue on the walls, and the way it was set out.
>
> (M12, tourist)

> The environment, because it's green. I think I'm a colour person ... I react strongly I think to colours and it's a very colourful place.
>
> (G7, local resident visiting alone)

> There's red walls down there that I find really kind of irritating.... Red and black is like really angry kind of colours, don't you think, and a yellow wall ... it's like warning signs, those colours.
>
> (M19, local resident)

Quiet environments were experienced as relaxing. Noisy environments introduce distractions and require effort in order to maintain directed attention. Tourists in particular appreciated the opportunity to find respite in a quiet place:

> I find the whole place really relaxing when you walk in, it just gives you that feeling ... this is very quiet, there's lots of people around, but you wouldn't know, it was very relaxing.
>
> (M4, day tripper)

> The noise levels were certainly conducive to being able to experience the exhibits without any distractions.
>
> (M16, tourist visiting alone)

> It's nice and quiet like.... It's just so peaceful. There are no distractions around or anything. It's just really relaxed. There's no one bothering you and no traffic or any of that.
>
> (G4, tourist)

We've been in Sydney and Brisbane now and it's nice to come somewhere where it's a lot quieter. Because even the coastal areas, they can be very busy and quite hectic ... so here's the first place where it has been really, really quiet and it's just nice to come here and relax.

(G9, tourist)

Peaceful sounds, however, were also seen as a positive aspect of the sensory environment. Treasure (2007) suggests that natural sounds such as wind, water and birdsong are not only aesthetically pleasing, but restful because of their associations with life and safety:

The high ceilings, so there's kind of a dull murmur that kind of happens ... I like the sound of it, the big open feel, the quiet feel.

(M19, local resident)

I'm sitting here listening to the bamboo clunking away.

(G16, local resident visiting alone)

You can hear the flow of the water there, that's very relaxing too, water flowing is a very meditating type experience, isn't it?

(G18, local resident)

Just the tranquillity of it all, the peacefulness ... it's all quite therapeutic I think and also the sound of nature, the birds, the ducks, all of that and the trees and the wind.

(G3, tourist)

Much like low noise levels, subdued lighting was experienced as relaxing as it reduced the distractions caused by high intensity light (including sunlight). Visitors preferred lighting levels that were neither too bright nor too dark:

I think it was the lighting that really gets to you. It is very soothing.

(M1, local resident visiting alone)

I just think it's the lack of intensity of light.... In a lot of museums that we would be used to visiting, the light is very intense and you get very sweaty and hot and you want to be out. I just think that the whole ethos here, the whole environment here is one that induces a kind of calmness.

(M17, tourist)

So just sitting in the shade and looking at the water.

(G7, local resident visiting alone)

Stillness creates a positive feeling of calm and supports a sense of being away, both physically and psychologically:

> I guess the water more than anything else.... The stillness. It's not moving. It's calm,... There is nothing interfering with it so I don't feel like there is anything interfering with me.
>
> (G19, tourist)

> Nature is settling for the mind. I think we need natural influences around us to stay relaxed I suppose. You can have too much motion around you, I think that may be part of it.
>
> (G18, local resident)

Within limits, however, gentle motion engages the visitors' attention and supports a sense of fascination or engagement without effort:

> I like this area, watching the ducks ... just sitting watching these ducks going along.
>
> (G13, local resident)

> The birds and when you see the turtle every now and again pop his head up.
>
> (G15, local resident)

> The waterfalls they pump up the hill and it all runs back, I like them ... they're just moving, watering the trees.
>
> (G17, local resident visiting alone)

Social environment

Aspects of the social environment were noted as either contributing to or detracting from the restorative experience. Interviewees spoke of observing others, avoiding or escaping others, but at the same time needing others. Although a sense of psychologically 'being away' often included escaping or avoiding other people, no-one wanted or expected to be completely alone. The need to feel safe and secure emerged as another possible distraction which, if not addressed, prevented visitors from fully engaging in a restorative experience. On balance, the presence of other people in the environment appeared to be a positive factor for most people, unless through their behaviour or numbers they became a distracting influence that disturbed the restorative process.

Observing other people relaxing and enjoying themselves contributed to creating an environment conducive to restoration:

> It kind of makes it that little bit better because you see all the kids enjoying actually learning which is quite nice.
>
> (M1, local resident visiting alone)

> There's not people rushing around everywhere and everyone's sort of moving at the same pace.
>
> (M12, tourist)

Restoration in museums and botanic gardens 211

> There's a nice atmosphere around ... everybody here is relaxed and just chilling.
>
> (G4, tourist)

> I like watching people enjoying themselves here too ... people look very content and no one's rushing out of the place.
>
> (G7, local resident visiting alone)

Escaping or avoiding others was, for many visitors, a necessary part of being away and thus contributed to the restorative process. When such escape was not possible due to overcrowding or lack of behavioural control, visitors reported feeling distracted or even stressed:

> Wouldn't it be nice if they had an adults only sort of time where you could go to the museum and actually explore without children getting in your way and touching things they're not meant to touch ... It can get stressful if there's too many kids and they're just naughty all the time.
>
> (M7, tourist)

> No one hassles you or annoys you ... yeah, it's relaxing.
>
> (M10, day tripper visiting alone)

> We're trying to get away from people basically.
>
> (G6, local resident)

> You can always find a spot where there is no-one there and just sit there and enjoy the time.
>
> (G8, local resident visiting alone)

Some visitors, however, acknowledged needing other people to provide a sense of belonging and security. This is consistent with Herzog and Rector's (2009) finding that the perception of danger reduced the judged likelihood of restoration:

> I can sit by myself but have people around – that's why museums are nice for this. It's ideal for me. There's people around so I can do a little people watching, but I can sit and do my own thing.
>
> (M19, local resident)

> There are people around ... people are around you so if you are on your own you don't feel lonely or anything ... you can come here and feel part of the world.
>
> (G13, local resident)

> It's nice to have a space big enough so that you can get away on your own in the world, in the environment, in creation, but without sort of feeling

isolated, as such, in terms of personal safety and vulnerability ... So the fact that there is still a smattering of people within cooee but then I can have a bit open space essentially to myself.

(G16, local resident visiting alone)

I think as a tourist and walking about the city you're always thinking about your bag. Whereas in here it does feel a bit more secure ... because it's not a busy place.

(G9, tourist)

Cognitive environment

At both the museum and the gardens, the provision of information was considered an important element in facilitating engagement. Visitors did not see cognitive activity as antithetical to a relaxing, restorative experience. However, in order for such engagement to occur without effort, and so allow directed attention to recover, the style of information presentation should facilitate ease of comprehension. Information needs to be provided carefully and 'gently' so that it is easily digested and appropriately structured. In particular, the availability of choices allows visitors to engage to their preferred extent, without feeling 'attacked' by the information.

Information should be easy to digest:

> Well I like it if you can just look at something that doesn't have too much to read and yet you still feel you've got something out of it ... you could digest it quickly ... you just wander and look and then you find interesting things. So that's just nice and relaxing.
>
> (M12, tourist)

> Just looking and just gently receiving information ... not like when you study and it's information overload.
>
> (M20, local resident)

Information should be appropriately structured:

> Normally when you look at a panel they can be very detailed and they can be distracting and tiring. But what I found about the panels I looked at, is I could absorb quite a lot without necessarily having to read on, that the information that was contained in the opening paragraph or two was sufficient to give you a flavour.
>
> (M17, tourist)

> It's very well planned out, everything sort of flows into one another. I mean if you want to take time to read the signs they are there, but they're not in your face.
>
> (G19, tourist)

Variety and choice are important to visitors:

> There's lots of stuff to look at and lots of things to read but it wasn't like overwhelming right in your face, you could sort of make your way over to something or you could completely bypass something if you didn't want to, didn't feel like it was attacking you.
>
> (M9, tourist)

> This is a natural tendency to want to read, if I choose to read the things ... Because I think human nature, anything that you feel you're doing because you want to do it, you take a whole different attitude towards [than if you] have to do it. This is like a treat.
>
> (G7, local resident visiting alone)

Temporal environment

Time pressures act as another possible distraction that threatens to disrupt the restorative process. Visitors talked of the importance of making time for the visit, being able to determine their own pace and losing track of time. Tourists in particular found it difficult to escape the tyranny of time. Although time issues are generally under the control of visitors themselves rather than designers and managers, it may be possible for designers and managers to influence visitor expectations regarding what is achievable or recommended during a short visit, and to educate visitors about the need for restorative experiences and how they might be achieved within a particular site.

Making time for the visit enabled visitors to experience the site without being hurried or rushed, and was thus an important component of being away:

> I believe when you come to a museum ... that you make sure you have time to do it, at your own leisure.
>
> (M11, tourist visiting alone)

> We're not in a hurry at all. I think it has an influence on you, that you do come in and just spend as much time as you want; there's no rush about the place.
>
> (G9, tourist)

When time could not be forgotten, for example, for tourists on a tight schedule, it detracted from the restorative process:

> I wanted to catch as much of things that I can while I am in the city. So I definitely had in the back of my mind what is the better use of my time, to go to a different museum or stay in this one. That is [why I] chose to rush through things I wanted to see.
>
> (M2, tourist)

> There's just so much to see that if you stop and read some things, you won't get time to even look at the other things.
>
> (M9, tourist)

Visitors appreciated not only being unhurried, but also being able to exercise some control over their own pace:

> You can do it at your own pace.... It does relax you because you can go at your own pace so you do not have to go a million miles an hour.
>
> (M1, local resident visiting alone)

> There was no one to rush you along, so that was really good ... I certainly wouldn't have loved to be with a group, with a guide saying well here you go, this is this and then say come on we're going to the next exhibition.
>
> (M13, tourist visiting alone)

> If you want to spend time by yourself and not feel you're being rushed out of the place or anything, you can kind of take your time ... I guess because nobody here is really rushing around.
>
> (G19, tourist)

Losing track of time, which is also a characteristic of the 'flow' experience (Csikszentmihalyi and Rathunde, 1993), was reported in this context as part of a 'being away' experience:

> Sometimes I get a bit engrossed in this sort of thing and read a lot ... I just suddenly had a thought that I didn't know how long I had been here ... I'd lost track of time. So I wasn't sure if I'd been here half an hour or two hours.
>
> (M4, day tripper)

> Well I've probably been here, wow, probably two hours, I didn't even know ... I was unaware of the time.
>
> (M11, tourist visiting alone)

> What I find here is that it's not so much that time goes quickly, it's that I'm not aware of the passing of time ... in the time that I'm here, it's a sense of being away from time and the hassles that that creates.
>
> (G1, local resident)

Restorative attributes in museum and botanic garden environments

Visitors' comments provided confirmatory evidence that the restorative attributes or components identified in the literature, mainly in relation to natural environments, can also operate in these tourism and leisure sites. As outlined above, these include *fascination* or being engaged without effort; a sense of *being away* from one's everyday environment; the perception that the *extent* of the environment is sufficient to engage the mind; and a sense of *compatibility* between one's purposes or inclinations and the affordances of the environment. Although only a few interview excerpts are presented below to illustrate these processes, words like 'taking my mind off', 'being away', and 'entering another world' were quite common throughout the interviews.

Fascination

Visitors explained that because they were focused on the objects or elements within the environment they were able to 'take their mind off' other things:

> If you're in a museum looking at stuff and reading the text about all these things, then you're absorbed in that, you're not thinking about other stuff.
> (M7, tourist)

Being away

Visitors talked about how their visit was like entering a completely different world. They were able to switch off or leave behind the outside world, adopt a different frame of mind and lose themselves in their own thoughts. Both local residents and tourists felt the need for such periods of respite:

> I just lose myself, I'm in a totally different frame of mind ... when I come in here I leave the outside world outside.... It just refreshes my mind ... when I come in here, I put everything to the back of my mind and I just shut everything out and when I come here I feel really relaxed.
> (M18, city worker visiting alone)

> It's like ... a little quiet oasis that's in the midst of all that busyness ... a little magical land in the middle of all that hustle and bustle that you can just sort of step into and take a deep breath before you go back and join it all again.
> (G16, local resident visiting alone)

> Just to get away from it, there are only so many buildings you can see in a day. You kind of need to get away for a while.
> (G19, tourist)

Extent

Both museum and gardens visitors mentioned the need for an environment that was big enough to be able to spend a reasonable amount of time in, without feeling that you had exhausted the possibilities. For some visitors, this was more noticeable when it was absent:

It just was not enough to keep me ... There just was not the quantity of things.

(M2, tourist visiting alone)

There are [other] little parks where it's not quite the same ... when there's a bigger place to walk around, you can spend more time here.

(G15, local resident)

Compatibility

The idea of compatibility was perhaps the least frequently mentioned of the four restorative attributes. In most tourism and leisure contexts, people choose which site they will visit based on its compatibility with their needs. The issue then becomes one of whether or not the site meets their expectations. Providing a range of experiences within the site is one way to increase the likelihood of compatibility with the needs of individual visitors.

It's what we wanted to see and we enjoy it and I suppose that sort of makes it relaxing.

(M4, day tripper)

There's lots of ways of looking at things and people have different perspectives on what they want to do and what suits them.... Depends on what you're looking for at the time, you know, you probably select something that may calm you I think.

(G18, local resident)

Visitors' accounts of the restoration experience

The ways in which visitors described the restoration-related outcomes of their visit was noticeably different for museum and gardens visitors and are reported separately below.

Only a minority of museum visitors reported feeling 'relaxed' or 'calm' as a result of their visit. Some who had arrived feeling tired or upset felt refreshed or soothed by the visit. One tourist (see M7 on the following page) felt more energised and ready to continue his sight-seeing schedule. Some visitors reported that the visit had led them to reflect more deeply on issues. This, according to some theorists, is one of the benefits of a restorative experience (Herzog *et al.*, 2003), but was not necessarily recognised as such by visitors themselves.

I was tired when I got here and I thought, 'Do I really want to go in there and walk around?' but now I feel heaps better.

(M1, local resident visiting alone)

It's very calming for me and yeah I feel really good ... I've been lifted up ... I actually do feel a lot more refreshed.

(M18, city worker visiting alone)

> Before we came in here we were sort of quite tired and my legs were aching and I was thinking, 'Oh I'm not going to bother going anywhere else', but now I'm actually raring to go visit other places.
>
> (M7, tourist)

> I kind of like to dwell on what I've seen or think about what I've seen ... I don't have to meet anyone, so I don't have any communication to break my line of thought.
>
> (M11, tourist visiting alone)

Botanic gardens visitors reported a much broader and richer set of restorative outcomes. They talked about being relaxed, refreshed and rejuvenated, about de-stressing, slowing down and getting in touch with themselves. They reported a deeper sense of inner peace and contentment, greater energy, and a new perspective on life. A number of visitors mentioned that they now felt more ready to return to their everyday life with a new sense of energy, creativity or inspiration.

> Just de-stressing, just sort of slowing your mind down, taking a big deep breath.
>
> (G16, local resident visiting alone)

> It gives me a real calmness ... you're looking for that peacefulness, that peace within and ... you know you've got to quiet yourself and still yourself and I found that you can do that here, you can still your soul.
>
> (G2, local resident)

> I think it just makes you go at a slower pace. It slows you down ... it just puts a different perspective on the busy-ness of the world ... I know some things I've got to do today, but because I've come here I feel that I will do those things more likely than had I just gone home and thought, 'Gees I don't want to do those things'.
>
> (G7, local resident visiting alone)

> I suppose I've taken a little rest, when you leave the place you feel ready to rush around again.
>
> (G19, tourist)

Conclusion

The aim of this study was to explore, from the perspective of visitors, the circumstances that facilitate and enhance restorative experiences in tourism and leisure contexts, and the ways in which visitors experience the restorative processes identified in other literature. The findings in this regard are summarised in the following section.

Circumstances that facilitate and enhance restorative experiences in tourism and leisure contexts

Visitors identified a number of environmental features, including aspects of the physical, sensory, social, cognitive and temporal environments that supported, enhanced, or were seen as necessary for restorative experiences to occur. These might be seen as component parts that contribute to the total visitor experience, and as such, are consistent with the framework offered by Pearce (2011). The following are features that managers of tourism and leisure sites might consider building into their facilities to meet visitors' needs for restoration.

Physical environment

- Provide an environment that is open or spacious
- Design areas of refuge or escape
- Provide seats and rest areas
- Incorporate features that facilitate ease of movement and way-finding

Sensory environment

- Incorporate aesthetic elements (beauty and design)
- Use colour to create relaxing spaces
- Provide a quiet or natural soundscape
- Provide areas of subdued lighting
- Provide opportunities for visitors to experience stillness or gentle motion

Social environment

- Provide opportunities to observe others relaxing and enjoying themselves
- Provide opportunities to escape or avoid others
- Create awareness of the presence of others for belonging and/or security

Cognitive environment

- Provide information that is easy to digest
- Provide appropriate structure
- Provide opportunities for visitors to choose their own level of engagement

Temporal environment

- Provide opportunities for visitors to explore the site at their own pace
- Encourage visitors to allow sufficient time for the visit, or to adjust their expectations of the visit to the time they have available

Ways in which visitors experience restorative processes in tourism and leisure contexts

Visitors' comments illustrate the ways in which the unique environments encountered at museums and botanic gardens facilitate restorative processes. Visitors experienced fascination by being engaged in cognitive experiences (especially at the museum) or sensory experiences (especially at the gardens). These experiences gently and comfortably held visitors' attention without the need for mental effort. However, if distractions were present, either their attention would be broken or effort would be required to maintain it, thus interfering with the restorative process. Tourism and leisure sites have many potential distractors that incrementally add to visitors' stress levels and prevent them from experiencing fascination. These include confusion, clutter, overcrowding, overstimulation, noise, light, excessive movement and safety concerns. Removing these increases the likelihood that visitors will have a restorative experience.

Some visitors felt that their tourism or leisure experience was akin to leaving their everyday lives and entering a different world. They were able to take their minds off the concerns and worries that they may have arrived with, and gain a new perspective on life. After even a short time in such an environment, visitors left feeling more equipped to deal with the things they had been worried about. Providing entrances, exits and visible boundaries that signal and reinforce this sense of being away might help to prepare visitors for a restorative experience.

Although there was less evidence for restorative processes that relied on extent and compatibility, some visitors spoke of the need for an environment that was extensive enough to keep them occupied and diverse enough to meet a range of different needs. The use of techniques that ensure visitors have a choice regarding the nature and level of their engagement could be helpful in this regard.

Finally, it should be noted that museum and gardens visitors gave quite different reports of their experience of restoration. Museum visitors were more likely to talk about environmental features that reduced the distractions or removed the obstacles to a restorative experience, while gardens visitors were more likely to talk about environmental features that were positively restorative. As a result, the restorative experiences reported at the gardens were broader and deeper than those at the museum. As noted by Hartig and Staats (2003), in designing restorative environments it is necessary to not only eliminate the physical, social and temporal conditions that impose unwanted demands, but also to introduce those characteristics that promote restoration.

It is not the intention of this chapter to suggest that all visitors should be expected to seek or to attain a restorative experience, or that all tourism and leisure sites should provide a purely restorative experience. At many such sites, this will not be visitors' main focus. Indeed, different tourism and leisure sites are likely to offer different types of restorative experiences, and appeal to visitors with different sets of needs and interests. Thus, for example, museums may offer a restorative experience for visitors with a high need for cognition

(Cacioppo and Petty, 1982; Packer and Ballantyne, 2002) while gardens may offer a restorative experience for those with a greater sense of connection with nature. Cultural differences may also influence the types of environments visitors find restorative, and indeed in the present study a number of visitors specifically commented on the appealing sense of design and aesthetics in the Japanese garden. Frequent visitors to a site are more likely to both seek and experience restoration at that site, while first-time or infrequent visitors are more likely to be seeking novelty and stimulation – experiences that may be incompatible with a restorative experience (Packer and Bond, 2010). However, even in the midst of more intense and stimulating experiences, many visitors feel the need for times of respite and recovery. Tourism and leisure sites that make provision for these needs are likely to be experienced by visitors as more satisfying.

Schmitt (2003) and Pine and Gilmore (1999) suggest that it is the experiential dimensions surrounding the provision of goods and services that matter to guests. They highlight the marketing power of providing experiences that are engaging, personal, sensation-rich and memorable – experiences that instil a sense of wonder, beauty and appreciation. By providing such experiences, tourism and leisure providers convey to their visitors that they care about them and take their needs seriously.

Tourism and leisure sites that cater specifically to the need for restorative experiences play an essential role in our increasingly urbanised and fast-paced world. Such sites might even be considered to be health resources as they enable visitors to more effectively cope with the normal 'wear and tear' associated with everyday life (Hartig, 2004). The benefits of a restorative experience include recovery of directed attention capacity, enhanced ability to reflect on issues of importance, improved problem-solving ability and task performance (Herzog *et al.*, 2003; Kaplan, 1995). Increased access to restorative environments in tourism and leisure contexts will thus 'have positive effects on the health of the population as a whole, if not on every individual within the population' (Hartig, 2004, p. 4).

References

Ballantyne, R., Packer, J. and Hughes, K. (2008) 'Environmental awareness, interests and motives of Botanic Gardens visitors: implications for interpretive practice', *Tourism Management*, 29 (3): 439–444.

Cacioppo, J. and Petty, R. (1982) 'The need for cognition', *Journal of Personality and Social Psychology*, 42: 116–131.

Cimprich, B. (1993) 'Development of an intervention to restore attention in cancer patients', *Cancer Nursing*, 16: 83–92.

Crompton, J.L. (1979) 'Motivations for pleasure vacations', *Annals of Tourism Research*, 6: 408–424.

Csikszentmihalyi, M. and Rathunde, K. (1993) 'The measurement of flow in everyday life: towards a theory of emergent motivation', *Nebraska Symposium on Motivation*, 40: 57–97.

Hartig, T. (2004) 'Toward understanding the restorative environment as a health resource', www.openspace.eca.ac.uk/conference/proceedings/summary/Hartig.htm [Accessed 20 August 2012].

Hartig, T. and Staats, S. (2003) 'Guest editors' introduction: restorative environments', *Journal of Environmental Psychology*, 23: 103–107.

Hartig, T., Evans, G.W., Jamner, L.D., Davis, D.S. and Gärling, T. (2003) 'Tracking restoration in natural and urban field settings', *Journal of Environmental Psychology*, 23: 109–123.

Herzog, T.R. and Rector, A.E. (2009) 'Perceived danger and judges likelihood of restoration', *Environment and Behavior*, 41 (3): 386–401.

Herzog, T.R., Maguire, C.P. and Nebel, M.B. (2003) 'Assessing the restorative components of environments', *Journal of Environmental Psychology*, 23: 159–170.

Hill, J.M.M. (1965) *The Holiday: A Study of Social and Psychological Aspects with Special Reference to Ireland*. London: The Tavistock Institute of Human Relations.

Iso-Ahola, S.E. (1980) *Social Psychology of Leisure and Recreation*. Dubuque, IA: William C. Brown.

Kaplan, R. and Kaplan, S. (1989) *The Experience of Nature: A Psychological Perspective*. New York: Cambridge University Press.

Kaplan, R., Kaplan, S. and Ryan, R.L. (1998) *With People in Mind: Design and Management of Everyday Nature*. Washington, DC: Island Press.

Kaplan, S. (1987) 'Aesthetics, affect, and cognition: environmental preference from an evolutionary perspective', *Environment and Behavior*, 19 (1): 3–32.

Kaplan, S. (1995) 'The restorative benefits of nature: toward an integrative framework', *Journal of Environmental Psychology*, 15: 169–182.

Kaplan, S., Bardwell, L.V. and Slakter, D.B. (1993) 'The museum as a restorative environment', *Environment and Behavior*, 25: 725–742.

Korpela, K. and Hartig, T. (1996) 'Restorative qualities of favorite places', *Journal of Environmental Psychology*, 16: 221–233.

Korpela, K.M., Ylén, M., Tyrväinen, L. and Silvennoinen, H. (2008) 'Determinants of restorative experiences in everyday favorite places', *Health and Place*, 14: 636–652.

Laumann, K., Gärling, T. and Stormark, K.M. (2001) 'Rating scale measures of restorative components of environments', *Journal of Environmental Psychology*, 21: 31–44.

Ouellette, P., Kaplan, R. and Kaplan, S. (2005) 'The monastery as a restorative environment', *Journal of Environmental Psychology*, 25: 175–188.

Packer, J. (2006) 'Learning for fun: the unique contribution of educational leisure experiences', *Curator: The Museum Journal*, 49 (3): 329–344.

Packer, J. (2008) 'Beyond learning: exploring visitors' perceptions of the value and benefits of museum experiences', *Curator: The Museum Journal*, 55 (1): 33–54.

Packer, J. and Ballantyne, R. (2002) 'Motivational factors and the visitor experience: a comparison of three sites', *Curator: The Museum Journal*, 45 (3): 183–198.

Packer, J. and Bond, N. (2010) 'Museums as restorative environments', *Curator: The Museum Journal*, 53 (4): 421–456.

Pearce, P.L. (2011) *Tourist Behaviour and the Contemporary World*. Bristol: Channel View Publications.

Pearce, P.L. and Lee, U.-I. (2005) 'Developing the travel career approach to tourist motivation', *Journal of Travel Research*, 43: 226–237.

Pine, J. and Gilmore, J.H. (1999) *The Experience Economy: Work is Theater and Every Business a Stage*. Boston: Harvard Business School Press.

Schmitt, B.H. (2003) *Customer Experience Management*. Hoboken, NJ: John Wiley & Sons.

Scopelliti, M. and Giuliani, M.V. (2004) 'Choosing restorative environments across the lifespan: a matter of place experience', *Journal of Environmental Psychology*, 24: 423–437.

Snepenger, D., King, J., Marshall, E. and Uysal, M. (2006) 'Modeling Iso-Ahola's Motivation Theory in the tourism context', *Journal of Travel Research*, 45: 140–149.

Staats, H., Kieviet, A. and Hartig, T. (2003) 'Where to recover from attentional fatigue: an expectancy-value analysis of environmental preference', *Journal of Environmental Psychology*, 23: 147–157.

Treasure, J. (2007) *Sound Business*. Cirencester, UK: Management Books.

Ulrich, R.S. (1979) 'Visual landscapes and psychological well-being', *Landscape Research*, 4 (1): 17–23.

Ulrich, R.S. (1984) 'View through a window may influence recovery from surgery', *Science*, 224: 420–421.

13 A blueprint for tourist experience and fulfilment research

Sebastian Filep and Philip Pearce

Both in communicating research ideas and in planning further studies it is useful to have succinct rubrics or blueprints to guide action. These summary devices can take many forms. Formal theories are usually considered to be the pinnacle of scientific and social science inquiry because they both integrate and direct action (Smith and Lee, 2010). Models, road maps, frameworks, taxonomies and other analogous summary terms are less powerful but also serve as valuable integrative devices. The construction of these way-finding devices does however require abstracting generalisations from the details of the knowledge base. There are some recurring questions underlying this process. How is it possible to seek generalisations about tourist experiences and fulfilment through the lenses of positive psychology when we know there are one billion diverse tourists and numerous specific ways to seek fulfilment through tourism? Is it possible to seek cohesion in our studies when, for example, the research reported has been approached through positivist as well as non-positivist lenses? By identifying common threads in the available studies in this book, it is argued that some useful steps towards building a blueprint for further work are indeed possible.

Seeking cohesion

The challenge of seeking cohesion among seemingly disparate concepts and ideas in the hope of developing a theoretical or integrative model has been present in tourism studies for some time (Echtner and Jamal, 1997; Ren *et al.*, 2010; Tribe, 2006, 2010). Echtner and Jamal (1997) listed five key dimensions necessary for the evolution of tourism studies: generation of theoretical body of knowledge; use of diverse methodological approaches; theory and methodology clearly explicated; interdisciplinary focus; and holistic, integrated research.

A holistic, integrated body of knowledge is clearly desirable yet hard to achieve (Smith and Lee, 2010). In tourism studies, as in positive psychology, researchers have traditionally relied on established, positivist ways of building theoretical models. Blalock's (1967) three elements of theory building to develop tourism knowledge have been widely used (Pearce, 2005). These elements include: specification of assumptions; specification of relationships among factors or variables; and articulation of propositions to integrate or predict outcomes (Blalock, 1967). As shown however by Dann *et al.* (1988), while Blalock's elements have been used for theory building in our field, there are other ways we can develop informative summaries of tourist behaviour. Dubin (1969) and Silverman (1973) offer alternative perspectives to building theory and these approaches are neither less rigorous nor inferior to Blalock's (1967) elements.

One of the less ambitious approaches to seeking cohesion has been to develop typologies that integrate and/or relate seemingly disparate themes. Typologies in tourist behaviour studies essentially offer a classification of diverse images of tourists into tourist types, such as the drifter type, the explorer type and so on (Cohen, 1988). Yet, typologies are problematic from the standpoint of generalisation about a phenomenon. Franklin and Crang (2001) remark that researchers in tourism studies have been predisposed to offer finer subdivisions and more elaborate typologies as though hoping that this effort might eventually form a classificatory grid in which tourism could be defined and regulated. Typologies can become rigid and outdated. Due to these challenges, we decided not to develop a new typology or create a theoretical model of tourist experience and fulfilment; we chose instead a less ambitious approach to seek inductively derived generalisation among our studies. In essence the approach adopted amounts to a listing, albeit a listing where the items are identified on the basis of their apparent importance. Additionally, and benefiting from our exposure to the studies in positive psychology, we then link these listed themes to an existing classification scheme. It is an approach which resonates with the perspective that emerging topics of inquiry initially need organisation and an appreciation of the range of the phenomenon rather than premature attempts at theory building or highly differentiated taxonomies.

Tourist experience and fulfilment: core themes

The central concerns of this book have been to emphasise the personal benefits which people may realise through tourism. The use of theories and methods from positive psychology help inform the special focus of this work (Seligman and Csikszentmihalyi, 2000). In the following section we group these benefits in the hope of arriving at a more coherent view of tourist experience and fulfilment. The list of the themes serves to highlight the benefits but is not exhaustive in its representation of all of the tourists' positive benefits. The synthesis strongly reflects themes that emerged in more than one chapter.

Enhanced pleasure

First, we identified the personal benefit of enhanced pleasure through engaging in tourism. In De Bloom *et al.*'s Dutch study, it was found that vacationers experienced high levels of pleasure from their vacation activities: mean scores of pleasure ranged between 7.9 (during short vacations) and 8.1 (during winter and summer longer vacations). Their findings showed that vacation activities associated with experiences of pleasure and relaxation were also related to improvements in physical health. Similarly, Panchal's study revealed enhanced pleasure through tourist spa experiences: high degrees of relaxed feelings, peacefulness and calmness were reported. The work on humour too adds credence to the fact that people enjoy the pleasures of their multiple tourist host contacts. A cynic might counter that this is all to be expected and hardly needs studies to demonstrate the point. Nevertheless building a cadre of studies which document what commentators expect is not always possible, and as this field emerges, it remains worthwhile to provide evidence about the expected as well as the counter-intuitive points.

Positive relationships

The value of relationships and the associated social contexts was another strong theme in the studies. The findings of Saunders *et al.* revealed that interpersonal relationships as well as an awareness of the needs of others lead to personal growth outcomes for long distance walkers. In Matteucci's study it was revealed the relationships with peers, instructors and the local community led to enhanced spirituality for flamenco tourists in Spain. Packer's results from her study of restorative visitor experiences in a museum and botanic garden setting also support this theme. Restorative experiences are those that facilitate recovery from mental fatigue and help us continue to meet the demands of everyday life. Packer found that the presence of other people in the environments studied was a positive factor for most people, though it was also noted that the presence of others may sometimes be distracting and disturb the restorative process. The specific cultural context in which this finding applies is a consideration. Cultural differences shaping tourists' experiences are highlighted subsequently.

Greater competence

Witsel's examination of travelling academics demonstrated that tourism is a vehicle for enhanced competence; she showed how the ability to adapt to changing environments when travelling leads to greater competence and learning. Similar conclusions were made by Alexander and Bakir in their examination of volunteer tourists in Africa. The findings revealed increased self-confidence, reduced anxiety and depression levels following the tourist experience. The study also showed that volunteer tourists were more likely to become involved and absorbed in artistic events following a volunteer tourism experience, hence increasing their competence.

Flow

Rátz and Michalkó's study highlighted that the tourist experiences they investigated typified flow – a state where one is totally involved in a voluntary activity that is highly rewarding (Csikszentmihalyi, 1990). Flow experience consists of nine dimensions: challenge-skill balance, action-awareness merging, clear goals, unambiguous feedback, task concentration, sense of control, loss of self-consciousness, time transformation and autotelic experience. Panchal also revealed flow in her study of tourist spa goers in India, Thailand and the Philippines. A slight variation across the scores for each of the nine flow dimensions was observed but the results suggest some degree of endorsement for the spa activity as a flow tourist experience. Similarly, Pearce and Pabel's investigation of humour revealed that the experiences of humour by tourists led to enhanced concentration outcomes; this finding clearly matches the concentration on task dimension of flow.

Personal transformation

Personal transformation, which can be broadly defined as re-evaluation of one's values and belief system, was another core theme that emerged from the studies. Research efforts revealed that the experience of challenge (defined as sacrifice and hardship by Matteucci) led to personal transformations. Ross's review of narratives revealed that those narratives that contained themes of adjusting to challenging life transitions were much more likely to emphasise personal growth and transformation. Alexander and Bakir's study showed that volunteer tourism represents a proactive catalyst for altering our perspectives and subsequently our actions. But they similarly point to the challenges of attaining this personal transformation through volunteer tourism by citing Csikszentmihalyi (1997): 'the best moments usually occur when a person's body or mind is stretched to its limits in a voluntary effort to accomplish something difficult and worthwhile' (p. 3).

Improved fitness levels

Our sixth tourist experience and fulfilment theme is improved fitness. The studies in the book convincingly demonstrate that engagement in tourism sometimes leads to improved fitness levels of tourists. Saunders *et al.*'s study showed that, despite the tired muscles and blisters, the act of engaging in long-distance walking as a voluntary leisure and tourist activity was personally rewarding and led to increased fitness levels of the participants. Similarly, Alexander and Bakir showed that volunteer tourists in their study were more likely to return from their trip feeling energetic. Many volunteers improved their fitness as a result of the physical nature of their volunteer tourist activities.

Better overall quality of life

This was the last theme we identified and can be seen as our overarching theme. It includes judgements about life satisfaction and judgements about physiological benefits of tourism. In Hagger and Murray's examination of Australian retirees who engage in tourism, it was shown that tourism can contribute to positive ageing – increasing overall life satisfaction. They showed that tourist satisfaction is a significant indicator of life satisfaction. Their respondents indicated a higher overall level of life satisfaction if they were anticipating future holidays. Multiple holidays increase the level of life satisfaction and this finding is independent of both income and perceived health. They argued that people who do not travel may be limiting their options to maintain their life satisfaction. The findings on physiological benefits of tourism also support the argument that tourist experiences lead to better overall quality of life. One example of this physiological benefit is De Bloom *et al.*'s results that vacations enabled their Dutch cohort of tourists to sleep longer than during their working times at home. It was sleep quality rather than sleep quantity that was linked to improvements in health and well-being across all types of vacations studied by the researchers. Similarly, Panchal's study revealed that one of the benefits of spa tourist experiences was the ability to sleep better.

Bringing the themes together

In summary it appears that the tourist experience and fulfilment themes resemble elements of Seligman's (2011) theoretical model of well-being – PERMA. The model was introduced and heavily employed by Saunders *et al.* in this book so the model is not re-evaluated here. The studies in the book however demonstrate that the benefits identified neatly fall under each letter of PERMA. P for positive emotions (enhanced pleasure); E for engagement (flow and greater competence); R for relationships (positive relationships), M for meaning (personal transformation) and A for achievement (improved fitness levels and better overall quality of life). Some readers may have used PERMA as a personal or intuitive lens for studying tourist experiences. For example when daydreaming about an upcoming vacation, our positive emotions might increase. Next, when mindfully processing some of the environmental or architectural details of sites we visit, we feel engaged. Further, when laughing and joking with travel companions or host communities we bond and build relationships. Achievement as another outcome of importance might be a priority after bungee jumping or white-water rafting. Finally, when we witness extreme poverty on our trips we may question our meaning or sense of purpose in life. Previously, there has not been a compilation of empirical evidence to support this kind of musing. We are reluctant to state that tourist fulfilment with all of its complexities equals PERMA; in this book however we can tentatively tie the research themes we have identified to this well-being model based on the immediacy of the research evidence. In addition to these exciting links, it can be argued that some progress has been made in addressing previously identified knowledge gaps.

Knowledge gaps and ideas for the future

In an earlier book (Pearce *et al.*, 2011) we identified what we then believed to be areas of inattention or ignorance in linking positive psychology and tourist behaviour studies. Among other gaps, we noted two key areas where further research was required: first, the need to better understand positive experiences of diverse cohorts of tourists (particularly non-Western contemporary tourists); and second, the desirability of undertaking more research on health benefits of tourism – such research was seen as complementing initiatives in the positive health research field (Seligman, 2008).

This book has addressed these two gaps. The researchers in this book have conducted work with both Asian tourists and less traditional samples of Western respondents. The research tools and approaches have been diverse. For example we learned about personal benefits of Hungarian tourist experiences from Rátz and Michalkó and we found out about the motives for and outcomes of spa experiences for Indian and Philippino tourists in Panchal's investigation. Second, the research reported by Hagger and Murray, De Bloom *et al.* and Packer offers some solid, mutually supportive, preliminary work addressing the health research gap. Thus far, limited research existed on the impacts of tourist experiences on physical health (Gump and Matthews, 2000). On this note, Jafari (2005) lamented that the tourism field and medical professionals have not joined forces to explore and advance the proposition that tourism is good for health. By way of contrast travel medicine studies are often dauntingly depressing as to the dire consequences which may befall tourists. Through the research endeavours of our authors we are managing to work towards a better understanding of the relationship between tourist experiences and positive health.

There are nonetheless, remaining research opportunities relevant to the investigation of tourist experiences and fulfilment. These are noted in the following sections. We can group the remaining knowledge gaps under four broad sections; the section headings reflect new ranges of inquiry for tourism studies informed by (positive) psychology (Pearce and Packer, 2012):

Greater social focus and attention to cultural contexts

Much of current work on tourist experience from a positive psychology perspective is still confined to examinations of individual functioning, drawing from Western theories of well-being; future research attention to the social contexts and group processes can enhance the value of the work. For example in Japanese culture, the self or *jibun*, implies that the self is not necessarily separate from the social realm. *Jibun* literally means self part – that is, a part of the larger whole that consists of groups and relationships (Christopher, 1999); this revelation may have implications for the way we understand personal transformation through travel experiences of Japanese cohorts of tourists. Similarly, the concept of a harmony ties together many of the ways Chinese tourists experience their holiday worlds. The concept applies to within group, out group and person-environment interactions and produces surprising moments of happiness when revealed in these interactions (Li, 2008). It is hoped that future researchers can more readily acknowledge the importance of the cultural frames influencing their findings, while also endeavouring to forge international partnerships for more comparative studies.

More emic perspectives

The perspective taken by researchers in studying tourist experiences and fulfilment should be explicitly acknowledged. The emic perspective is often more qualitative and allows for deeper investigation of the ways tourists see their experiences, while etic perspective uses established categories and assessments. Both are valuable and this book contains both etic and emic research. Future investigations could however include further emic examples (as these are currently underrepresented); by so doing we could more thoroughly understand conditions for and consequences of fulfilling tourist experiences.

More domains of enquiry

Our book has predominately focused on exploring psychological benefits of tourism. There is value in also exploring other domains (e.g. physiological effects) to better understand how people flourish through vacations. To map out optimal human functioning in a holistic manner, there is a need to further assess multiple domains of inquiry (Seligman, 2008); for example, assessments of physical capacity such as flexibility, walking speed and physical indications of balance, endurance and fitness could complement the exploration of tourist subjective well-being. Similarly, there is an opportunity to expand the domain of inquiry by further investigating how negative experiences could give rise to more positive experiences; for example, do regularly stressful experiences of travelling build resilience amongst tourists to deal with problems in their daily life?

More longitudinal studies

The last idea for future research is to conduct more longitudinal studies to better understanding the impact of tourism on quality of life over time. Our research in this field has typically investigated processes happening at one point in time. For example particular cohorts of tourists and their perceived well-being in specific settings at specific points in time are often examined (Deery *et al.*, in press; Filep *et al.*, in press; Pearce *et al.*, 2011); future investigations could track tourists' experiences over a longer period, certainly over weeks and months, and possibly years, to better understand themes such as personal growth, meaning and positive memory.

Concluding thoughts

Moscardo (2009) reminds researchers that tourism is not always good for the individual. She observes that tourism can lead to negative outcomes by exposing them to health risks and a greater chance of injury. Holiday travel can also sidetrack career endeavours, cost money that could be invested in other areas and disrupt tourists' social networks. It may also enhance feelings of incompetence generated by negative travel experiences. We accept that these may be consequences but reject their inevitability. As one single instance which forms a counter view, the work on 'The University of Travel' which records positive learning experiences among backpackers can be noted (Pearce and Foster, 2007).

We do acknowledge the negative effects of tourism on the individual but we now hope that future researchers will weigh these negative effects against the emerging studies of positive tourist experiences that have been presented in this book; a more holistic representation of tourist experiences is important so that tourism studies do not become a litany of woe. Positive psychology was borne out of a need to study optimum human behaviour so we could better understand what makes people flourish (Seligman and Csikszentmihalyi, 2000). Much of clinical psychology research prior to the birth of positive psychology in 1999 was heavily focused on 'dark topics', alleviation of depression, anxiety, trauma and harm, and very little was known about conditions for a good life. Psychologists knew how to bring people from –8 to 0, but not how to bring them from 0 to +8. We side with Samdahl (2000) and Stebbins (2011) in arguing that in order for studies in our interest areas to survive and thrive we must develop a robust body of knowledge on 'positiveness'.

To accentuate the positive impact of tourism, future tourist behaviour and positive psychology scholarship may need to be linked more closely to the relevant research developments in other fields. These study areas include some of those already mentioned in the Introduction: transformational tourism research (Reisinger, 2013), peace through tourism investigations (Blanchard and Higgins-Desbiolles, 2013), hopeful tourism (Pritchard *et al.*, 2011) and most directly, health and wellness tourism research (Voigt and Pforr, 2013). Links too can be built with research clusters exploring equality and justice (Higgins-Desbiolles and Whyte, 2013). Additionally, there are opportunities to develop partnerships with researchers from outside the tourism field such as those who have conducted vacationing studies in psychoanalysis (Hymer, 1993; Rhoads and Rhoads, 1995) and the positive sociology research community (Stebbins, 2011). Optimism perhaps is the positive psychology value we most need as tourists, as researchers and as individuals. It is optimism that helps us believe that what we are doing is worthwhile for ourselves, for others and for our communities. Optimism and a dash of Panglossian naïveté perhaps, encourage us to adopt a line from the quintessentially tourism linked film *The Best Exotic Marigold Hotel*:

> Everything will be alright in the end ... and if it is not alright, it is not the end.

It is the kind of mantra which can both help tourists survive lost luggage and researchers adhere to their task of building studies in positive effects of tourism.

References

Blalock, H. (1967) *Theory Construction: From Verbal to Mathematical Formulations*. Englewood Cliffs: Prentice Hall.

Blanchard, L. and Higgins-Desbiolles, F. (2013) *Peace Through Tourism: Promoting Human Security Through International Citizenship*. New York: Routledge.

Christopher, J.C. (1999) 'Situating psychological well being: exploring the cultural roots of its theory and research', *Journal of Counseling and Development*, 77: 141–152.

Cohen, E. (1988) 'Authenticity and commoditization in tourism', *Annals of Tourism Research*, 15 (3): 371–386.

Csikszentmihalyi, M. (1990) *Flow: The Psychology of Optimal Experience*. New York: Harper Collins.

Csikszentmihalyi, M. (1997) *Finding Flow: The Psychology of Engagement with Everyday Life*. New York: Perseus Book Group.

Dann, G., Nash, D. and Pearce, P. (1988) 'Methodology in tourism research', *Annals of Tourism Research*, 15 (1): 1–28.

Deery, M., Filep, S. and Hughes, M. (in print) 'Exploring well being in parks and nature reserves', in Pforr, C. and Voigt, C. (eds), *Wellness Tourism*. New York: Routledge.

Dubin, R. (1969) *Theory Building*. New York: The Free Press.

Echtner, C. and Jamal, T. (1997) 'The disciplinary dilemma of tourism studies', *Annals of Tourism Research*, 24 (4): 868–883.

Filep, S., Klint, L., Dominey-Howes, D. and DeLacy, T. (in print) 'Discovering what matters in a perfect day: a study of well being of adventure tourists', in Taylor, S., Varley, P. and Johnston, T. (eds). *Adventure Tourism: Meanings, Markets and Learning*. Abingdon, Oxford: Routledge.

Franklin, A. and Crang, M. (2001) 'The trouble with tourism and travel theory?' *Tourist Studies* 1: 5–22.

Gump, B. and Matthews, K. (2000) 'Are vacations good for your health? The 9-year mortality experience after the multiple risk factor intervention trial', *Psychosomatic Medicine*, 62: 608–612.

Higgins-Desbiolles, F. and Whyte, K.P. (2013) 'No high hopes for hopeful tourism: a critical comment', *Annals of Tourism Research*, 40. 428–433.

Hymer, S. (1993) 'An alternative to the "traumatizing" vacation: the enriching, expansive vacation', *American Journal of Psychoanalysis*, 53 (2): 143–157.

Jafari, J. (2005) 'Bridging out, nesting afield: powering a new platform', *Journal of Tourism Studies*, 16 (2). 1–20.

Li, F.M.S. (2008) 'Culture as a major determinant in tourism development of China', *Current Issues in Tourism*, 11 (6): 492–513.

Moscardo, G. (2009) 'Tourism and quality of life: towards a more critical approach', *Tourism and Hospitality Research*, 9 (2): 159–170.

Pearce, P.L. (2005) *Tourist Behaviour: Themes and Conceptual Schemes*. Clevedon: Channel View Publications.

Pearce, P.L. and Foster, F. (2007) 'A "university of travel": backpacker learning', *Tourism Management* 28 (5): 1285–1298.

Pearce, P.L. and Packer, J. (2012) 'Minds on the move: refreshing the links from psychology to tourism studies', *Annals of Tourism Research*, DOI:101016/j.annals.2012.10.002.

Pearce, P.L., Filep, S. and Ross, G. (2011) *Tourists, Tourism and the Good Life*. New York: Routledge.

Pritchard, A., Morgan, N. and Ateljevic, I. (2011) 'Hopeful tourism: a new transformative perspective', *Annals of Tourism Research*, 38 (3): 941–963.

Reisinger, Y. (2013) *Transformational Tourism: Tourist Perspectives*. Wallingford: CABI.

Ren, C., Pritchard, A. and Morgan, N. (2010) 'Constructing tourism research: a critical inquiry', *Annals of Tourism Research*, 37 (4): 885–904.

Rhoads, E. and Rhoads, J. (1995) 'The benefits of vacation/interruptions in psychoanalysis', *Journal of Clinical Psychoanalysis*, 4 (2): 209–222.

Samdahl, D.M. (2000) 'Reflections on the future of leisure studies', *Journal of Leisure Research*, 32: 125–128.

Seligman, M.E.P. (2008) 'Positive health', *Applied Psychology: An International Review*, 57: 3–18.

Seligman, M.E.P. (2011) *Flourish*. Sydney: Random House.

Seligman, M.E.P. and Csikszentmihalyi, M. (2000) 'Positive psychology: an introduction', *American Psychologist*, 55 (1): 5–14.

Silverman, D. (1973) 'Methodology and meaning', in Filmer, P., Phillipson, M., Silverman, D. and Walsh, D. (eds), *New Directions in Sociological Theory*. Cambridge, MA: MIT Press, pp. 183–200.

Smith, S. and Lee, H. (2010) 'A typology of "theory" in tourism', in Pearce, D.G. and Butler, R. (eds), *Tourism Research: A 20–20 Vision*. Oxford: Goodfellow, pp. 28–39.

Stebbins, R. (2011) 'Leisure studies: the road ahead', *World Leisure Journal*, 53 (1): 3–10.

Tribe, J. (2006) 'The truth about tourism', *Annals of Tourism Research*, 33 (2): 360–381.

Tribe, J. (2010) 'Tribes, territories and networks in the tourism academy', *Annals of Tourism Research*, 37 (1): 7–33.

Voigt, C. and Pforr, C. (2013) *Wellness Tourism*. New York: Routledge.

Index

Page numbers in *italics* denote tables, those in **bold** denote figures.

academics: benefits of travel 41–8; cultural backgrounds 43–4; transnational teaching 48–9; *see also* work-related travel
achievement and challenge, long-distance walking 133–5
actions, religious meaning systems 101
active citizenship, volunteer tourism 154
active recovery mechanisms 169–70
activity levels, volunteer tourism 158–9
activity, volunteer tourism 153
adaptation 38
adventurousness, volunteer tourism 154, 159
aesthetic experience 77
aesthetics 65–6
affiliative humour 32–3
aggressive humour 32
Alave, K.L. 76
Alexander, Z. 147, 148, 153–60
Allostatic Load Theory 168–9
altruism, volunteer tourism 154
antecedent conditions, long-distance walking 138–9
anticipation: and life satisfaction 193–5; and memory 189
anxiety, volunteer tourism 155
appreciation 45
Argyle, M. 97
Aristotle 56
arousal: flamenco 116–19; and spirituality 112
artistic interest, volunteer tourism 154, 157
Asian spa study: conclusions 84–5; context and overview 72; flow and tourist experience 77–8; flow dimensions from spa experiences 79–81; flow experience – spa activity vs other physical activities *81*; implications of research 84–5; liminality and thresholds 82–4; market size 75; measuring flow in tourist experiences 78–9; perceived benefits 82–4; positive tourism 72; respondent profile 79; spa practices 75–7; traditional practices 75–6; wellness and Asian spa industry 72–7; *see also* spa tourism
Attention Restoration Theory 202
Australia: long-distance walking 129–30; *see also* retirees
authentic happiness theory 56, 68
authenticity: experiential 117, 122; of self 119
autonomy, personal 95
autotelic experiences 117
Ayurvedic tourism 76

backpackers 104–5
Bakir, A. 147
Barrow, R. 40
Barzun, J. 40
Basu, P. 95
Bauer, J.J. 99, 103, 104
Beardsley, M.C. 77
beauty 65–6
being away 202, 215
belonging 63–4; long-distance walking 135–6
Benjamin, M.R. 99
bizarreness, and memory 32
Blalock, H. 223–4
body resonance 117
Bonanno, G.A. 103
Bond, K.E. 117, 118
Bond, N. 203
bonding 178

234 *Index*

book: concluding thoughts 229–30; place in research 1–2; research challenges 2–5; research problem 1–2; research team 5–10; structure 10–12
boredom 38
botanic gardens: restorative attributes 214–16; *see also* restoration
Bowen, G.A. 26
Bridges' change process 142
Bridges, W. 128
Broaden-and-Build Theory 32, 170, 178
bushwalking 127
Butler, T.S. 130

Cacioppo, J.T. 99
Campallo, Rafael 117
Cantor, N. 103
carefreeness 61, **62**
Carson, S.H. 24
Celtic spirituality 96
challenge: flamenco 115–16; and spirituality 112
challenge and achievement, long-distance walking 133–4
challenges, benefits of 38
change of environment 61–2
Chapman, J. 75
Character Strengths and Values Handbook (Peterson and Seligman) 91
Chinese spa treatments 76
Christian travel 93–4
Christopher, J.C. 38, 56
Clawson, M. 82
cognitive environment, restoration 212–13, 218
cognitive function, and humour 32
cognitive journeys 49–50
Cohen, E. 77–8, 93
cohesion, in research 223–4
collectivism, and humour 19–20
Collett, Peter 17
Collicut, J. 92
Collins-Kreiner, N. 93, 102
comfort, and humour 21, 28
commercialism, and well-being 4
communitas 113, 135
compatibility 202–3, 216
competence 225
concentration, and humour 21, 30–1, 33
concept-driven coding 28
confidence: long-distance walking 141; volunteer tourism 159–60
connection: and humour 21, 29–30, 32; long-distance walking 137–8

Connell, J. 74
Conservation of Resources Theory 169
consumption, and well-being 4
contingencies, religious meaning systems 100
Couper, G.E. 39
Crust, L. 130–1
Csikszentmihalyi, M. 38, 67, 77, 78, 120, 123, 155, 156, 161
cultural backgrounds, academics 43–4
cultural contexts 228
cultural stereotypes 43
cultures, experience of 42–3

dagdagay 76
Daniel, Y.P. 117, 122
Dann, G.M.S. 196, 224
data-driven coding 26
data saturation 26
Deci, E.L. 169
Delphi 91
Den Breejen, L. 130
depression, volunteer tourism 157–8
destinations: dream destinations 66–7; selection of 60
Dewey, J. 118
Diener, E. 2–3, 187
Digance, J. 129
Dillon, M. 96–7
dimensions of flow 79–80
directed attention fatigue 202
diversionary mode 77
diversity, value of 47
domains of enquiry 229
dream destinations 66–7
Dubin, R. 224
Durrell, Lawrence 190
dutifulness, volunteer tourism 154–5

Echtner, C. 223
education, happiness in 40
Effort-Recovery Theory 168
Eklund, R.C. 78, 81
emic perspectives 229
Emmons, R. 112
emotional arousal, humour 32
emotional engagement, long-distance walking 141–2
emotional happiness 38
emotional states, religious meaning systems 101
emotionality, volunteer tourism 158
emotions, volunteer tourism 154
empathy 117

empowerment 141
enarratives 105
engagement: concept of 147; long-distance walking 139–41; volunteer tourism 147–8, 156
Engagement Theory 159; volunteer tourism **153**
enhanced pleasure 224–5
enjoyment, transnational teaching 48–50
environment: flamenco 113–15; and spirituality 112
eudaimonia 56, 68, 119–20; and spirituality 123; vs. hedonism 39
Event Experience Scale 78
existential mode 77
expectations, religious meaning systems 100–1
experiences, autotelic 117
experiential authenticity 117, 122
experiential mode 77
experimental mode 77

Faisse, L. 97
family, travelling with 62–3
fascination 202, 215
Filep, S. 39, 56
Finlayson, M. 99
first independent trip 65
fitness 226; long-distance walking 136–7, 141; volunteer tourism 158–9
five modes of tourist experience 77–8
flamenco: arousal 116–19; challenge 115–16; conclusions 121–3; context and overview 110–11; dimensions of the spiritual experience **122**; environment 113–15; flow 120; ineffable 116–19; method 111; music 114; respondentsí spiritual experiences *112*; as sacred 122–3; self 119–21; spirituality 111–21; transformation 115–16, 121
flow 3, 38–9, 67, 225–6; dimensions of 79–80; flamenco 120; long-distance walking 130, 140; restoration 214; and tourist experience 77–8; in tourist experiences 78–9; volunteer tourism 155
flow experience – spa activity vs. other physical activities *81*
Flow State Scale (FSS-2) 78
Foucault, M. 113
Frankl, V. 156–7
Fredrickson, B.L. 20, 32, 170
freedom to travel 65
Freud, S. 98
Frew, E. 31

fulfilment, defining 2

Gannon, M. 43
Gibbs, G.R. 26
Gilmore, J.H. 128
Giuliani, M.V. 203
Glastonbury 95
Global Spa Summit Committee 73
goals: personally valid 189; religious meaning systems 100–1
Goldstein and Coyle Hospitality Group 83
good life 39, 56
growth themes 104

Hall, M. 74–5
Hampden-Turner, C. 46
happiness: definitions and conceptions 2–3, 37–8; in education 40; experience of 3–4; factors 55–6; research approaches 55–6; and tourism 55–8; transnational teaching 48–50; types of 38; and well-being 37–8; *see also* travel-related happiness
health 21; long-distance walking 136–7, 139, 141; as tourism product 73
health and ageing, and tourism policy 196–7
hedonism, vs. eudemonia 39
Hehl, F.-J. 19
Herodotus 91, 92
heteropias 113
Hickinbottom, S. 38, 56
Higgins-Desbiolles, F. 196
Hills, P. 97
hilot 76
Hobfoll, S.E. 169
Holt, J. 2
Hom Cary, S. 117, 122
Horowitz, M.D. 74
humour: appreciation 18–19; attitudes to 17; blog humour ratings **25**; as character strength 31; and cognitive function 32; collectivism vs. individualism 19–20; comfort 21, 29; communication 27–8; concentration 21, 30–1, 33; conclusions 33; connection 21, 29–30, 32; content of humorous travel experiences 26; context and overview 17–18; discussion 31–3; episodes that can happen to everyone 27; findings 26–31; implications of research 33; and individual differences 18–19; literature review 18–21; and nationality 19–20; observant tourists 28; outcomes 21, 28, 31; and personality 19;

humour – *contd.*
   and positive psychology 20–1; production 18; provided for tourists *23*; research and methodology 21–4; selection of blog entries 24–5; sexual 19; social influence and control 27–8; study of provided humour 22–4; travel blog study 24–5; travel essentials 26; *see also* sense of humour
humour style model 32
Hungarian Central Statistical Office 57
Hungary: conscious perception of travel-related happiness 61–7; context and overview 54–5; destinations 60–1; discussion and conclusions 67–8; happiness-inducing role of life events and situations **58**; method 58–9; perception of happiness 56–7; results 60; spatial aspects of travel-related happiness 60–1; tourism and happiness 56–8

identity, as ëseriousí traveller 190–1
ikigai 186
India, Ayurvedic tourism 76
individual differences, and humour 18–19
individualism: and humour 19–20; and spirituality 96
ineffable: flamenco 116–19; and spirituality 112
Inoue, T. 32
integrative growth 104
interactional temperament model 158
intercultural competence 48
International Spa Association 74
internationalisation 47
interpretive phenomenological analysis (IPA) method 149, 151, 152
intrinsic growth 104
intrinsic motivation 121
intrinsic motivational values 104

Jackson, S.A. 78, 80
Jamal, T. 223
Janky, B. 55
jibun 228
job stressors, effects of 167–8
joke appreciation, and nationality 19
Jonah complex theory 156
joy, transnational teaching 48–50

Kaplan, R. 202–3
Kaplan, S. 202–3
Kaufmann, E.L. 74
Kazarian, S.S. 19–20
Kelly, E.W.Jr. 111–12
Kesebir, P. 2–3
Kihlstrom, J.F. 103
Knetsch, J.L. 82
Koenig, H.G. 97
Korpela, K.M. 203
Kosek, R.B. 97
Kottler, J. 128

Langer, E. 118–19
laughing, effects of 20
Layard, R. 38
Lean, G.L. 129
Lee, U.-I. 82
Lengyel, Gy. 55
Li, B. 121
life events 57–8; happiness-inducing role **58**
life satisfaction 55; and anticipation 193–5
liminality 82–4, 113
Little, D.E. 121
local people 67
long-distance walking: aims of study 131; antecedent conditions 138–9; Australia 129–30; challenge and achievement 133–4; conclusions 143–4; context and overview 127–8; emotional engagement 141–2; enduring change 141–3; engagement and reflection 139–41; flow 130, 140; health and fitness 136–7, 139, 141; literature review 128–31; meaning and connection 137–8; method 127; motivation 138; and pilgrimage 129; preparation 138; relationships and belonging 135–6; research participants 130, 131–2; study context 131; themes 132–8; therapy and problem solving 132–3; tracks and trails 131; transformation 141–2, **142**
longitudinal studies 229
Lutterbie, S.J. 38
Lyubomirsky, S. 38, 43, 92

Mahoney, A. 122–3
Makiguchi, T. 40
Marks, N. 55
Martin, A.A. 19–20
Martin, R.A. 18
Maslow, A. 155–6
McAdams, D.P. 99, 102–3, 104
McCullough, M.E. 97
McEwen, B.S. 168

McGehee, N. 154
McGowan, K. 39
McIntosh, A. 154–5
meaning: and happiness 39; long-distance walking 137–8
meaning making 99–100; and religious expression 100–2
meaning systems: and narratives 102–3; *see also* religious meaning systems
meaningful life 56
medical tourism 74
Meijman, T.F. 168
memories 177–8, 188
memory, and anticipation 189
mental health: long-distance walking 136–7, 139; volunteer tourism 153, 155, 157–8
Michalkó, G. 57, 58, 60
Miller, J.W. 73
Mills, A.S. 130
mindfulness 118–19
mindset happiness 38
Minnaert, L. 196
mixed methods 148–9, 191
Mohan, K. 123
Moscardo, G. 229–30
motivating values 104
motivation 4; long-distance walking 138
Mueller, H. 74
Mueser, R. 130
Mulder, G. 168
multi-paradigmatic approach 148–9
multicultural teaching environment, benefits of 47
multiple cycles of tourism experiences 188–91; *see also* retirees
museums 203; restorative attributes 214–16; *see also* restoration
music 114
mutual care 50
mutual tuning-in relationship 114–15
Myers, D.G. 98–100

Nakamura, J. 155
narratives: and meaning systems 102–3; online 105; transformative 103–5
Nash, D. 129
nationality, and humour 19–20
Nawijn, J. 39
negative outcomes 229–30
New Age 95
nine elements of enjoyment 79–80
Noddings, N. 40
Noy, C. 104–5

Olsen, D.H. 99
openness to experience 97, 98, 138–9
optimism 18, 230
other spaces 113
otherness, exposure to 44
outcomes, negative 229–30

Packer, J. 203
Pargament, K.I. 111, 122–3
Park, C.L. 121
parks 203
passive recovery mechanisms 168–9
Pearce, P.L. 67, 72, 82, 119
pedagogy of intercultural experience 43
perception of extent 202, 215–16
PERMA 39, 45, 128, 131, 138, 143, 187, 227
personal attitudes, volunteer tourism 154
personal autonomy 95
personal change: long-distance walking 141–3, **142**; *see also* transformation
personal reconstruction 189–90
personal responsibility 156–7
personal transformation *see* transformation
personality, and humour 19
personally valid goals 189
Peterson, C. 123
Philippines, spa treatments 76
philosophy of life, and happiness 38
physical environment, restoration 206–7, 218
pilgrim-tourist dichotomy 92, 93–4
pilgrimage: flamenco tourism 111–21; and long-distance walking 129; religious and secular 94–6
Pine, J.B. 128
pleasant life 56
positive psychology: defining 72; and humour 20–1; scope of 5; in tourism studies 230
positive relationships 225
positive-tourism 72; *see also* Asian spa study
Power, R. 96
preparation, long-distance walking 138
privilege 4–5
problem solving and therapy, long-distance walking 132–3

quality of life 55, 226–7

Rátz, T. 58, 60
Reader, I. 94–6
recreational mode 77

reflection, long-distance walking 139–41
Relate–Dedicate–Donate 147, 159
relatedness 169
relationships, long-distance walking 135–6
religion: and social support 99; tradition in 94–6
religious beliefs, and values 96–7
religious expression: forms of 96–8; and meaning making 100–2; and well-being 98–100
religious meaning systems 100–2; *see also* meaning systems
religious shrines 91
religious tourism: attitudes to theory 93; Christian travel 93–4; context and overview 91; issues and perspectives 92–6; models 93–4; motivation 104–5; pilgrim-tourist dichotomy 92; transformative narratives 103–5
religiousness 97
responsibility, volunteer tourism 156–7
restoration: accounts of experience 216–17; attributes and effects of environments **205**; cognitive environment 212–13, 218; concept of 202–3; conclusions 217–20; facilitating circumstances 218–20; favourite places 203; interview questions 204; modes of experience 219–20; physical environment 206–7, 218; research study overview 204–6; role of tourism and leisure 203–4; sensory environment 207–10, 218; slowing down 203–4; social environment 210–12, 218; temporal environment 213–14, 218
restorative attributes, museums and botanic gardens 214–16
retirees: aims of study 191; anticipation and life satisfaction 193–5; anticipation and memory 189; conclusions 197–8; consumer satisfaction 190; context and overview 186; demographics 192–3; engagement with life 187; findings 193; identity as ëseriousí traveller 190–1; limitations of sample 191–2; method 191; multiple cycles of tourism experiences 188–91; personal reconstruction 189–90; personally valid goals 189; tourism experience 188; tourism policy, health and ageing 196–7
Ricard, M. 5
Rinschede, G. 92, 93
Robbins, S. 45
romance 64–5

Ron, A. 93–4
Roof, W.C. 98
Rosenweig, J.A. 74
Ruch, W. 19
Ryan, R.M. 169
Ryckman, R. 158
Ryff, C. 39

sacred 100, 122–3
Saldanha, A. 118
Santos, C. 154
Saroglou, V. 97
Scherer, K.R. 117
Schmidt, C. 121
Schütz, A. 114–15
Scollon, R. 46
Scollon, S.W. 46
Scopelliti, J. 203
Sedona 95
self: flamenco 119–21; and spirituality 112
self-actualisation 64
self-awareness 46
self-confidence, volunteer tourism 159
self-defeating humour 32–3
Self-Determination Theory 169
self-development 128
self-directed change 128
self-efficacy 141; volunteer tourism 154
self-enhancing humour 32–3
Seligman, M. 39, 45, 56, 91, 92, 123, 128, 187
sense of belonging 63–4
sense of humour 18; *see also* humour
sense of purpose 186
sensory environment, restoration 207–10, 218
Shah, H. 55
Sharpley, R. 3–4, 5, 37, 121
Sheldon, P. 39
Shikoku 94
Silberman, I. 100–2
Silverman, D. 224
Sin, N.L. 92
Singer, B. 39
Smith, V.L. 93
social change, and spirituality 94
social comic relief theory 31
social environment, restoration 210–12, 218
social focus 228
social integration, volunteer tourism 157–8
social support, and religion 99
South Africa, volunteer tourism 148
spa tourism: description and definition

74–5; origins 74; *see also* Asian spa study
spaces 113
spatial aspects, of travel-related happiness 60–1
spiritual transformation 123
spirituality: Celtic 96; dimensions of 112; features of 97–8; flamenco tourism 111–21; and individualism 96; psychological perspectives 111–12; and social change 94; and sociality 99; and well-being 123
Sri Aurobindo Ashram 121
Stanford Research International (SRI) 73
stereotypes 43
Stinson, S.W. 117, 118
Stone, P. 3–4, 5, 37
storytelling 188
stress-related growth 121
stress, work-related 167–8
study-abroad students 56
subjective well-being theory 56
Sundaram, P. 121

Takahashi, M. 32
temple of Apollo at Delphi 91
temporal environment, restoration 213–14, 218
the sea 63
therapy and problem solving, long-distance walking 132–3
three elements of theory building 223–4
thresholds 82–4
tourism: as academic subject 37; and happiness 55–8
tourism policy, and health and ageing 196–7
tourism studies, developmental dimensions 223
tourist experience and fulfilment research: cohesion 223–4; knowledge gaps and future research 227–9; overview 223; PERMA 227; themes 224–7
tourist experiences: five modes 77–8; flow in 78–9; variability 3–4
tourist moment 117, 122
tradition, in religion 94–6
trait happiness 38
transformation 226; constraints 129; flamenco 115–16, 121; long-distance walking 128–31, 141–3, **142**; spiritual 123; unintentional 129; volunteer tourism 153–60
transformative narratives 103–5

transition 128
transnational teaching 48–9
travel career pattern (TCP) model 82–3
travel, personal impact 39
travel-related happiness: conscious perception of 61–7; dimensions 61–8; spatial aspects of 60–1; *see also* happiness
Trompenaars, F. 46
trust, volunteer tourism 154, 155–6
Tugade, M.M. 170
Turner, V. 113

vacation, definition 167
vacations: active recovery mechanisms 169–70; activities 172–3, 174–6, 178–9; bonding 178; context and overview 167–8; contributions to recovery 168–70; discussion 177–81; future research 180; health and well-being 172, 173–4, **174**, *175*, 177–8; measures 172–3; memories 177–8; negative incidents 176–7; passive activities 176; passive recovery mechanisms 168–9; pleasure 173, 176; practical suggestions 180–1; procedure 171; recovery 173, 177; research questions 170–1; results 173–7; sample 172; sleep 173, 176, 178; strengths and limitations of study 179
Values in Action Inventory of Strengths (VIA-IS) 31
values, motivating 104
Van Dierendonck, D. 123
variability, of tourist experiences 3–4
Venice **66**
volunteer tourism 56; active citizenship 154; activity levels 158–9; adventurousness 154, 159–60; altruism 154; anxiety 155; artistic interest 154, 157; conclusions 160–1; context and overview 147; depression 157–8; discussion 153–60; dutifulness 154–5; emotionality 158; emotions 154; engagement 147–8, 156; Engagement Theory **153**; fitness 158–9; flow 155; limitations of study 160; literature 148; mental health 153, 157–8; personal attitudes 154; qualitative analysis 151; quantitative analysis 150–1; research design 148–9; responsibility 156–7; results **151**, 151–3; sample 149–50; self-confidence 159–60; self-efficacy 154; social integration 157–8; trust 154, 155–6

Waterman, A.S. 119
Weiner, E. 60
well-being: definitions 3; five elements (PERMA) 131, 138, 142, 187; *see also* PERMA; and happiness 37–8; within psychology 91; and religious expression 92, 98–100; social-emotional 104; strategies 92; subjective and objective 55; theories of 3
wellness: characteristics 73; concept of 72–3; as tourism product 73
wellness industry 72–3
Wink, P. 96–7, 98
Wiseman, R. 19
Witsel, M. 43
Wood, M. 91
work, and happiness 38, 39
work/life satisfaction 186
work-related stress 167–8
work-related travel: cognitive journeys 49–50; conclusions 50–1; context and overview 37; essential and beneficial activity 41–8; happiness, enjoyment and joy 48–50; implications of research 51–2; knowledge and skill development 45–7; literature review 37–40; major themes 41–50; method 40–1; mutual care 50
Wuthnow, R. 98

yoga, flow 81
younger travellers 104–5

Zahra, A. 154–5
Zentner, M.R. 117